CHILDCRAFT
YOUR YOUNG CHILD

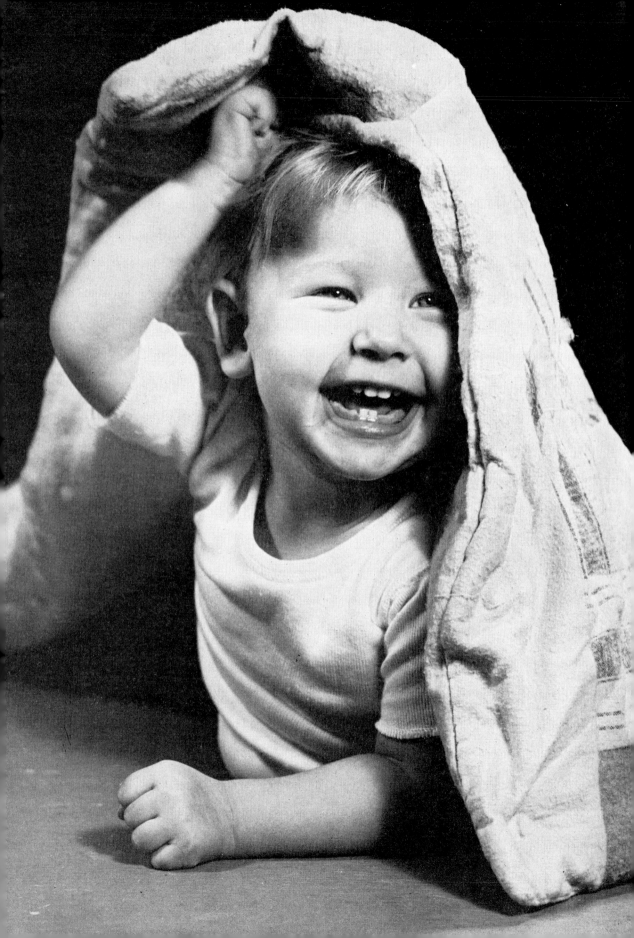

Childcraft

IN FIFTEEN VOLUMES

●

VOLUME THIRTEEN

YOUR YOUNG CHILD

FIELD ENTERPRISES EDUCATIONAL CORPORATION
Merchandise Mart Plaza · Chicago 54, Illinois

1961 Edition

CHILDCRAFT
(Reg. U.S. Pat. Off.)

CONTENTS

These Are the Authors

Mary M. Aldrich

in "MY CHILD DOESN'T LIKE TO EAT" (page 177), points out how good appetites can be cultivated so that mealtime will be relaxed and pleasant. The author and her late husband, Dr. C. Anderson Aldrich, made an intense study of this subject and wrote *Feeding Our Old-Fashioned Children* and *Babies Are Human Beings.*

Carmen Stone Allen

in TRAVELING WITH YOUNG CHILDREN (page 226) tells how to provide for the needs of babies and toddlers traveling in trains, planes, ships, or automobiles. In this chapter, the author gives other mothers the benefit of her own experience in raising her family.

Evelyn M. Beyer

Director of Nursery School, Sarah Lawrence College, Bronxville, N. Y. Her chapter HIS LANGUAGE IS RICH AND FLUENT (page 111) describes how children grow in ability to use words and how parents can encourage them.

Gertrude E. Chittenden

in WHAT DOES HIS "NO, NO" REALLY MEAN? (page 85) explains why young children often seem contrary, and suggests how these unco-operative tendencies can be handled. She was formerly head of the Child Development Department of Iowa State College, Ames, Iowa. She is author of *Living with Children* and of many articles.

Roberta Collard

with affectionate humor in HE'S A GREAT PRETENDER (page 117), tells how children grow through the use of their imaginations. She has been a nursery-school teacher and a child psychologist. She has had a broad experience in dealing with children who have emotional problems.

Charlotte del Solar

Formerly Assistant Professor in Psychology and Education at the Child Study Center, Yale University, brings a rich background to BEFORE THE BABY ARRIVES (page 3). She is particularly familiar with questions which concern a mother-to-be. In her chapter she sets forth some of the ways a baby can be given a good start before birth.

Arnold Gesell, M.D.

has made an invaluable contribution to the understanding of child development. His work has made his name a household word, not only in North America but also in other lands. His chapter GUIDING HIM TACTFULLY (page 90) emphasizes basic principles. Doctor Gesell is Research Consultant of the Gesell Institute for Child Development in New Haven, Connecticut. He co-authored *Infant and Child in the Culture of Today.*

Cornelia Goldsmith

author of OTHER CHILDREN BECOME MORE IMPORTANT (page 130), is Chief, Division of Day Care and Foster Homes, New York City Department of Health. Her knowledge of young children's behavior in groups makes this an unusually helpful chapter for every parent.

Christine M. Heinig

in HE GETS ALONG BETTER WITH HIS PLAYMATES (page 169), tells how parents can help children of kindergarten age play together happily. The author organized and taught nursery schools in the United States and in Australia before becoming Childhood Education Associate for the American Association of University Women.

Pauline Hilliard

has made children's literature her special interest. In the chapter STORIES FOR YOUNG CHILDREN (page 290) she recommends the kind of tales the smallest ones will enjoy, and ways of telling them. She is Associate Professor of Education at the College of Education, University of Florida.

Frances R. Horwich

points out how you can recognize a good nursery school in WHAT NURSERY GROUPS OFFER (page 231). Long before she became beloved as Miss Frances of the popular television program, Ding-Dong School, she was a leader in developing nursery schools. She is a former Chairman of the Department of Education at Roosevelt College, Chicago, and has served as President of the National Association of Nursery Education.

Frances L. Ilg, M.D.

tells how parents can give toddlers suitable opportunities to be independent, in THE AGE OF "ME-CAN-DO" (page 73). Her name is honored wherever there is real concern for the welfare of small children. She is the Director of the Gesell Institute of Child Development, New Haven, Conn., and co-author, with Dr. Arnold Gesell, of *Infant and Child in the Culture of Today*.

Edith B. Jackson, M.D.

is a pioneer in the plan of keeping new-born babies in the hospital room with their mothers. In ROOMING-IN (page 15) she explains how this plan works. She also tells why those who have been part of rooming-in units are enthusiastic about the idea. Doctor Jackson was formerly Professor of Pediatrics and Psychiatry at Yale University.

Mary Elizabeth Keister

heads the Department of Child Development and Family Relationships at the University of Tennessee, Knoxville. In CAUTION—TODDLER AT WORK HERE (page 79), she advances solutions to that worry of parents of two-year-olds: How can we give a youngster the chance to explore and still protect him from harm?

Ethel Wright Kunkle

in the chapter EXCURSIONS FOR YOUNG CHILDREN (page 304) suggests the kind of simple experiences near home that three-, four-, and five-year-olds delight in. She is the author of *Saturday Walk, Saturday Ride*, and *Saturday Flight*, and is a former Executive Director of the Winnetka Community Nursery School, Winnetka, Illinois.

Mary Fisher Langmuir

gives parents an understanding of the sources of children's fears and some ways of handling them, in WHEN CHILDREN ARE ANXIOUS (page 209). The author is a former Chairman of the Department of Child Study at Vassar College. She has also served as Director of the Vassar Summer Institute on Family and Community Relations.

Milton I. Levine, M.D.

is co-author with Jean Seligmann of HE LEARNS ABOUT DIFFERENCES BETWEEN BOYS AND GIRLS (page 123). Here is practical guidance for parents who want to know how to answer children's earliest questions about sex. Doctor Levine, who is Associate Professor of Pediatrics at the New York Hospital, Cornell Medical Center, is also co-author

with Jean Seligmann of *The Wonder of Life* and *A Baby Is Born*.

Donovan J. McCune, M.D.

in HE DISCOVERS HIS OWN BODY (page 55) explains how a baby learns that he is a separate individual through the discovery of his hands, his feet, and his ability to reach, grasp, and kick. Doctor McCune is a pediatrician with the Permanente Medical Group in Vallejo, California.

Mary E. Mercer, M.D.

has put study and effort into reducing fear and anxiety in small children who must be hospitalized. This is the topic she discusses in IF YOUR CHILD GOES TO THE HOSPITAL (page 267). She is psychiatrist in the Department of Health, New York City.

Lynette M. Messer

gives a picture of what kindergartners like to do and what may be expected of them, in HE IS READY FOR NEW EXPERIENCES (page 143). The author is a former Assistant Professor of Education and Director of Education at San Francisco State College.

Marjorie Momyer

discusses the question WHEN ARE CHILDREN SPOILED? (page 135). She points out that either feeling unloved and unwanted, or being hovered over constantly, can produce the disagreeable behavior we call "acting spoiled." The author is Chairman of the Child Study Department at Stephens College, Columbia, Missouri.

John C. Montgomery, M.D.

is a pediatrician and the author, with Margaret J. Suydam, of the highly regarded *America's Baby Book*. KEEPING A BABY COMFORTABLE (page 32) by these two authors gives useful suggestions for baby's sleeping arrangements, for his bath, and for selecting and caring for his clothing and equipment. Doctor Montgomery's counsel considers Mother's needs as well as Baby's.

Richard W. Olmsted, M.D.

is especially interested in helping new parents get a good start in parenthood. In FOR FATHERS ONLY (page 20) he tells about ways a husband can give his wife the encouragement and help she needs before the baby comes, as well as during the early months of motherhood. Doctor Olmsted is a former pediatrician and Clinical Instructor in Pediatrics at the Yale School of Medicine.

Eveline B. Omwake

is Associate Professor at the Child Study Center, Yale University, and one of the outstanding authorities on the behavior of small children. Her chapter Difficulties in Living with Others (page 201) offers definite help in guiding children from angry, unco-operative behavior toward more desirable ways of working out problems.

Mary R. Osborne

knows from her experience as a mother and as a trained nurse what patience and skill are required to keep a sick child contented and occupied. Her Keeping a Convalescent Child Happy (page 273) contains suggestions mothers will find invaluable. The author lectures on Marriage and Family Life at Sarah Lawrence College in Bronxville, N. Y., and at Columbia College, New York City.

Lili E. Peller

brings years of study and experience to He Learns Through Activities and Toys (page 65). She knows how babies and small children play in many different situations. Mothers will find original and useful her ideas on playthings. The author is a Lecturer at the City College, New York City.

Frances C. Perce

is Chief Psychologist, Institute for Juvenile Research, Chicago, Ill. In Early Growth Is Swift and Dramatic (page 27), she describes the way a baby grows in size, in ability to co-ordinate his muscles, and in how he responds to others. She also suggests the surroundings that promote good growth.

Maria W. Piers

in He Has a Conscience (page 162), traces the development of a child's conscience and explains how we can create the atmosphere in which conscience will become serviceable, yet not overstrict. The author is a child-guidance consultant who has written extensively for parents.

Sally Ann Provence, M.D.

in Keeping Your Young Child Healthy (page 247) stresses the kind of surroundings and routines that keep a child well, and how some illnesses can be prevented. She is Assistant Professor of Pediatrics at the Child Study Center, Yale University.

Julius B. Richmond, M.D.

in The Doctor and the Dentist—Your Child's Friends (page 254), tells why a pleasant relationship with the child's physician and dentist promotes health. He also tells how parents can further such friendliness. He is Chairman of the Department of Pediatrics, College of Medicine at the State University of New York, Syracuse.

Nina Ridenour

points out in He Asks Endless Questions (page 149) that parents need to listen for the "question behind the question." If they do this, they can help children grow. She is Secretary, Ittleson Family Foundation.

Jean H. Seligmann

is co-author with Milton I. Levine of He Learns About Differences Between Boys and Girls (page 123). In this chapter, the authors guide parents who want to know how to answer children's earliest questions about sex and the differences between the sexes. The Wonder of Life and A Baby Is Born are among their books.

Milton J. E. Senn, M.D.

directs the Child Study Center at Yale University. In Some Children Have Trouble Sleeping (page 185), Doctor Senn discusses some causes of sleep disturbances, and ways that parents may improve children's sleeping arrangements. Doctor Senn co-authored All About Feeding Children.

Emma Dickson Sheehy

in Young Children and Music (page 297) suggests musical experiences small children can enjoy and parents can easily provide at home. She is Associate Professor of Education, Teachers College, Columbia University, New York, and is responsible for planning Childcraft's Volume 11, Music and the Family. She is the author of There's Music in Children.

Rowena M. Shoemaker

gives parents detailed and practical help in Toys and Play Materials (page 283). She also gives directions for acceptable homemade substitutes for many of the toys in the stores. As Assistant Director of Play Schools Association in New York, the author became thoroughly familiar with the kind of play materials children like best and use best.

J. H. Sillman, D.D.S.

in Your Child's Teeth (page 261) explains what parents can do to care for children's teeth, and how dental difficulties can be reduced. As Associate Visiting Dentist, Bellevue Medical Center, New York, and a Consultant at New York Infirmary, he has given special attention to such questions. He is the producer of an educational film, *The Child and His Thumb*.

Mollie S. Smart

gives a picture of the nursery-school child in HE LIKES TO BE BUSY (page 105). She suggests, too, how parents can channel his "busy-ness" so it will be constructive and less troublesome. She is also the author of many lively, readable books for parents, including *Babe in a House*. With her husband, Russell C. Smart, she wrote *It's a Wise Parent* and *Living and Learning with Children*.

Terry Spitalny

is a former director of the nursery school and member of the faculty at Sarah Lawrence College, Bronxville, N. Y. In WHAT DOES HE LIKE TO DO BEST? (page 97) she discusses how, with what, and with whom toddlers enjoy playing, and how parents can provide what they need for play.

Virginia Messenger Stapley

author of WHAT LEAVING HOME MEANS TO A SMALL CHILD (page 221), explains why being away from home and Mother upsets many children, and how the separation can be made easier. She is professor and head of the Department of Family Relations and Child Development, Oklahoma State University of Agriculture and Applied Science.

Celia Burns Stendler

in WILL MY CHILD BE READY FOR FIRST GRADE? (page 309) discusses how parents can help children be ready to learn to read, to work and play in a group, to listen to others, and to speak up. The author is Professor of Education at the University of Illinois, and is a distinguished teacher. She is the co-author of *Child Development*.

L. Joseph Stone

author of HE STILL LEARNS THROUGH HIS PLAY (page 156), is Chairman of the Department of Child Study at Vassar College. He explains how thinking and imagination, as well as ability to use muscles and to get along with others, are furthered through play.

Margaret Jane Suydam

is Home Economist for the Family Service of Cincinnati and Hamilton Counties. She is co-author with Dr. John C. Montgomery of KEEPING A BABY

COMFORTABLE (page 32), where the parent can learn how to simplify baby care.

A. Genevieve Trainham

has supplemented her experience as a trained nurse with study of children's behavior. As a consultant in the development and problems of infants and children, she is keenly aware of the tension spots in bringing up children. Her chapter HELPING YOUR CHILD LEARN TO USE THE TOILET (page 47) explains what learning to control elimination means to a small child, and how parents can help.

Gustave F. Weinfeld, M.D.

in SOME CHILDREN RESIST THE TOILET (page 193), gives practical suggestions for helping children acquire control without undue strain and tension. Doctor Weinfeld is on the staff of the Institute for Juvenile Research and of Children's Memorial Hospital in Chicago, and the staff of the Highland Park Hospital, Highland Park, Ill.

Anna W. M. Wolf

in MOTHER AND CHILD ARE DOING NICELY (page 9) points out how the mother-baby couple can get off to a good start. The author is on the staff of the Child Study Association of America, and is Child Care Editor of the *Woman's Home Companion*. She is also author of *The Parent's Manual*.

Katherine M. Wolf

has taken part in important studies on the effect on personality of the early relationship between Mother and Baby. In HE FINDS OUT WHO IS IMPORTANT TO HIM (page 60), she applies these to the care of babies in a down-to-earth way. She is an Associate Professor at the Child Study Center, Yale University.

Richard E. Wolf, M.D.

is Director of the Pediatric Psychiatry Clinic of the Children's Hospital, Cincinnati, Ohio. His FEEDING HAS MANY MEANINGS (page 40) explains how satisfactory early feeding experiences contribute to healthy personality in childhood. He also gives suggestions for starting a baby on the road to a happy disposition and a good appetite.

Elizabeth L. Woods

in IF YOU WANT A PLAY GROUP (page 237) explains how parents can co-operate in organizing and carrying on different kinds of nursery groups. As president of the Southern California Association of Nursery Schools, she has had a close connection with co-operative nursery schools. She is also the author of *Care and Guidance of Children*.

THE BABY IS BORN

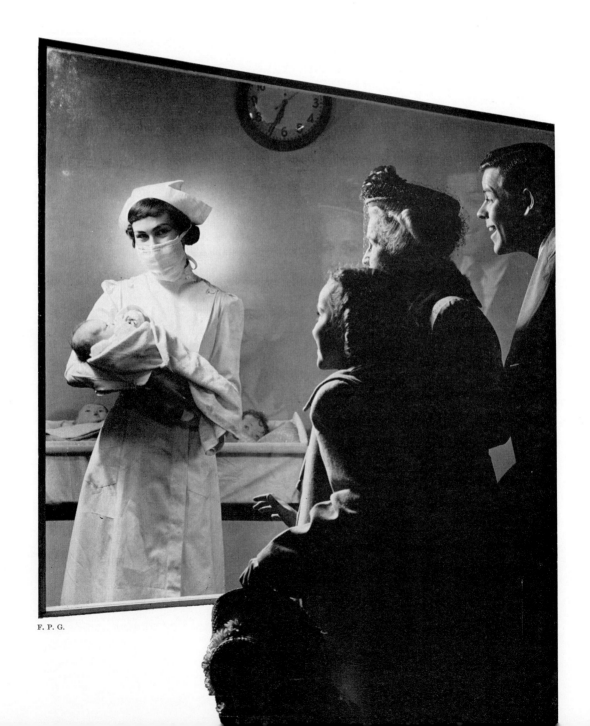

F. P. G.

Husbands and wives usually share the joys and responsibilities of parenthood during the months before the baby arrives. Joint preparations for making the baby part of the family, and in planning for his care, can draw husband and wife even closer together.

Family life will tend to go more smoothly when a married couple know what they may expect of themselves during the period of pregnancy, and what the baby will be like during the early months. Nor should they shut their eyes to discouragements and difficulties which can inevitably be expected.

This is the time to learn how medical science is being used to increase the comfort and well-being of mothers and babies, so that the new family unit may have a good start.

A warm, close relationship between mother and baby is the foundation of a healthy personality for the baby. But it is the husband's affectionate and understanding encouragement of his wife which make that warmth and closeness possible.

BEFORE THE BABY ARRIVES

CHARLOTTE DEL SOLAR, Ph.D.

Formerly, Assistant Professor of Psychology and Education,
Child Study Center, Yale University,
New Haven, Conn.

Your feelings and attitudes about parenthood began many years before you ever dreamed of having a child of your own. As children you played at being parents. A four-year-old girl says to her boy playmate, "I'll be the Mommie and you be the Daddy. I'll make the baby quiet so you can work." Throughout childhood, by observing and imitating your parents and other parents, you learned what it means to be a mother or to be a father.

Most husbands and wives become more acutely aware of the meaning of parenthood as they await the birth of their first child.

It Is Hard to Wait

You see in parenthood the fulfillment of your marriage, but you also wonder what this new arrival is going to do to your lives. You expect parenthood will be fun, and rewarding. During pregnancy, expectant parents usually daydream about what is going to happen once the baby arrives.

Most parents naturally want to do everything possible to insure the best growth and development of their new baby. Nevertheless, they realize they cannot influence many important developments of the baby's prenatal life. Expectant mothers may express the conflict they feel by becoming impatient during the last months of pregnancy.

One mother said, "I could wait forever if only I knew for sure everything is all right. It's like baking a cake. When the cake is half done, you like to take one quick peek." During pregnancy there is no quick peek! Although you cannot observe the prenatal growth of your own babies, there is much you can learn about prenatal development in general. Knowledge concerning the process of reproduction and childbirth may serve to decrease some of your doubts and fears.

Development Before Birth

Take a quick look at growth and development before birth. At the moment of conception, when a sperm enters an egg, or *ovum*, the hereditary gift of each parent is bestowed on this tiny individual. The sex of your new baby was determined by his father. For convenience, throughout our discussion we will speak of your new baby as a boy, with humble apologies to all girl babies!

Most of this baby is egg. The sperm is so small that ten billion can be held easily in a small-sized thimble. The egg cell is fertilized in a Fallopian tube which connects the uterus and the ovaries. The cell immediately begins to divide. The fertilized egg, which is called an *embryo*, moves toward the uterus through the Fallopian tube. Five or six days after conception, the embryo embeds itself in the wall of the uterus. The uterus is prepared for the embryo, because menstruation was arrested at the

time of conception. The uterus retained rather than expelled the rich lining of blood cells and is prepared to nourish the embryo.

Within the first four weeks of prenatal existence, the foundations of life are formed. During the third week the heart begins to beat. During the fourth week the beginnings of the digestive and

H. Armstrong Roberts

Good medical care can keep you more comfortable. It is the best health insurance for you and your baby, too.

nervous systems are traced out. The placenta and umbilical cord are formed. These organs will transfer nourishment from the expectant mother to the embryo, and carry the embryo's waste materials back to the mother.

An infinite number of miraculous changes take place during the first four

Learning some of the tricks of the trade before the baby arrives prevents that "all thumbs" feeling when you are face to face with a squirming, slippery baby.

weeks of prenatal life. The important thing to remember is—never again will the baby grow so fast! Through these swift changes, parents are not even dimly aware that a new baby is on the way.

The Baby Gets Ready for Birth

By the end of the third month of prenatal life, your baby has begun to look like a human being. Until this time he resembled a large-headed seahorse. At three months he is about two and one-half inches long from head to rump. His head still represents one third of his total body length. He has ears, a flat nose (the nose stays flat so it will not get in the way at the time of birth), a mouth, arms, hands, fingers, legs, feet, and toes. He moves, but his mother may not feel his movements until the fourth month.

At the end of six months, the expectant mother is carrying a baby who is almost ready to live outside of her uterus. In fact, with special care, a baby born at the end of the sixth month may live. He can breathe, suck, grasp, and cry. He no longer feels to his mother like a light flutter somewhere inside her. He kicks and churns around so that she knows he is really there. He weighs only two pounds, on the average, and in the next three months of his life his main job will be to get some flesh on his bones and to gain strength. He badly needs some more fat, but it should be remembered that he is capable at this early age of performing activities such as breathing, digesting, and crying. In the last three months of prenatal existence, the baby seems to take it easy. He becomes well prepared for the process of birth and for his new life outside of his mother.

There is a lesson for you as parents in Nature's arrangements. In a world of speed and hurry, you sometimes get the false notion that you can even hasten the growth of your children. From time to time, children need a quiet period to consolidate new abilities and accomplishments.

Meet the Newborn

At birth, the average boy baby weighs seven and one-half pounds and the average girl is a half-pound lighter. Depending on your point of view, the brand new baby is wonderful and even beautiful, or a funny-looking, squirming thing that has great potentialities but certainly is no beauty. The baby is well equipped to nurse, to cry, and, most important of all, to show discomfort and satisfaction. It will be these first signs of satisfaction and dissatisfaction that will be your guides in learning how best to care for the new baby.

Care for the Expectant Mother

The first, and by far most important, duty of the expectant parents will be to obtain good medical care and supervision for the expectant mother. As soon as a woman suspects she is pregnant, she should visit her doctor or the prenatal clinic in her community. Medical supervision of pregnancy is the best insurance for a healthy and happy pregnancy and delivery. The monthly or even more frequent visit to the doctor during pregnancy can be an encouraging and pleasant experience.

Many mothers enjoy their trip to the doctor because here is one place where they can talk to their hearts' content about how they have been feeling. They may talk with the doctor or the nurse, or perhaps with other pregnant women. Possibly a pregnant woman's best audience is another expectant mother. People who are not pregnant (including mothers, mothers-in-law, and even husbands) find it difficult to realize how odd it seems not to see your feet as you walk down the street. Or how reassuring and good it feels to have the baby kick vigorously inside you.

Some women may find it difficult to accept the many tests and examinations the doctor may find neccessary to perform. If one has never had an obstetrical examination, it may be downright embarrassing to be stretched out on the table in anything but a modest position. In addition to embarrassment, an expectant mother may even resent her doctor and the people who are presumably trying to help her.

One mother said, "I sometimes wonder who's having this baby—me, the doctor, or my husband. Why, they treat me as if I was just a convenient container! The doctor pokes at me, the nurse tells me how to eat, sleep, and eliminate, and my husband tells me to do what they say."

Frequently the expectant mother's complaints have some justification. In our zeal to keep her healthy and well, we may forget that she is the most active and important participant in this event. Often the expectant mother's angry complaints mask fears and apprehensions concerning her own and her baby's welfare. If you understand your own feelings and the purpose of the tests and examinations, you may find it easier to accept what is done for you.

Must Childbirth Be Painful?

Most of you have assumed that childbirth must necessarily be an extremely painful experience. In modern times, effort has been spent on discovering anesthetics and other ways of reducing pain, to relieve the mother without harming her baby. It seemed to doctors and mothers alike that the pain of childbirth was inevitable, and our primary goal was to relieve it or block it from the mother's conscious experience. This, of course, has meant that many mothers are not fully conscious during the process of childbirth.

Although the general trend has been toward the assumption that childbirth is painful, here and there doctors and nurses have observed women who did not appear to experience great pain in childbirth. It was not until Dr. Grantly Dick Read wrote *Childbirth Without Fear* that there was serious consideration of the possibility that childbirth need not be accompanied by overwhelming pain. Dr. Read observed that women who were not afraid of childbirth, and who had learned how to relax during labor, did not find unbearably painful

Philip Gendreau

the contractions which force the baby from the uterus. Some mothers assured him they felt no pain at all. Other mothers felt some pain, but it was far from unbearable. Dr. Read and his followers have named their method of delivery "natural childbirth."

What Advantages in Natural Childbirth?

The greatest psychological advantage of natural childbirth is the conscious and active participation of the mother in the process of childbirth. She has been waiting nine months to see her baby and hold him in her arms. It would seem only just for her to feel and see her youngster at the moment his head and shoulders emerge from her body. Mothers who have seen their babies born tell us there is no joy comparable to that first glimpse of their offspring.

Natural childbirth has met with varying degrees of acceptance by obstetricians. An expectant mother should discuss with her obstetrician the advisability and feasibility of her obtaining training for natural childbirth.

Understanding Reduces Fear

We know that fear and anxiety are archenemies of the expectant mother. Our task is to diminish the strength of these destructive forces. We have at least three strong allies with which to combat these enemies. First, we may increase the mother's knowledge and understanding of the reproductive process. To most young women, the functions of their reproductive organs are strange and baffling mysteries. For many moth-

Let the girl you married know she is still the girl you love. Listen to her fears, share her hopes, admire her, and she will thrive as a mother-to-be.

ers, merely to become acquainted with the process of reproduction and of labor and delivery is enough to dispel their feelings of dread and apprehension. Some mothers will gain confidence from studying the many excellent books and pamphlets concerning human reproduction.

It is doubtful that any book or pamphlet can answer all the reasonable and ridiculous questions which pop into an expectant mother's mind. This is particularly true for what mothers often call their "silly questions." They start out, "Doctor, I know this is silly but so-and-so told me the other day . . ." Or a mother may ask her doctor during the eighth month of her pregnancy if her baby is "still alive." Both she and her doctor knew they had just felt the movements of the baby and heard his heart beat, and yet for *this* mother at *this* time more reassurance was needed. She wanted not only to feel, but also to hear from someone she trusted and respected, that her baby was alive.

She asked for the kindly support and reassurance of another human being. That reassurance is the expectant mother's second ally against fear.

Support Diminishes Anxiety

The pregnant woman has the right to expect support and reassurance from people close to her. Fear and doubt feed on loneliness and lack of companionship. One of the major principles of natural childbirth is the insistence that, during labor and delivery, a mother never have the sense of being left alone to carry through the task of childbirth.

During pregnancy, some mothers find the support and companionship they need within their families. Possibly the compliments which husbands seem particularly good at inventing are the greatest morale booster. A woman toward the end of pregnancy likes to hear that she looks pretty cute waddling down the street like a duck. She may also wish to hear that her size is not disfiguring in the eyes of her husband, but a grand and glorious sight. Childbearing is a family affair, and a woman need not feel weak or ashamed when she asks for support from those who are meant to share in her reproductive task.

The Baby Himself Is Reassurance

The third ally is the baby himself. An expectant mother may notice that she feels happiest and least troubled when she is thinking about her new baby or making preparations for him. Some mothers shy away from buying clothes and other necessities in the dread of a possible mishap during pregnancy or delivery. But most mothers are willing to take a chance and prepare for the baby, because of the pleasure and fun involved. These preparations serve to increase the reality of the baby's existence. Bit by bit, as husband and wife make ready for their child, the baby takes on an individuality all its own. On the eve of its birth, both expectant parents are not awaiting the birth of just any old baby, but are looking forward to meeting *their own special child*.

It seems, therefore, altogether possible to combat fear and anxiety. But there is much to be done before excellent medical and psychological care are offered to all expectant families. Communities might well consider it a worthwhile goal to give every family the opportunity to lay the cornerstone for a secure and happy parenthood through the best of care for the expectant mother and father.

MOTHER AND CHILD ARE DOING NICELY

ANNA W. M. WOLF, B.S.

Child Study Association of America;
New York, N. Y.

Lois Hobart, Cushing

Joy at the baby's safe arrival will remain always one of life's deepest experiences for a mother. Yet there is often a puzzling admixture of other feelings, too. This doesn't mean that the joy is less real, but that human emotions are more complex than we realize.

The baby's here at last! Everything went off normally enough, yet somehow, perhaps, he isn't quite what you expected. The baby does not seem quite real, quite your own yet. Some of your feelings puzzle you, too. Where is that great rush of maternal tenderness you had expected? These doubts and conflicts are hard to take when you are totally unprepared for them; much harder if they make you feel that you are unnatural and unworthy.

This Is Your Baby

The truth is that many women, even those who turn out to be the best of mothers, sometimes have to *learn* to love their babies. This is worth knowing, so you will not feel guilty. Equally important is the faith that as you get to know your baby, and as you care for him and tend him with increasing confi-

dence, love will come inevitably, even though it may, for some mothers, not have been love at first sight.

Hospital routines vary in their details. It is a good idea to ask your doctor in advance just what is going to happen. This applies not only to your labor and delivery but also to the care of the baby. Most doctors now know that it is worth taking the time to explain both the *what* and the *why* of infant care. As with any new experience, a mother with her first child is less anxious if it is the expected rather than the unexpected that happens.

What Is a Newborn Like?

No matter how much you have been told, the appearance of a newborn infant can come as a shock. Often he is red and scrawny. Instead of smiling, he

9

grimaces. He may have some temporary blemishes from the pressures and stresses of the birth process. Even though these usually disappear quickly, they can be distressing if you do not know how usual they are or what they mean. Yet you are likely to find him truly fascinating. You will watch in rapt absorption the strange weavings and wavings of the pink clenched fists. The soft spot on his head throbbing with life, the workings and smackings of his lips, the sudden yawns, the profound sleep, the violent crying are all a source of wonder and delight.

You have made these beginnings of a human life. You will be privileged to watch, every step of the way, as the whole organism becomes more and

more unified. Finally, you discover a special, unique personality. You look without tiring at the ten fingers and the toes with their midget nails that already need cutting, at the beginnings of lashes and eyebrows, at the soft hair. Everything is there. You have done well. You know it, and pride overwhelms you. Soon these feelings crowd out all others, and, when that happens, you find you are ready to take over entirely.

How Do You Become Acquainted?

This relationship between mother and baby requires time and leisure to grow. Women sense that they will need quiet and closeness to their babies from the beginning. Many do begin this great new venture with full consciousness during the birth experience itself. Many mothers want the baby in the hospital room, too—at least at those times when they feel rested and able to enjoy him. In spite of the excellence of scientific

Your baby looks mighty good to you, even though she is no prospect for a beauty contest right now. She'll soon get over that "new" look.

Ten little fingers and ten little toes! A baby is miraculous to his mother, and Mother has every right to be proud of herself when she finally holds him in her arms!

formulas, many mothers prefer breast feeding. Through all these basic contacts, a mother learns the ways of her baby down to the last detail. As she learns, the baby becomes truly her own, and her pride and self-confidence grow by leaps and bounds.

Off to a Good Start

A hospital is not the only possible place to have a baby, but for most families at the present time it is probably the safest and simplest.

Because of limited space and nursing staff, it has become more or less the custom for hospitals to discharge a patient on the sixth day after the baby's birth. Hospitals cannot consider what a mother may be going home to in the way of household responsibility, or whether she is emotionally ready. When the patient or the patient's family sense that she would be better off for a few more days in the hospital, they will be wise to throw their weight toward a longer stay. This investment in time and money will pay off in the end.

There is an additional reason why the sixth day is a poor choice for going home. It is the day when the breasts are likely to be at their most uncomfortable stage from the coming-in of milk. If a mother can remain quiet and inwardly at peace for a few more days, the chances are excellent that the flow will be well established, and that she will have clear sailing from then on.

New Mothers Need Help

A mother needs help and support for herself at this time, even though she is not always aware of it. When she feels emotionally sustained and mothered a bit by her husband, her doctor, and the nurses at the hospital, she most rapidly

gains in the capacity to give mothering to her baby.

At home, during the early weeks, if a baby is wakeful at night, if he is a fussy feeder, if he breaks out in a rash,

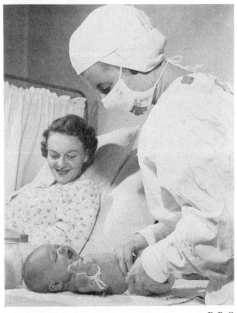

F. P. G.

You feel good as you bask in the glory of your great achievement. You watch your baby go through his paces and are glad to have help in caring for him.

if his digestion seems upset, if he cries a lot, it is a relief to have someone around who knows from experience what to do, and who shares the responsibility. All these minor crises may turn out to be trivial, but at the moment they may loom large. The best person is perhaps a mother, mother-in-law, or other relative. But nobody is the right person unless the new mother herself feels at ease with her. New mothers often need reassurance. No blood relationship, efficiency, or experience with babies can possibly make up for inability to bring about a sense of peace in the new mother. The truly skilled helper is the person who has the knack of building self-confidence. Her job is well done only when she succeeds in making both parents happy, relaxed, and, finally, independent.

Why Breast Feeding?

In spite of the excellence of artificial feeding, why is the best medical opinion still in favor of breast feeding when possible?

An increasing number of reports show that breast-fed infants are better able to cope with the hazards of the first weeks of life. They seem to be better armed against later infections and illness. Breast-fed infants appear to get more complete satisfaction from suckling, have less pain with their digestive processes, relax and fall asleep more contentedly. There is evidence, too, that later "feeding problems" are fewer in the breast-fed baby.

Is Breast Feeding a "Must"?

For those mothers who want it, their pleasure and satisfaction in nursing the baby are vital factors. If they gain a heightened sense of fulfilment and a deepened feeling of maternal love, it is surely worth the day or so of discomfort, the slight amount of extra trouble for doctors and nurses to get the breasts to do their job. If a mother has no such feeling, then any attempts to urge her into breast feeding can do nothing but harm. If she hesitates, friends and relatives will do both mother and child a favor if they refrain from giving the impression that she is less of a woman and mother if she prefers giving a bottle.

There are sometimes real reasons for not nursing a baby. The commonest of these is actual failure of the milk to flow, in spite of the best efforts to produce it. There are times, too, when inverted nipples cannot be corrected and the baby has nothing he can really suck on. Among other reasons for bottle feeding are the appearance of breast abscess, or chronic illness of certain kinds in the mother. Such obstacles are unfortunate but they are certainly no reflection on a woman's love for her child.

For those who want to nurse their babies, the co-operation of fathers will be necessary, for fathers who do not like breast feeding can subtly influence their wives against it. Mother and father must be backed wholeheartedly by the hospital "team." This means obstetrician, pediatrician, and nurses. Once they really work for it, it is amazing what substantial results they get.

Know-How in Breast Feeding

Success in breast feeding takes persistence and a refusal to be discouraged by initial obstacles and discomforts. During the first few days, a baby should not be too long at the breast. This allows time for the nipples to toughen up instead of getting sore. If the nipples show a tendency to crack, the best treatment is to wash them with soap and water and cover them with sterile gauze after each feeding. This seems to be more helpful than salves. Inverted nipples, if treated by massage before the baby's birth, can sometimes, but not always, be brought out.

There are additional tricks and know-how that the skillful nurse discovers and teaches the mother. She does not urge the baby to suck every minute. If he falls asleep she wakes him gently, with-

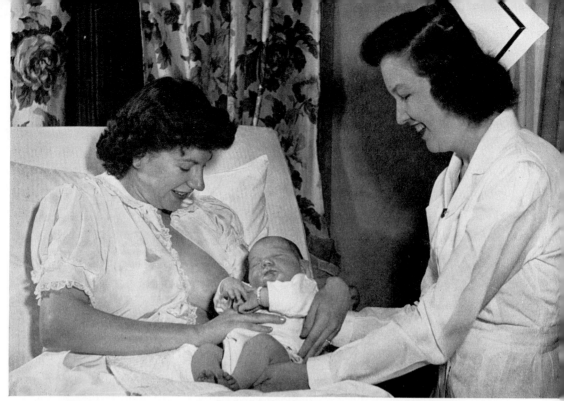

Eileen Darby, Courtesy *Woman's Home Companion*

Nothing like a snooze after a big meal! Nurses know how to keep nursing mothers comfortable, and how to encourage babies to feed vigorously.

out jiggling him or flipping his face or feet. She knows how to encourage the baby to "root" at the breast, to nuzzle and feel around for the nipple. Soon it is the mother, not the nurse, who helps him find it. The mother learns, too, that the baby should have whatever time he wants; there is no hurry.

Since vigorous sucking stimulates the flow of milk, it is best to give water from a bottle, but no formula, during the whole period of the first six days. This will make the baby really eager for food when put to the breast. The best insurance for a good milk supply is a hun-

Your baby counts on you to come to his rescue when he signals S.O.S. by setting up a first-class howl.

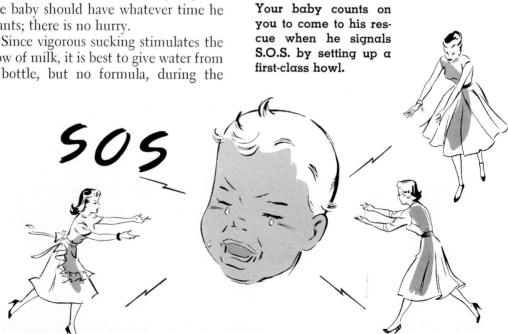

gry baby who has to work for it. Later, after the flow is well established, he may have a supplementary bottle if he seems to want it. It is normal for him to lose weight during the first week of his life.

What Is "Demand Feeding"?

Another tremendous aid to successful breast feeding is the "self-demand," instead of the old-fashioned fixed schedule. A baby should be put to the breast day and night during the first six days, whenever there is a chance that he might be hungry. Between the fourth and the sixth days, this may be often. It requires willingness and time on the part of nurses! But if a hospital feels it is vital, routines can almost always be adapted. A mother can then go home with a baby whose food supply is assured and who, once the milk comes in strongly, will accept longer intervals between feedings. The chapter on FEEDING HAS MANY MEANINGS, in this volume, discusses other aspects of feeding a baby.

What About Crying?

Even when they are first born, and increasingly as time goes on, babies have distinct personalities. Some are placid and good-natured, others are inclined to be tense and troubled. Some cry a great deal, others little. Sometimes a baby is fussy and discontented for the first three or four months, then straightens out and becomes all joy and smiles. We do not yet understand fully the reasons for these differences, or what they may mean for the future. We do know that it is best to do everything we can to get a baby to be as contented as possible as soon as possible.

Crying is an S O S, and an appeal for help should never be ignored. There are many tricks for restoring peace that a mother soon learns. A crying baby usually responds to rhythmic motion, to being held tight to his mother's body, to having his head stroked, to gentle pressure against the soles of his feet. A meal, even one that is "off schedule," may be worth trying, for some babies get hungry quickly. He may be too hot, too cold, or otherwise uncomfortable. He may need a change of position.

Does Attention Spoil a Baby?

Attention to a baby's real needs has nothing to do with spoiling. Babies do not profit by long periods of "crying it out." Hospitals that have kept records of babies' crying report that if the things previously suggested are done promptly, babies cry less, not more.

But no matter what we do, crying is often a difficult problem for a household. After we have tried everything, we must sometimes resign ourselves to just doing the best we can, in the faith that time itself will come to the rescue.

Other Family Members

A mother and her baby are living in a family. How some of the other members of the family feel at this time is important, too. The chapters FOR FATHERS ONLY in this volume, and SOMETIMES RIVALS, SOMETIMES FRIENDS, in Volume 12, give a picture of the feelings of the father and of other children in the family. GRANDPARENTS AND OTHER RELATIVES, in Volume 12, may be helpful in sorting out ideas about parents and parents-in-law. The mother-baby combination is immensely important, but mother and baby together get along best if the whole family setting and the relationships of the adults make for as much peace of mind and contentment as possible.

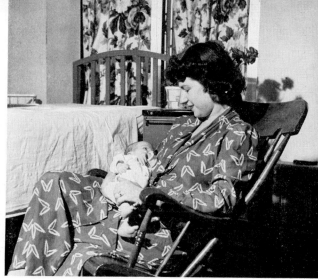

ROOMING-IN

EDITH B. JACKSON, M.D.

Former Professor of Pediatrics and Psychiatry,
Yale University School of Medicine,
New Haven, Conn.

Rooming-in is a way of hospital maternity care in which the infant's crib is placed by the mother's bedside, at least during the day. Ideally, the same nurses take care of both mother and baby. The mother can watch her child to her heart's content, and may hold him when he seems to want to be cuddled or fed. She can observe the nurse taking care of him.

When the mother feels ready, she may herself clean and change him, with the nurse standing by to help. In some hospitals, when the father visits he may also be given the pleasure of holding his child. If he chooses, he also may learn some practical points of baby care. Many parents who have thoroughly enjoyed this type of experience with a new baby have asked, "Why is rooming-in new?" "Why was it ever any other way?"

Why We Have Hospital Nurseries

Answers to these questions call for some explanation of the development of the hospital nursery. A "central nursery" for all newborn infants has been the custom in the United States. It was first tried out toward the end of the last century. It is supposed by those who have looked into the records that the main reason for such a plan was to protect infants from exposure to infection, and possibly also to protect mothers from unnecessary disturbance. In the old days, the majority of mothers stayed at home to have their babies. Those who went to the hospital for childbirth usually had some complication or illness, or an unfortunate home situation.

For many reasons, going to the hospital to have a baby became the accepted practice during the first quarter of the twentieth century. There were public-health rules and codes for regulating maternal and infant care in hospitals. A nursery for newborns was regarded as a necessity. By 1940, doctors and nurses had been trained in this tradition for almost a generation.

Obstacles to Rooming-in

The suggestion for rooming the baby in with his mother was made independently from three widely-separated medical centers in this country between 1942 and 1945. It is not surprising that it was not immediately accepted elsewhere. For some hospitals it required rearrangement, if not remodeling, of existing facilities. It required a definite change in

YOU AND YOUR BABY
BECOME ACQUAINTED

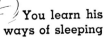

You play with him
if he feels sociable

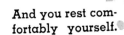

You learn his
ways of sleeping

Still you know a nurse is
near by to give helpful
pointers or take over

And you rest com-
fortably yourself.

Eileen Darby, Courtesy *Woman's Home Companion*

Father dresses for the part and gets into the act. He soon discovers what a tight grip a baby can get on you!

the assignment of nurses, and a change to a different type of nursing care. It is indeed remarkable that the rooming-in idea, with so many reversals of routine procedures, took hold as quickly as it did. Between 1945 and 1950, approximately twenty hospitals had rooming-in facilities in more or less continuous operation. Approximately twenty other hospitals had private or semiprivate rooms which were used occasionally for rooming-in, when mothers wanted it and their doctors recommended it.

The Purpose of Rooming-in

The first rooming-in arrangements were planned primarily around the needs, comfort, and satisfaction of mother and infant in relation to each other. Mothers were given the opportunity of choosing whether they wanted their babies to be in the hospital nursery or in the room with them. Some mothers, it was assumed, would not want the rooming-in plan, and would prefer to keep to the familiar, well-known way. In addition, the illness or attitude of other mothers, or anything wrong with the babies, could make it inappropriate.

The main consideration was to establish a natural, friendly, homelike situa-tion, where the baby could be fondled and fed as he needed it. It was felt that in this way the mother could gain confidence in her ability to give good care to her child. She would also feel free to ask help or advice about any matter. Finally, an arrangement where the father could feel included, too, was needed. The goal was to achieve all this without losing the protective advantages of the hospital. It was considered important to instruct nurses and doctors, before they started to work in rooming-in, about appropriate methods and attitudes for taking care of mother-infant couples on a flexible schedule. This type of care is quite different from the separate routines of maternal and infant care.

Do Doctors Approve?

The daily visits of the hospital physicians took on vitality in the rooming-in units. Doctors attending the mothers and infants gained increased awareness of the value of letting parents know ahead of time what to expect next about themselves, and about the baby's behavior. They found that, in addition to individual conferences with mothers, a group discussion with several mothers almost ready to go home was also helpful. This proved to be a mutual educational experience. They found that professional suggestions, seasoned with practical comments from experienced mothers, offered particular satisfaction to first-time mothers.

An interest in revising hospital management of pregnancy, labor, and delivery in the direction of greater naturalness was developed on the part of some doctors shortly after rooming-in programs were started. This interest was prompted by a visit to this country in 1947 by Dr. Grantley Dick Read, under the auspices of the Maternity Center Association of New York. In some teaching centers, natural childbirth and rooming-in programs were unified. They are based on similar ideas of step-by-step guidance for mothers. Parents' classes during pregnancy were adopted as part of an over-all hospital or medical-guidance program for parenthood.

Rooming-in and the Overcrowded Hospital

A few hospitals originally undertook rooming-in from a different point of view. It seemed to be a partial solution to the dilemma of too many babies and too few nurses in the nursery. Overcrowding resulted from an increased birthrate following World War II. Some large hospitals had to solve this problem by letting mothers and infants go home on the second or third day, where they could have rooming-in, original style. In other hospitals, department chiefs decided to place infants beside their mothers' beds soon after delivery, rather than run a possible risk of epidemic infection among the newborn in overcrowded nurseries. In such instances, existing hospital accommodations, without any alterations, were used, and infants were left with their mothers both day and night.

In rooming-in accommodations where overcrowding has not been a constant factor, there is usually some provision for small nurseries next to the mothers' rooms. Here the babies can be kept at night (or at any other indicated time) under the supervision of a nurse. In new plans for maternity buildings, it is expected that the accommodations will include small adjoining nurseries adaptable for rooming-in use or otherwise, as the need may be.

Rooming-in and Rest

What about the rest that mothers get, or do not get, in rooming-in? That always seems to be a burning question. Fear that they will not get enough rest

Questions are answered and worries forestalled as the doctor talks to a group of mothers ready to go home.

Cobb photograph, Courtesy *Baby Talk* Magazine

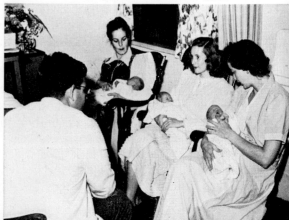

is the reason most generally given by mothers who do not want rooming-in. The fear is based, usually, on a misunderstanding of the type of care offered in rooming-in. Mothers are afraid of being left alone to take care of the baby without help from a nurse.

Mothers who have had both types of care have been almost unanimous in saying that they felt more rested and contented with the baby beside them than in a room where the baby was brought in only at feeding time. In many hospitals, mothers can hear the babies crying in the nursery. Each mother is sure that it is *her* baby crying, and that he is not getting proper attention, and that makes for worry. With her own baby beside her, a mother feels contented and assured, and then the crying of other babies rarely disturbs her.

How About Schedules?

Babies who are with their mothers, and are fed soon after they indicate hunger, cry relatively little. For this reason, and because nothing has to be done at any exact time, the general atmosphere of the rooming-in unit is peaceful. The general hospital timetable is followed in regard to mealtime, nap time, and visiting hours; but there is a comfortable degree of latitude. Sometimes the baby may be hungry when the mother's tray is brought in. The nurse may then hold the baby until the mother has eaten, or she may keep the mother's meal warm while the baby finishes his. If the mother is asleep, she is not wakened for any routine procedure. It is necessary to awaken her only if her baby needs to go to breast. Mothers in the usual setup in a hospital are roused for one routine after another, and

seldom succeed in finishing out a nap. Interrupted sleep is a possible drawback to rooming-in, if the baby is left with the mother all night. Mothers usually express a sense of relief when the babies are removed for the night under a nurse's watchful eye.

"How does having your baby in the room with you at the hospital affect your strength after you get home?" is a question mothers often ask. Some mothers have so great a sense of well-being when they leave the hospital that they may be overambitious in spite of the note of caution the nurses have sounded. Fatigue equally affects those who have had the baby in the same room and those whose babies have been in the central nursery.

How About Visitors?

In the early stages of rooming-in development there have been various modifications of arrangements, according to the individual hospital rules and the distribution of the nursing staff. There are differences in visiting rules. In general, fathers are allowed to visit with wife and child together, but a few hospitals have regulations which make this greatly-appreciated privilege impossible.

Various Rooming-in Plans

The babies may be placed with their mothers right away in some hospitals. In others, mother and baby are together after 24 hours; in still others, not until the second, third, or fourth day. By this time the mothers are up and about, and feel able to take care of their infants.

The baby may be left with his mother just for prolonged periods during the day. There may be a nurse in constant attendance, or nurses may make rounds several times a day to help the mothers

When the baby is beside you, you can watch him. You are more contented for you do not imagine every cry you hear in the distance is his, and you relax.

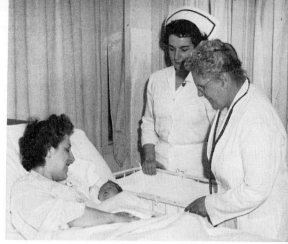

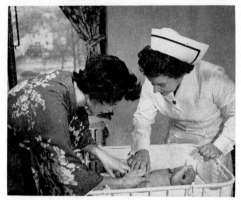

David Linton, Courtesy McGraw-Hill

You can gain practice and confidence in the fine points of baby care while a nurse stands by to lend a hand.

and give practical demonstrations of infant care.

The rooms may be private, or semi-private with anywhere from two to eight beds. These and other details have been regarded as of less importance than the co-operative attitude of the doctors and nurses, and the measure of time and patience that can be allotted to easing the early days of adjustment of mothers and newborns to each other.

Baby Thrives on Rooming-in

Actually, all the early accounts of rooming-in, regardless of the particular plan, are in essential agreement on major points. They all report no infection among the infants. Rooming-in arrangements of one to eight beds seem to be safer for the babies' health than large central nurseries. They all report that these infants receive better and more appropriate care, and appear quieter and more contented than infants in nurseries. Mothers are said to be appreciative of the opportunity to come to know their babies. They enjoy learning how to handle them without "fear of breaking them" before leaving the hospital. Experience has proved that the medical and nursing staffs, once they become accustomed to the change, find working relationships in the rooming-in units more gratifying.

If You Want Rooming-in

The indications are, accordingly, that the rooming-in idea is fundamentally sound. It is more than a passing fancy. Because of past education, and because of a tradition that is built into long-standing structures, the change-over cannot be expected to come overnight. The best thing for you to do if you want rooming-in is to see your doctor about it. Find out his attitude and the rules of the hospital(s) in the community. Explain your reasons for wanting to have your baby with you. Abide by what your doctor has to suggest. If it proves that the community situation is not yet ready for rooming-in, you and your friends with similar ideas may find you can interest hospital boards or administrators before the arrival of your next baby.

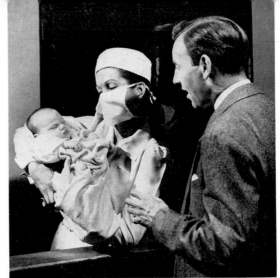

FOR FATHERS ONLY

RICHARD W. OLMSTED, M.D.
Former Instructor in Pediatrics, Yale School of
Medicine, New Haven, Conn.

Pregnancy, delivery, and the first few weeks of a baby's life would, thirty or fifty years ago, have been primarily woman's concern. But medical knowledge has taught us that the husband's interest in the beginnings of his child's life is of the utmost importance.

If we are to raise healthier, happier, and better-adjusted children, fathers need to understand both the mother and the baby. If a woman knows she has her husband's backing in the crucial moments of family life, many troubles can be avoided. Fathers in the United States are showing more and more interest in these matters in an attempt to make themselves better fathers and husbands.

Pregnancy Is a Partnership

Having a baby is one of the greatest and most satisfying experiences of a woman's life. It can, and should be, equally satisfying to the father. You need to be willing to accept your role as a father from the time of conception on, if you are to find it rewarding.

The realization that a baby has been conceived naturally brings feelings of joy and anticipation to both husband and wife. Many times, too, there are moments of anxiety and concern when you think of the complex job of child-rearing ahead of you. Accepting these responsibilities together, and working out the problems on a partnership basis, often brings husband and wife closer than they have ever been before.

Authorities agree that children reared in a family where love and understanding between husband and wife are present have a good start toward being happy and well adjusted. If the period of pregnancy is shared equally and happily between husband and wife, love and understanding grow and become stronger.

What Changes During Pregnancy?

Pregnancy is a period of life requiring certain adjustments on the part of both man and wife. The physical changes of pregnancy are striking, even to the uninitiated father. These changes are most marked during the first three months and the last month or two. During the first three months, so-called "morning sickness" is quite common, and may be an extremely uncomfortable and unpleasant experience for your wife. The sudden feeling of nausea, and the vomiting that accompanies it, can make life rather miserable for a while. Your wife may not seem so "glamorous" to you at these times. Fortunately, the condition tends to stop about the third month of pregnancy. A little sympathetic understanding during this period is always appreciated. Cooking and the odors of foods may be disagreeable to a pregnant woman. Anything you can do toward helping her to avoid the kitchen might be wise and helpful.

"Pregnant" Means "Heavy"

During the last two months, the marked change in a woman's figure and the weight of the baby may bring much fatigue and physical discomfort. If there are other children to care for, particularly if there are small ones to lift, the strain on her may be quite marked. This is the time when your wife really needs your help with heavy work around the house. Scrubbing floors, emptying heavy garbage pails, carrying heavy loads, any tasks that involve lifting or reaching may be hard on some women in the later months of pregnancy. It is well to remember, too, that your wife may not feel much like going out, or having company in to visit, when she is so tired.

Many mothers have definite feelings of being conspicuous on account of their changed appearance. Some women may

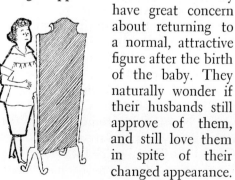

have great concern about returning to a normal, attractive figure after the birth of the baby. They naturally wonder if their husbands still approve of them, and still love them in spite of their changed appearance.

This concern is not only due to the physical change but also is connected with doubts the wife may have that her husband truly wants the baby.

Wives Need Affectionate Support

Women often have definite concern, perhaps even fear, about labor and delivery. This is true for mothers who have had other children as well as for the new mother.

Feelings of apprehension about the task of rearing a healthy baby are often keenly felt by the mother during the course of pregnancy. She realizes that a large part of the responsibility will rest upon her. She may become a little bewildered when she is bombarded with advice from all sides by relatives and friends.

Unless there are special reasons why her doctor has restricted her activity, a normal, active life is good for a woman, and most women prefer it. It is not sympathy, but understanding and encouragement, your wife needs.

Each woman may show her reaction to all these changes in a different way. She may never have felt better in her life one day. The next day she may be "blue" and "down in the dumps." Tears may come more readily. She may be more irritable some days than others.

During these periods of up-and-down emotions, a little extra attention is appreciated. Planning a special "date" together, or bringing small treats or presents from time to time, will go a

Occasional surprises and treats do as much for the mother-to-be as rest and the right kind of food will do.

Your help can save your wife's limited strength and bolster her morale on days when she is not feeling her best.

is able to be happy and contented and that she will return to her usual self-reliant, cheerful self soon after delivery.

How Can You Show Your Interest?

Try to bring up the subject of the baby as often as you can. Do not be

long way toward relieving some of her "blue" feelings.

Despite many articles written on the subject, there are no set rules for you to follow in handling these changes. More than anything else, your wife needs to know that you are solidly behind her and that you approve of all that is taking place. She wants to know that you are interested and that you are trying to understand.

A good many men may hesitate to show their true feelings during pregnancy. Perhaps they are bashful. Some think it is not the masculine thing to do. But the father who does try to get his feelings across to his wife will be well rewarded. He will probably find that she

afraid to discuss your own ideas of how to raise and care for the baby. Arrange to read books or articles on the subject of babies together with your wife. Let her know that you will be happy with either a boy or a girl. Enjoy the fun of naming the baby.

Many men hesitate to discuss whether the baby will be bottle fed or nursed. This is an extremely important decision for your wife. Even if you do not know much about the subject, your wife will be pleased if you are interested. One excellent way to show your interest would be by doing something for the new baby. Fixing up a room or making a cabinet for the baby's clothes are among the practical jobs that need a man's skill.

Your wife would be proud to say, "My husband did this for the baby."

Talk to Your Wife's Doctor

Arrange a talk with the doctor you and your wife have selected to deliver the baby. Here is another way of showing your interest. This is also an excellent opportunity for you to learn more about some of the peculiarities of pregnancy. Your doctor will welcome the opportunity to talk to you, even if he is a busy man. Such a conversation would give a good opportunity to discuss financial arrangements with him. Your doctor can also tell you about the necessary sexual adjustments to be made when normal sex relations are interrupted during pregnancy. This is an important consideration.

Many of the attitudes men have toward pregnancy and delivery may have been unconsciously developed through childhood observations in their own families. It would be helpful to discuss any of your worries about childbirth with your doctor.

Many communities are now offering courses in family relations and child care, for husbands and wives. If such courses are available in your community, they would be most worth while. Here again you would be accomplishing a double purpose by showing your wife you are interested. At the same time you would be gaining understanding. Taking the course together draws you closer, too.

"I Never Lost a Father"

This grim and worn-out little joke is a falsehood. Fathers are all too often "lost" in many ways when the baby is born. After the anxious nine months of waiting, the actual moment of delivery

23

Sometimes you feel you are the Little Man Who Isn't There

may be a letdown for the father. Unfortunately, most hospitals make little or no provision for the father-to-be as part of the delivery. But many modern doctors are recommending that husbands be allowed to stay with their wives during labor.

Those husbands who have had the feeling of sharing all along are less likely to feel left out when the baby is born. It usually happens, too, that a wife

"This man knows what the score is"— that's a good feeling for a baby to have. Here may be the beginning of a beautiful friendship and a lot of fun.

David Linton

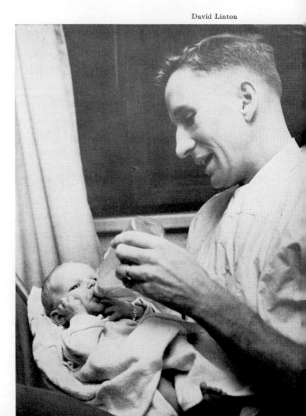

who has had constant encouragement and understanding from her husband will feel less alone and worried at the time of delivery.

Does a Husband Take Second Place?

Occasionally a husband may feel that his wife is more interested in the baby than she is in him, or a woman may think her husband shows more affection for the baby than for her.

Some new mothers seem quite attached to the doctor who delivers the baby. At least they talk about him with great enthusiasm for a while. His professional skill takes on a magical quality for them. This does not mean that they think any less of their husbands. It is usually a temporary feeling, and passes quickly.

How Does Father Meet Baby?

You may be disappointed when you find you are unable to see and handle the new baby in the hospital. Many hospitals are working on plans to allow the mother and father to have the baby with them at least for some parts of the hospital stay.

You may be disappointed, too, in the appearance of your baby. Newborn babies are not always the attractive and endearing creatures they become in a month or two. Don't worry if, in those first days, your son or daughter is less thrilling than you had anticipated.

Good Husbands Make Good Fathers

There are no set rules to follow in attempting to become a good husband or father. Your understanding and encouragement are still essential to your wife after the baby arrives, if she is to develop fully her capacities for enjoyable motherhood. Even under the best of circum-

stances, it is not uncommon for the mother to become somewhat easily discouraged and "blue" during the first few days and weeks after delivery. This feeling is commonly known as the "baby blues." If this low-spiritedness continues steadily a week or more, you should report it to your doctor.

Father's Share in Baby Care

In most instances, it is a matter of practical necessity for the father to help with the care of the baby. Nothing brings more of the true feeling of knowing and understanding children than working with and for babies right from the start.

Most doctors feel that the newborn baby actually senses and feels the presence of the father. The baby needs a father's love and understanding to develop his own personality. Men who help care for their new babies, who learn how to handle them and enjoy them, are not "sissies" in the eyes of other men.

It is a common experience that fathers enjoy the second and third children more than they did the first child. This is true because so often they have been reluctant to care for and handle the first one at an early age.

Fathers who help care for the baby during the first few weeks of life understand better how time-consuming such work is. They will never protest that the mother who is home alone with the children has "nothing to do all day."

If some of these suggestions seem difficult to carry out in the daily struggle of trying to support the family, remember that they are merely suggestions. They need to be fitted to your own special situation. How you feel about what you do is more important than what you do in any of these situations.

THE INFANT

Rae Russell

5. EARLY GROWTH IS SWIFT AND DRAMATIC

6. KEEPING A BABY COMFORTABLE

7. FEEDING HAS MANY MEANINGS

8. HELPING YOUR CHILD LEARN TO USE THE TOILET

9. HE DISCOVERS HIS OWN BODY

10. HE FINDS OUT WHO IS IMPORTANT TO HIM

11. HE LEARNS THROUGH ACTIVITIES AND TOYS

More exciting changes take place in the first year or year and a half of the child's life than will ever occur again in the life of an individual.

During his first year he acquires enough control of his body to change from one position to another, to go after things he wants, and, often, to get from one place to another.

If his experiences with feeding and toileting are satisfactory, and if his mother and father care for him tenderly and lovingly most of the time, he learns to recognize and to trust them. Out of this trust grows confidence in other persons.

Through his exploration of his own body, the baby becomes aware of himself as a separate person. Through his activity and his playthings he learns something of the world around him, and develops his sense of touch, of sight, of hearing, of taste, and of smell. All these important changes come about naturally as a baby lives with those who love him.

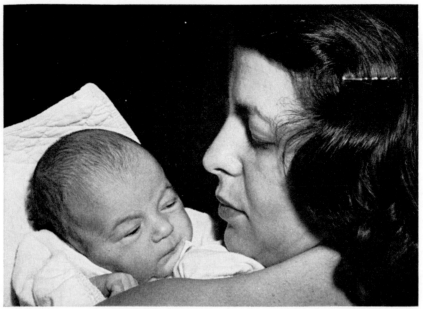

EARLY GROWTH IS SWIFT
AND DRAMATIC

FRANCES C. PERCE, M.S.

Chief Psychologist, Institute for Juvenile Research, Chicago, Ill.

PARENTS who have an idea of what to expect as their babies grow during the first year usually find that they enjoy their babies more. They find, too, that knowing something about growth and development keeps them from expecting too much of their baby. They are not unduly distressed if he takes new steps later or earlier, or more or less willingly, than the other infants on the block.

At no time during your child's growth are there so many rapid changes as during the first year. This is not only true in weight and measurements, but also in muscular control. Muscular control is a matter of orderly progression. It begins with the head and neck. Control of shoulders, arms, and, finally, legs, follows later. A baby's mental growth cannot be separated from physical growth and maturation. For example, he cannot learn to play until he has the ability to control his larger muscles sufficiently well to maintain himself in an upright position.

How Do the Senses Develop?

Although his hearing is acute and he will respond with a start to a loud noise, the baby cannot locate sounds. A ringing

"Hear that? Said 'daddy' plain as day—eleven and a half months old."

"Eight months old —walks."

bell makes him stop and listen, but he does not know which way to turn his head to locate the source of the sound. Eye co-ordination develops gradually. For many months there may be times when one eye looks crossed.

During the first weeks, your baby's crib is his environment. His eyes move in a small arc as he turns his head at random from one side to the other. His world is a horizontal one. He sees his hands only when he is able to bring them above his head and in direct line with his eyes. Even when you hold him for a few minutes, he has little freedom to move because of his need for support. Until he develops sufficient eye—hand co-ordination, he is unable to reach for objects he would like to have. Until he has the muscular development to sit, to reach, and to crawl, he has to be content in his crib or on the floor where he can only turn over. His normal but progressive physical development sets the limits to what he is able to do.

Developing Muscular Control

In the first three months, a baby gains some control of the larger muscles used in maintaining his head in an upright position and in manipulating his hands. Toward the end of this period, he will focus his eyes on objects, and approach them with both hands. In the beginning, his fists will be tightly closed. He will grasp a rattle handle so firmly that it will be necessary almost to force his fingers open to remove it from his grasp.

As weeks go on, you will observe that his hands are held open for longer periods of time, and are not so tightly closed around an object. But it will be some time before he will be able to release a toy at will. It is much easier for him to reach out and grasp an object than it is to get rid of it once he has hold of it. During this early period, toys as such are not of prime interest, because there is so little that he can do with them. But they should be available and offered to him. Before toys intrigue him, he would rather watch his hands in motion. He learns to bring them to his mouth, and into contact with each other. Later, as he gains control of his legs and feet, these also become important and he pulls his feet up so that he can watch and play with them.

If Your Baby Is Left-Handed

Parents sometimes wonder if they should make an effort to teach their baby to use his right hand. As he grows up, you may feel it would be more convenient if he were right-handed. But there are many left-handers whose preference is so definite that they resist any attempt to change. Hand preference may appear as early as six to eight months with some infants. Others may continue to use either hand well during the early preschool years. Children differ in the definiteness of the preference too.

Let your baby use his hands in the

way that is natural for him! Left-handed children who are forced to use their right hands are under a strain. This strain may create more difficulties than left-handedness itself.

He Needs to Use His Muscles

It is important for you to anticipate and make possible each developmental step. For the most part, good common sense will tell you what is right for your baby. You will know when he is able to sit with support without discomfort. As you hold him, you can feel the amount of control he has over his head, shoulders, and back. You will sense the difference when he is ready to be bolstered up in a high chair or in the corner of an adult chair. Watch him carefully when he starts sitting up. He should not be allowed to become fatigued or to fall.

It is not necessary to wait until he sits unsupported to remove him from the confines of his crib, for he will have started moving around before this. You can place him on the floor on a blanket or, better still, in a play pen, so that he will have more space to move around. He can enjoy a change from his room. You will not be spoiling him if you move his play pen around so that he can watch you and hear your voice. As he gains control, he will use the sides of the play pen for pulling himself up. That is how he learns what his legs are for.

After he has become fairly expert at pulling himself to a standing position, he may try a few sidewise steps, hanging on to the playpen rail. He will practice walking in this fashion for weeks or even months before he is ready to walk alone. Until he is ready, there is no use hurrying him.

Now he will have a larger area for play with toys. If you put him in a play pen before he has learned to enjoy the freedom of crawling, he will have play space and yet not be exposed to dangers or need constant watching. If he does not learn to enjoy the play pen before he can crawl, you may find that later he rebels when he is restricted. If the location of the play pen still isolates him from companionship with the rest of the family, he may resist being confined in it. A baby wants to be near his mother or other members of the household. He is happier in a walker that permits wider range.

The Beginnings of Speech

Language development begins long before any individual words are used with meaning. Your baby needs to be talked to for the sake of his development, and particularly for his speech. He wants and should have attention, and he gets it in a satisfactory way when someone is talking to him. Then, too, he will learn to talk by imitation. During the first three months, his responses will be cooing and smiling with a show of excitement and pleasure when he recognizes attention directed toward him. It is important for him not only to be able to hear you, but also to see you when you talk and smile.

When Will My Baby Talk?

Gradually, his cooing and squealing will develop into recognizable vowel sounds. Toward his eighth month, you will probably be hearing vowel-consonant combinations such as "da." When he has a variety of sounds at his command, he will often seem to be practicing these over and over, and getting considerable enjoyment from his own vocalizations. During the second half of his first year, certain sound combina-

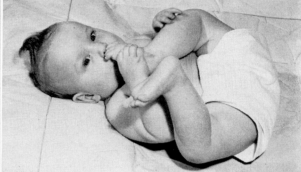

It is a good sign that a baby is developing satisfactorily when something new to look at, to listen to, or to feel, gets an enthusiastic response.

tions may be repeated in relation to persons or things, so that your child has "words."

While words are being developed, he will jabber with inflections as if he were talking, and will continue to pick up new sounds through imitation. During this same period, he is learning to respond to definite sound combinations and the words you use frequently when you are with him. These may be his own name or simple requests, such as waving "by-by" or patty-caking. He will respond by waving by-by when you wave at him. Say "by-by," and gradually he will be able to associate just your spoken word with your request, and will not need your demonstration.

During this first year, your baby will probably have progressed from an infant who could cry when uncomfortable or hungry to one who is responding to words and is beginning to have some way of employing language for his own use. His first words are exciting and will bring pleasure to him because you will be so pleased.

Why Are Some Babies Slow in Talking?

Some babies will be much slower than others in adding to their vocabularies. They may show you their growth and gains through their interest in handling objects. They are developing perfectly well but are not going to be great talkers for a while. It may be frustrating and irritating to such babies to be pushed to talk earlier than their own pattern of growth and development would impel them to. Words, phrases, and sentences come to a baby when there is reason and need, but some babies may not get the same amount of pleasure that others do out of talking. If too much pressure is placed on the infant, with urging and cajoling to repeat words, he may refuse to talk and develop resentment toward the person urging him. This, in turn, would not make him a happy baby.

Touch and Taste Are Teachers

During this first year, along with control and development of his hands and of his senses, your baby will investigate everything within his reach. The right kind of toys will help him develop. The chapter HE LEARNS THROUGH ACTIVITIES AND TOYS, in this volume, suggests useful toys. In the beginning, his way of learning is to carry everything to his mouth. This "mouthing" usually reaches its peak at about six months. After that, the baby's pleasure is centered around what and how he can manipulate, rather than on how objects and toys "taste."

Obviously, if everything is going to his mouth, it is important to remove from his reach objects that may hurt him or that are so small he might choke on them. Toys should be kept reasonably clean. But, after your baby has begun to crawl and progress from place to place, there is no way to have only washed and immaculate toys at his disposal.

He has come a long way from his early activity of watching his hands and moving his head from side to side, to the activity of using objects for his own pleasure. First, play may be no more than bringing one object against another for banging. The baby may get some considerable delight from hitting a spoon against his high-chair tray, waving a rattle, or transferring an object from one hand to the other. As he approaches nine to ten months, he will combine objects better and more frequently. He may bring two blocks together, take crumbs from his high-chair tray and put them in his cup, and then remove them.

Baby's Feelings Develop

Along with physical and mental development, your baby's emotional growth is of great importance during this exciting first year. His world should be a friendly one, full of love. Remember that he is a person, with definite emotional needs. Love and attention will give him a sense of security, of belonging. Of course you will always try to be sensitive to these needs and wise in meeting them. But some mistakes will occur, since parents cannot always be perfect. Fortunately, babies are flexible. In an atmosphere of affection and understanding, they can accept frustration and, as they grow up, learn also to accept reality. The chapter HE FINDS OUT WHO IS IMPORTANT TO HIM, in this volume, discusses how a baby learns to recognize his mother, and what this recognition means.

In the early months, the baby will respond to attention from anyone who is friendly and satisfies his wants. He does not seem to distinguish between family and strangers. In the second half of his first year, he learns to recognize the members of his family. He shows his anxiety, stops activity, and withdraws when outsiders approach. Gradually, if he is allowed to make friends at his own pace and without being overwhelmed, he will accept strangers again.

At the end of the year, a degree of independence has gradually developed. Your baby has found that he can satisfy some of his needs and his curiosity with and sometimes without it. He is an explorer in every way. He is gaining a limited control of his surroundings, and also of you, his family. He has come a long way from that tiny, helpless infant of a year ago. He has established a tempo of growing, reacting, and living with others.

KEEPING A BABY COMFORTABLE

JOHN C. MONTGOMERY, M.D.

Pediatrician, Detroit, Mich.

and

MARGARET JANE SUYDAM, B.S.

Family Service of Cincinnati and Hamilton Counties, Cincinnati, Ohio

A BABY can be fed, changed, bathed, dressed, and put to sleep in a number of acceptable ways and places. Any one of them will keep him quite contented and happy, if he is sure that you love him, are glad to have him, and can be trusted to make him comfortable as soon as he lets you know he needs attention.

Your ability to respond to your baby's needs, to make him comfortable, will depend upon how comfortable you feel about yourself.

Comfortable parents do not set impossible standards of behavior for themselves or their babies. They choose a doctor to advise them, or take their baby to a well-baby clinic. They learn as much as they can about child development, and then they use their own common sense in applying what they have learned. They know that they will make some mistakes, but they also know that babies and young children are really pretty sturdy. A child may suffer briefly from mistakes, but he can bounce back again if his parents comfort him when he cries, feed him when he is hungry, or cuddle him when he seems restless or upset.

Understanding Baby's Ways

Your baby's crying is his first language, his first effort to do something for himself. He is telling you that he needs help. You can learn what his cries mean.

His first and most urgent cries are for food. When this need has been met, other causes for crying can be considered. His clothing or his covers may hold him too tightly in one position. He may have been frightened by a bright light, a loud noise, or sudden and abrupt handling. He may be expressing loneliness or boredom. Many tiny babies cry because they cannot see beyond the sides of the bassinet or baby carriage. When a baby's only accomplishments are looking and listening, he wants to use them. More than one baby has been quieted by the sound of soft music or the sight of a brightly colored ribbon waving in the breeze.

Babies who have had their wants satisfied when they were completely helpless will be the most trusting and most co-operative as they grow. Those who have been left to "cry it out" are the ones who cry often and long. They may grow up to be querulous, demanding children, still seeking the security they never have had.

If all his needs have been satisfied promptly until he is six months old or so, a baby should trust you and his world enough to begin to take gentle restrictions. After he has been fed and loved, he can be put to bed confidently in spite of a little fussing.

What Is Colicky Crying?

Colicky cries are piercing shrieks of pain that let you know the baby is suffering a spasm of his intestines. Since babies on all types of feeding may suffer from colic, doctors think the cause is not related to food. They know that excitement, tension in the family, and noise can make it worse. The colicky baby apparently is one who is finding his adjustment to the world difficult. First babies are more likely to have it than later babies in the family. Most babies outgrow it by the time they are three months old, and grow and gain well in spite of it. Get your doctor's advice on what to do. He may recommend an enema or a hot-water bottle, or prescribe

Your baby does not cry to be annoying. He has something to tell you. Soon you learn what his cries mean.

a sedative. It is likely that the most important thing you can do is to make your own life and the baby's as calm, quiet, and relaxed as possible. Feeding comfort for the baby is discussed in the chapters MOTHER AND CHILD ARE DOING NICELY and FEEDING HAS MANY MEANINGS, in this volume.

Why Do Babies Rock, and Bang Their Heads?

It is not uncommon for babies to rock their beds or bang their heads against the crib. They may find it a way to relieve tension or a way of putting themselves to sleep. The baby is not likely to harm himself, and eventually he will outgrow the practice. You might consider what you can do to make his daytime hours more relaxed, so that he will not build up so much tension. More cuddling, crooning, and quiet play, and more opportunities to do the things he is able to do, may help.

Elizabeth Hibbs

Sleeping Comfort for Baby

A smoothly-made bed of his own, in a reasonably quiet spot that can be darkened when necessary, gives the baby a comfortable place to sleep. Some babies will not object to sleeping in one place by day and being moved to another at night. Others are sensitive to change and will be quite unhappy about it. If a baby must share a bedroom with his parents at first, it is better, for a variety of reasons, to have him out of the room before he is a year old.

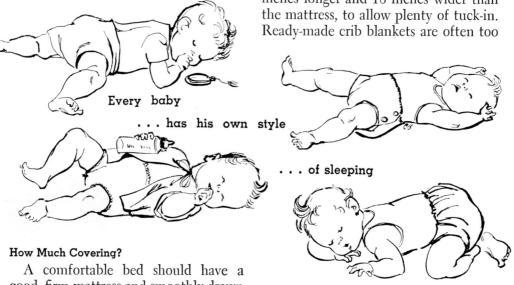

Every baby

. . . has his own style

. . . of sleeping

How Much Covering?

A comfortable bed should have a good, firm mattress and smoothly-drawn sheets. Covering for the baby will depend on the weather. A top sheet is not necessary for the young baby, unless it is used in warm weather as the only cover. Blankets should be lightweight and warm. Bedspreads are not required at all; in fact, they are a nuisance. Pillows are not recommended. Certain of the sleeping-bag arrangements made of blanket material are unsafe, because it is possible for a baby to choke or smother in them.

A crib is a better investment than a bassinet, for cribs can be used longer, and the baby can see out of the sides.

When you make your baby's bed, put a waterproof sheet over the mattress. Put a smooth muslin sheet over the waterproof sheet and tuck it in securely. Place a small waterproof pad where the baby's buttocks will be. Have at hand a top cover, suitable for the temperature, to cover the baby when he sleeps.

The little baby who does not roll around much will not require a full-size blanket to tuck in under the mattress. The older baby will need a blanket 10 inches longer and 18 inches wider than the mattress, to allow plenty of tuck-in. Ready-made crib blankets are often too small to allow for the baby's kicking and still tuck in. You can get the size you need, and save money, too, by cutting down an old blanket from an adult's bed, or making one out of wool flannel bought by the yard.

What Does He Wear for Sleeping?

Baby's sleeping garments will depend upon the weather. In summer a diaper may be all he needs. In many homes where an even temperature can be maintained, babies sleep all winter in shirt and diapers. Other mothers prefer night-gowns or kimonos. As the baby gets older, the two-piece "sleepers" are practical. Most babies are dressed and covered more warmly than they should be. Do not worry about hands and feet being uncovered in mild temperatures. They will not feel as warm as the rest of the baby's body. They are not supposed to.

When you put the baby to sleep, you can put him down on his stomach. It sometimes helps get up bubbles after a feeding. If he does not like sleeping this way, turn him over. Babies usually have definite ideas about the way they like to sleep.

The chapter SOME CHILDREN HAVE TROUBLE SLEEPING in this volume discusses problems in connection with sleep.

Can Babies Sleep Away from Home?

Taking baby with you wherever you go is a fine practice, if you do it in moderation. Subjecting a baby to an undiminished social whirl would scarcely be in his best interests. Some babies are perfectly happy sleeping in strange surroundings, with merriment not too far away. Others can become upset by it. You will have to gear your excursions with your baby to what he seems able to take. What he can take will vary with his age. All places may be alike to a four-month-old baby, but at a year he may become more aware of differences.

Comfortable Bathing for Baby

Bath time should be before a feeding. Have room temperature at about 75°. Then the baby will be comfortable without clothes. You need lukewarm water —too hot or too cold can be a shock to

Cushing

Time for a bath is time for fun, if the room and the water are pleasantly warm and mother is not hurried.

him. Use a mild soap that will not irritate his delicate skin. Be sure you have a good firm grip on him so that he will not be frightened by slipping in the tub.

The canvas and rubber bathinettes are the bathtub choice of many mothers. Others find a dishpan (not the one you use for your dishes!) convenient. The wash bowl may turn out to be the easiest place to bathe the baby.

After you have set a regular time for his bath, you will find the baby looking for it expectantly at the same hour each day.

For the first six weeks, one complete bath a week is as much as your baby needs. Too many baths for the young baby wash away protective oils from his skin, and leave it unnecessarily exposed to infection. After six weeks, a daily bath is a good idea. In hot weather, he will sometimes be happier if he has two.

Bath time can be a social time for the

family. Baby needs a chance to wriggle and stretch and kick a few minutes without any clothes. A baby who gets fussy in the late afternoon can be soothed by a bath. As he grows older, he takes delight in kicking and splashing. Water toys add to his pleasure when he is old enough to reach for them and grasp them. Dad and the older children will enjoy watching him.

How Should a Baby Be Bathed?

You will find it easier if, before you start the bathing, you collect clean clothes, towel, washcloth, and soap. Then have the water ready before you bring the baby to the bath. Use your elbow to test the temperature if you have no thermometer.

Before he goes into the tub, wash the baby's face and the outside of his ears with a cloth wrung out of clear water— no soap. Let nature take care of the inside of his ears and his eyes, nose, and mouth. Babies never did like mothers poking into them, and doctors no longer recommend doing it.

You will get the most secure grip on the tiny baby if you cradle him on your left arm, with his head at your elbow and your left hand under his buttocks. Then your right hand is free to wash him. (Reverse this order if you are left-handed.) You will find it easier to get soap into the creases of neck, arms, and legs if you use your hand instead of a cloth. He will be happier if you can bathe him in a leisurely fashion—not as though his bath were one more chore to be whipped through on schedule. After

you have rinsed off the soap, pat him dry with a big soft towel. Take care in both rinsing and drying that you get into those above-mentioned creases. Neither oils nor powders are necessary to his comfort unless too much bathing has deprived him of the natural oils in his skin.

Dressing is resisted by most babies. To a baby, clothes are a nuisance of the civilized world. To make the best of a bad situation, clothes should be as few as possible, simply made, and big enough to slip on easily.

What if Baby Objects to Baths?

If your baby objects to his bath, he has probably been frightened by some experience you may not recall. The best way to handle him is to build his trust in the bath situation over again. Do not force him to take a bath in the tub. Sponge him off on a towel in your lap

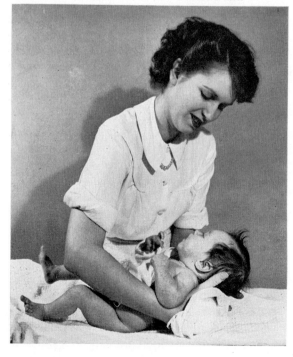

Elizabeth Hibbs

The easier it goes on the better. Perfect fit is less important than perfect comfort for the well-dressed baby.

And so to bed, comfortably sleepy after a relaxing bath. It's a great life!

for a few days, and then try getting him back to the tub by putting less water in it. Try a new toy in the bath, to make it attractive. Hold him securely and talk to him soothingly, pleasantly, and confidently. Gradually he may again be willing to think bathing is an acceptable routine. Never leave a baby alone in his bath, or leave within his reach pins or any other items he should not have.

Baby's Ways of Eliminating

Comfortable parents observe a baby's elimination, but do not worry about it

37

unless there is a real reason for it.

The new baby's elimination, like his heart beat and his breathing, is irregular in the beginning. Then, like these other processes, it settles down to a rhythm of its own. Several bowel movements, or none, may occur in one day, but, eventually, regularity develops. This may prove to be one or two movements a day, or one movement every other day.

Stools of breast- and bottle-fed babies are different. The bottle-fed baby's stool is the more solid. The breast-fed baby's movement is usually soft, almost runny, by contrast. Bottle-fed babies usually have more bowel movements than breast-fed babies. This is because the formula does not meet the baby's nutritional requirements as accurately as breast milk. Unused material in the formula is left to be eliminated. Breast milk may not leave enough waste material for a daily bowel movement.

The small baby's stools are yellowish in color, but take on a greenish cast when exposed to the air. When fruits and vegetables are added to the diet, both consistency and color may change. The stool may be softer and take on the red of beets, or blackish-green of spinach, a day or two after these vegetables have been eaten. Such changes are natural and no cause for alarm. Several loose stools in a day, or an unusually hard stool, should be reported to the doctor.

Constipation in a baby, if it occurs, is more likely to be caused by tension and overanxiety of the parents than by anything else. Tension in the parent handling the baby creates tension in the infant. Automatic alarm is conveyed from one body to the other. The muscles controlling elimination become tense, along with other muscles in his body, and the baby's elimination is affected in this way.

Elimination by the young baby is entirely automatic. It takes place without any control on his part. In this volume, HELPING YOUR CHILD LEARN TO USE THE TOILET discusses the toilet-training question.

Washing Diapers

The burdensome, daily diaper washing is often the reason Mother is so anxious to get Baby "trained." This is understandable. Commercial diaper services are worth even a sacrifice in the budget for the first months of a baby's life. Their use is a twofold gain. Baby's development can proceed in a natural, unhurried fashion that is vital to his emotional welfare, and Mother's strength is conserved as well.

If you wash diapers at home, wet diapers should soak in a covered pail until you wash them. (A step-on garbage can, purchased for the purpose, is a fine container.) Soiled diapers should have the stool dumped in the toilet before putting them to soak. (If you dip the soiled section into the toilet bowl and flush water through it, you can remove some stain, as well as the stool, while it is fresh.)

Diapers should be removed from the soak water and put into a hot suds. Suds should be made from a mild soap or special detergent designed for fine fabrics. The special detergent is best if your water is hard. Thorough rinsing is important. Baby's skin is delicate, and all soap curd should be removed lest irritation develop.

Drying in the sun or in a heated dryer is best. Unironed diapers are more absorbent than ironed ones. If you smooth and fold the diapers as soon as they are dry, you will have them ready for use. If your baby develops a diaper rash, ask your doctor about using one of the new chemicals in the diaper wash. These chemicals get rid of the bacteria which produce the ammonia that is not only irritating to your nostrils, but also to the baby's skin.

Clothing and Equipment

Clothing

3 to 6 shirts, 1 year size.

3 to 4 dozen diapers—largest size. (Need not buy if diaper service furnishes.)

2 or 3 waterproof panties.

3 to 6 nightgowns, 1 year size. (Optional. Some babies live in shirts and diapers.)

2 to 4 receiving blankets. (One yard square cotton flannel. Sometimes used in place of nightgowns on tiny babies.)

2 to 3 sacks or sweaters, 1 year size. (Optional. If used, should be large enough to fit over shirt or gown.)

1 cap or bonnet for cool-weather baby.

1 knitted shawl or bunting for outdoor wear for winter baby.

Unnecessary for the tiny baby: dresses, slips, socks, booties, and bibs.

Bedding for the Baby

2 waterproof sheets, size to cover mattress completely.

3 to 6 sheets. Lightweight, 128-thread count in muslin will be easy to wash, and quick-drying. Stockinette or gauze is preferred by some mothers.

2 or 3 small waterproof pads to be used on top of sheet.

2 blankets. More may be required for severe climates.

Bathing Equipment for Baby

Bathtub—may be folding fabric bathtub, enamelware, or even a large dishpan.

2 to 4 bath towels, 40″ by 40″ size.

2 to 4 washclothes, 12″ by 12″ size.

1 tray or baking pan to hold soap, cotton, and other items used for changing or bathing baby.

Soap—a pure, mild, unscented brand.

Furniture for the Baby (desirable, but not essential)

1 crib—large enough for the child until he is five or six years old.

1 mattress to fit crib.

1 chest of drawers for the baby's clothes.

1 comfortable chair for the mother, for feeding and rocking baby.

1 play pen, by the time the baby is four to six months old.

1 pad for play pen.

1 baby carriage or stroller.

1 highchair or low table and chair. (Latter is safest for feeding and play.)

1 diaper pail. (Necessary if not supplied by diaper service.) New step-on garbage pail serves purpose well.

1 rectal thermometer.

1 room thermometer. (Not essential—nice to have.)

1 bath thermometer. (Not essential—nice to have.)

CLOTHING

BEDDING

BATH

The well-dressed baby needs few clothes. Let simplicity be the keynote in selecting his wardrobe!

Korling

FEEDING HAS MANY MEANINGS

RICHARD E. WOLF, M.D.

Director, Pediatric Psychiatry Clinic,
Children's Hospital, Cincinnati, Ohio

FAR more than the mere intake of food is involved when a baby is fed. Nourishing a baby by offering him food is the first activity that involves him with another person. Mother feeds her baby through a *giving*, helpful activity. Baby receives the food through a *taking* activity. Since Baby's and Mother's first activity together centers around feeding, all human relationship begins around feeding and eating.

Food Stands for Love

Emotional and physical well-being has to do with happiness. It is therefore vital that this first relationship, around food, be a happy one. The chances of later human relationships being successful are good, when feeding and eating experiences in infancy are satisfactory.

What Does He Learn as He Eats?

During his feedings, a baby receives sensations from various parts of his body. These sensations tell him that the world, *his* world, is satisfactory, or that *his* world is uncomfortable and frustrating. If the latter is the case, he feels tense, and not satisfied.

He is *learning about his world* and the

40

people in it through impressions he receives while he takes in food. All attempts to acquire knowledge and learning are a "taking-in process." Satisfactory early feeding experiences become a forerunner of pleasurable and satisfactory learning experiences, not only in toddler days, but during school days, as well.

This is why mothers, fathers, and physicians are trying to help make these earliest, highly personal experiences pleasurable. Early feeding experiences sum up the maxim that it is good to give and good to receive.

How Does He Learn to Wait?

To a baby, food is the symbol of love, security, and well-being. Thus, the way he is fed contributes to the development of his sense of basic trust. Babies are so helpless that they need a sense of basic trust in other human beings if they are to achieve happiness in a human world.

A sense of basic trust means the ability to wait. The baby develops that ability gradually, but steadily. As he feels the need for something, and receives gratification of that need from his mother or his father, he discovers through the months and years that it is safe to wait. When he has learned that food will be forthcoming, he has taken a first step in emotional development. This lesson cannot be mastered completely in the first months of life.

Mother Spells Comfort

As a baby receives immediate gratification of his hunger, he builds up an im-

Eating is more than meat and drink to a baby. Eating is his work and his recreation. It takes the place of achievement and sociability in his life, and he eats with his whole being.

pression of Mother as a loving gratifier. At first it is the milk in his mouth and the stimulation of his lips that gives him pleasurable sensations as he sucks upon the nipple. In a little while, Mother's arms and voice and the infant's dawning realization of her face become fused and associated with this sense of well-being through a relationship with her. A baby needs to receive food-gratification fairly soon after he is aware of his need. Then he can build impressions of the world as a comforting place, of his mother as a comforting person, and of other human beings as contributors to his sense of trust.

How Often Shall Baby Be Fed?

Most babies set their own patterns for eating within the first six weeks of life. If Mother's emphasis is on her own peace of mind in the feeding experience, and on Baby's sense of well-being in his eating experiences, it matters little whether the intervals between feedings are constant or variable. As in so many other aspects of child-rearing, the *how* things go is more important than *what* is happening. With this as a goal, Mother and Father will conduct the

Korling

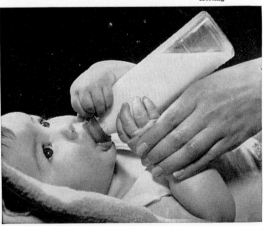

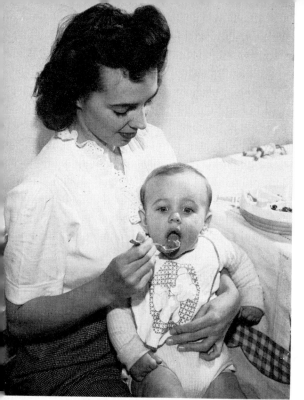

A. Devaney

Babies are conservative about accepting new flavors and textures in foods. Easy does it when you are introducing something new for His Nibs' dinner.

Babies are conservative about accepting new flavors and textures in foods. Easy does it when you are introducing something new for His Nibs' dinner.

early feedings with a respect for their own personality needs as well as the growing needs of the baby.

Some mothers and babies get along well by following the rhythms of Baby's hunger. This plan is called *demand-feeding*. Many mothers are more comfortable with a set but flexible schedule for the infant's eating. Many a mother needs to feel that, having fed her baby before she goes to bed, the chances are slight that he will awaken from hunger during the night. The understanding physician can help a mother decide whether a flexible schedule or following the baby's hunger rhythm harmonizes with her own personality. Some of the techniques of nursing a baby are discussed in the chapter MOTHER AND CHILD ARE DOING NICELY, in this volume.

When Do You Stop Night Feedings?

There is rhythm between the new-born baby's requirements for food intake and his sleep, just as there is a rhythm to all life. The baby sleeps, awakens with hunger, eats, and goes back to sleep. He is awake but a few hours out of the twenty-four. Gradually, with growth, he becomes more aware of his surroundings, and the rhythm becomes more complicated. He is now awake sometimes when he is not hungry. It is important for a young baby to learn that it is fun to be awake and to hear Mother's voice. He feels her arms as she rocks him or carries him about, and he finds there are other pleasures besides eating. Sleep should remain an independent activity that is enjoyed of and for itself, and for the passive relaxation that it brings.

It is important for parents to separate eating and sleeping practices for young children. Eating is one thing, and there is a time and a place for it. The relaxation of the nap or the night sleep is another activity. It is gratifying of itself, and should not require an accompanying bottle.

When a baby is able to take enough food during the day to meet his nutritional needs, and when he receives enough nourishment for his spirit and his emerging personality through his eating, he begins to sleep through the night. By this, he is telling you he is ready to stop night feedings.

If a baby is small, or for any reason unable to receive adequate food gratification during the day, night feedings may continue to be necessary. Your doctor can help you decide whether the continuation of the waking at night is really a need for food, or the expression of something else.

The Road to a Good Appetite

A physically healthy and well-developed baby has a healthy appetite. You can respect that appetite and offer enough food to gratify it. Baby eats for himself because it is fun.

"I can't get him to eat for me" suggests a disturbance in the personal relationship rather than in the appetite or need for nourishment. *One person cannot make another person eat!* Attempting to force food upon a baby or older infant robs him of the pleasure that there is in eating when he is hungry. At the same time, it brings unpleasantness and resentment into his relationship with the person offering him food.

Babies will be hungrier at one meal than at another, but a sudden loss of appetite bears looking into. It may be a sign of some kind of upset.

How Do You Introduce New Foods?

During your baby's first year, he learns to eat a variety of foods. His first experiences in eating revolve around the breast or the bottle, but it is not long before your physician, or your well-baby clinic, suggests introducing semisolid foods.

A baby who has enjoyed breast or bottle is ready to enjoy foods other than milk. But he needs time to learn how to enjoy food that is placed on a spoon and put in his mouth by someone else. To the baby, the spoon almost seems an obstacle to eating! The muscles of the mouth, face, and tongue are used in a different way in conveying food from a spoon to the back of the mouth than in making sucking motions on a nipple. Sometimes it looks as if the baby does not like the new semisolid food, because it keeps coming to the front of the mouth, rather than being carried back and swallowed.

If you spend some time in allowing your baby to *learn* new ways of eating, you are insuring a healthy attitude toward food. Again, the *how* that the foods are received is infinitely more important at the outset than the *actual amount* or the variety.

It is important to consider that even young children have food likes and dislikes. An infant may push aside a certain brand of puréed vegetable, and show pleasure over a competitive brand. As one mother said, "You'd think he could read the ads." If you are gentle and flexible as you experiment with new foods, if you are interested in keeping your baby happy and well-nourished, rather than in being able to brag about how many different foods he is eating, you will be fostering a good appetite.

Some babies are lazy eaters, but even such a baby should not be distracted and fed "when he is not looking." The

43

feeding should proceed of and for itself as long as Baby indicates he is still hungry.

What Does Change in Appetite Mean?

Sometimes you may notice a distinct change in appetite. Adult appetites vary from day to day, and even from hour to hour within the same day. Children are entitled to some variation in appetite, too. Variation does not mean a sudden loss of appetite. When Baby has a sudden loss of interest in food, it is important to determine whether this represents the onset of an acute illness, or whether something has happened in the feeding experience to cause him to push away food. He is not "trying to get away with something" when he does not eat. He may be sick or he may be troubled.

When Shall I Wean My Baby?

Your doctor or your well-baby clinic can help you decide when to wean your baby from the breast to the bottle.

Weaning is life's first frustration, just as nursing the breast or the bottle is life's first gratification. When Baby has been on the breast and starts to drink from a bottle, he begins to learn that someone other than Mother may be a source of gratification.

Many mothers need the security of knowing that their babies can take a bottle in place of a breast feeding and continue to do well. Your doctor may recommend occasional bottle feedings, even for a breast-fed baby. Many fathers need the opportunity to express their feelings of fatherliness and giving, through bottle feeding. Mother and Father can share the pleasure in giving to Baby. In doing so, they are also giving support and help to each other in a true partnership.

When Do You Start with a Cup?

You can begin to let a baby drink from a cup in early infancy. Some babies enjoy orange juice from a small cup when as young as six weeks. The bottle and the cup may be on the same bill of fare. Most babies are ready to give up the bottle or the breast as the only way of taking milk by nine to twelve months of age. Some babies seem to need the bottle longer. If Baby has had to depend more on his bottle for comforts, weaning should be postponed. Sometimes, other interests or problems have so occupied the mother that Baby's main source of gratification has been his bottle. Until other sources of gratification, such as his pleasure in Mother's or Father's company, can be increased, his bottle should not be taken from him. If he is over-dependent upon the bottle to get to sleep at night, or if the bottle is the only way he takes food, something may be troubling him. This is a situation where the doctor's help will be needed.

When a baby is weaned from the breast or bottle to the cup, he needs to be provided with many other sources of gratification. The chapter HE LEARNS THROUGH ACTIVITIES AND TOYS in this volume suggests what he can enjoy now. The question of thumb-sucking is discussed in the chapter HE DISCOVERS HIS OWN BODY in this volume.

Preparing Baby's Food

In our interest in attitudes toward infant feeding, the actual *method of making* a formula must not be overlooked. Actually, formula-making is so simple that every mother can do it correctly and easily. Ask your physician to *write out* the liquid ingredients for Baby's formula in ounces, and the sugar or sirup in tablespoons, to avoid confusion.

Bottles come in different shapes and sizes. Wide-mouthed ones are easy to wash and to fill. Narrow-necked ones take less storage space in the refrigerator. Larger bottles are useful for formula, smaller ones for water or juice. Each has a nipple guard.

Bottles and nipples must be thoroughly cleaned. Soak them in hot water and non-poisonous detergent to remove milk scum. Use bottle brush to get rid of any remaining milk rings.

Fifteen minutes of boiling in water bath in tightly covered kettle or pressure cooker sterilizes bottles and finishes a formula. Place bottles in rack or on towel to prevent breaking. Handle with care!

Most mothers find it convenient to prepare a twenty-four hour supply. You can save yourself steps if you keep together utensils and ingredients you use in making a formula.

The nursing bottles may be sterilized *first* by boiling in a large kettle. Or bottles containing the prepared formula may be sterilized *last* by placing them in a bath of water and allowing it to boil for 15 minutes. This is the method called "terminal sterilization." Since all formulas use boiled water, have the water boiling in the kettle before you start. As long as the milk used is pasteurized (evaporated, whole, or homogenized), there is no need to boil the milk. In fact, evaporated or homogenized milk should *not* be boiled. Whether bottles are sterilized first or last, whether formulas are refrigerated in individual nursing bottles or in bulk, makes no difference to your baby. The important thing is that the formula always be prepared carefully and refrigerated promptly.

What Is in a Formula?

All formulas consist of cow's milk or a milk-derivative in either liquid or powdered form; boiled water; and carbohydrate (sugar, corn sirup, or a commercially prepared brand of modified carbohydrate). If you have these ingredients ready, and the bottles prepared, it is a simple matter to mix the ingredients in a container by measuring first the appropriate amount of boiled water, then adding the sugarlike preparation, and, finally, the milk. If a powdered milk is used, add the boiled water and the sugar preparation to the powder and stir well. Once mixed, the total amount of formula may be divided into the appropriate number of nursing bottles and placed in the refrigerator. Sometimes it is more

convenient to store the day's formula in a sterilized quart bottle.

Heat the nursing bottle of formula by standing it in a bottle-warmer or a saucepan of hot water, just before feeding time. Test the temperature of the milk by allowing a few drops of milk to fall on your wrist. The holes in the nipple should be large enough to allow milk to drip freely when the bottle is turned over.

When Baby's Diet Broadens

The canned soups, vegetables, meats, fruits, and desserts have now so simplified feeding that you can have just that much more time to enjoy your baby. The canned baby foods are as nutritious, clean, and appetizing to the baby as any home-prepared food. There is little, if any, difference in cost when labor, gas, and electricity are considered. Cover any unused portion of baby food and return it to the refrigerator so that it can be used again. The old bugaboo about food left in metal cans becoming "tainted" is not valid, but all the baby's food should be refrigerated promptly.

Before the teeth he uses for chewing have come through, a baby handles puréed foods well. Later, when he has teeth for "choppers," he can have either commercially prepared chopped foods or foods from the table cut to "bite size."

Confidence to Grow on

Upon the firm foundation of gratification in feeding, of the giving and receiving of affection, is built a healthy personality that leads a child to develop into a happy, constructive individual. This process involves growth. Food and the experiences around eating provide the elements for the growth of personality as well as for the growth of the body.

Korling

HELPING YOUR CHILD LEARN TO USE THE TOILET

A. GENEVIEVE TRAINHAM,
R.N., M.A.

Consultant in Development and Problems
of Infants and Children, Detroit, Mich.

For the child, learning bowel and bladder control is an important experience in growing from babyhood to childhood. Achieved in an atmosphere of understanding guidance, it can be a natural step in the development of self-control, self-esteem, and a confident attitude toward all kinds of learning.

Relationship the Foundation

For a mother, this is another opportunity to guide her child's growth toward behavior and attitudes that our world finds useful and acceptable.

By the time your toddler is ready, and interested in using the toilet, you and he have had time to become warm, intimate friends. You can both find satisfaction in this new achievement, if you continue to respect him even in his early awkward and sometimes faulty attempts to gain this highly valued control.

"Learning," Not "Training"

A generation or two ago, mothers were in a great hurry to teach babies to stay clean and dry, but babies were in no way ready to learn. As a result, severe measures were often used in an attempt to impose this aspect of social behavior upon bewildered infants.

Now we know it is the baby's *learning* that is important, not a *training* imposed by Mother. Now we are told "wait until a child is ready."

As a rule, young babies do not find being soiled particularly unpleasant. Most people who have observed toddlers believe they have a different reaction.

Your toddler wants to do the grown-up

47

thing. He has found out that using the toilet is a distinct advance toward that desirable state of being more like the grownups he admires and wants to imitate. By the time he is a year and a half or two years old, occasionally earlier, he is likely to find being clean and dry more comfortable than being soiled or wet. He may often call your attention to the fact that he is wet or soiled. Now you will certainly want to consider whether he is ready to begin to learn control, and how you can give him opportunities to use the toilet.

Do Children Train Themselves?

Some mothers will tell you, "I just skipped the whole business, and one fine day Susie began using the toilet and that was all there was to it." Again you may hear, "Eventually they'll use the toilet, so why bother? Training a youngster is old-fashioned."

Both of these statements are inaccurate. Neglecting toilet training completely can cause trouble, just as overdoing it does. It is true that many children seem to acquire control easily and quickly, if you start them on the toilet when they themselves are really interested.

In teaching this control, just as in supporting other kinds of learning, it is a parent's job to *provide the opportunity to take the new step.* You can take advantage of the time when a child is ready to learn, and make it easier. It makes no difference whether it is a matter of learning to put on shoes, to read, or to use the toilet. Children rarely teach themselves.

Using the toilet is one of the ways children take on responsibility in our world. It is one of the big steps in the chain of responsibilities assumed in the course of growing up. Children need opportunities to practice being responsible. There is a sensible, middle-of-the-road course between intense, severe overemphasis on bowel and bladder control and complete neglect of any teaching. Either of the extreme courses is confusing to a young child who is trying to discover and fit into the pattern of life his parents follow.

Why Is Training So Important to Mothers?

Since the way you feel about your

With these aids you will do better. If work piles up, they see you through.

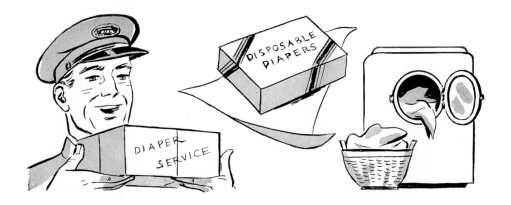

baby's control of his elimination plays a great part in his learning, it may be worth taking a look at your own feelings. In many neighborhoods and in many families, a baby who stays clean and dry at an early age is considered a credit to his mother. Every time one of your neighbors says, almost accusingly, "Still using diapers!" you begin to wonder whether you are a failure.

Cleanliness was undoubtedly drilled into you when you were small. It is hard to be relaxed about anything connected with elimination when your own upbringing said "keep clean, or be shamed."

The idea of time-consuming diaper washing may make it difficult for you to accept the idea of delaying toilet training. Between the commercial diaper wash, disposable tissues to use inside the diaper, and washing machines that wash and sterilize, the task of washing diapers has been cut down immeasurably for a great many mothers. If you cannot have one of these labor-saving devices, you can often have another, or you can at least make use of one or another when work piles up. The number of diapers the baby needs will gradually grow smaller, anyway. If you do make the diaper-washing period easier for yourself, and wait till your baby is ready to learn control, you may find it pays off in greater family happiness and in your child's taking full responsibility for his own toileting sooner. If you are washing diapers yourself, you will find helpful suggestions in the chapter KEEPING A BABY COMFORTABLE, in this volume.

Certainly, you can often catch the baby at the crucial moment, long before he understands what all the fuss is about. Then it is Mother who is being trained, not Baby! He may or may not be ready, even though you are succeeding in catching his body waste for *him*.

Behavior, Clue to Readiness

Usually, there is little gain in starting to put a baby on the toilet before he can

When a child is ready to learn toilet routines, he may become fascinated by the bathroom and everything in it.

He may want to play often with water.

He may even take you by the hand and lead you to the bathroom sometimes.

walk, although walking itself is not necessarily a sign of readiness. Often, when a mother has succeeded in keeping her baby from soiling before he learned to walk, she finds he is resistant to being placed on the toilet after he begins to run around. As every mother knows, when a baby begins to walk his concentration is almost entirely on his new achievement and the explorations now within his reach.

Your child may tell you *after* he has had a bowel movement, or has wet diapers, not *before*, but that is still a sign of progress. A great interest in playing in water, and in the toilet itself, is another frequent clue that the time to start using the toilet has arrived.

Some children squat to have bowel movements in their diapers. They, too, are advancing. They are aware of elimination. Many mothers report that a toddler will go to a certain corner of the room, or perhaps into a closet, and have a bowel movement in his diapers, or take them off and release the movement on the floor.

The ability to make himself understood in words, and the interest and willingness to take a large share in responsibility for toilet control, frequently occur at about the same time. This may be because a child's self-esteem is stepped up as he finds himself able to communicate as other persons do. The new attainment, speech, spurs him on to try yet another kind of learning, self-control of elimination.

Seeing other children go to the toilet is useful, if a youngster is to get the idea easily. Some children may be interested in watching, but show no interest in copying, the behavior for several months. It is advisable to give them an occasional opportunity anyway.

Why Are Girls Ready Sooner?

It is well known to those who have studied children that more girls are "fast growers" than boys. While some "fast growers" among the boys are ready to achieve toilet control as early as most girls, many more of them are later in their readiness than are girls. Similarly, a few slow growers among the girls may be relatively late in readiness for this learning. In the chapter How Do CHILDREN GROW?, in Volume 12, there is discussion of fast growers and slow growers.

If you take the baby or the toddler for regular check-ups, your doctor can help you in determining readiness.

Starting to Use the Toilet

A child who feels sure of his parents' love will tend to be friendlier and more ready for all kinds of learning. Trust in his mother is more important than anything else. Many other influences also enter in, as this chapter and the chapter in this volume, SOME CHILDREN RESIST THE TOILET, point out.

When you have decided, with the help of your doctor, that your toddler is ready to be introduced to toilet routines, watch to see when he usually has a bowel movement, if he has a regular time. Many babies have more than one bowel movement in the course of a day. Even with those who have no regular rhythm, one movement may occur at about the same time daily.

You can put the baby on the toilet at about the same time for a few days. Do not make him sit there more than a few minutes. If he protests, if he does not seem to understand, do not be disappointed. Your good-humored patience does much to further his progress.

About this time you may find your youngster waking up dry occasionally

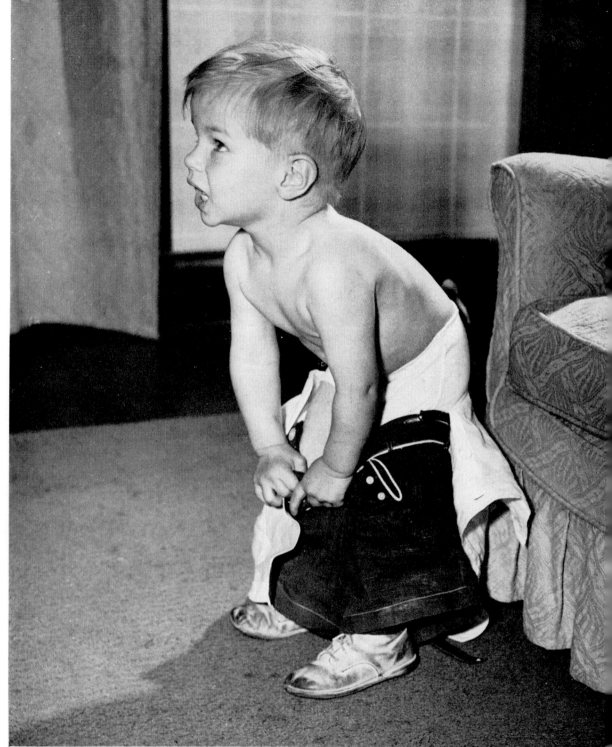

He is so proud of being on his own in toileting that he insists on undressing completely every time a trip to the bathroom is necessary. That, too, is progress!

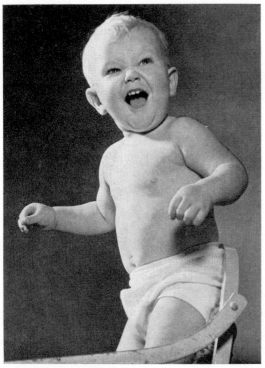
Korling

**Out of diapers and into training pants!
What a boost for two-year-old morale!**

after a nap. Put him on the toilet after a "dry nap." When you and your child are in the bathroom for other purposes, if he has been dry for a time, try putting him on the toilet. In this way you capitalize on the probability of his need to urinate, and you avoid creating resistance by interrupting his play.

It is helpful to use the same words each time. Words that the child will continue to use are preferable. Thus, the words, the time, and the place all become associated.

You may have to make several false starts before your youngster begins to use the toilet. Above all, do not give him the idea—and try to avoid the idea yourself—that using the toilet means "being good" and that failing to use it means "being bad." Success can be approved as

other kinds of successes are, but lack of success should never be a cause for disgrace or scolding. The exact steps you take will count less than a friendly, confident, encouraging attitude. At first, using the toilet for one bowel movement a day is enough to expect.

You might think that some mechanical means of getting a child to move his bowels at the desired time, such as a suppository, would be helpful. It is harmful, rather than a help, for he does not understand what you are trying to accomplish. In his second year a youngster is trying to become an individual capable of acting on his own. There is something overwhelming, confusing, and frightening in any situation that deprives him of this control. Never use a suppository or an enema, unless your doctor has told you to do so in a specific instance.

How Is Bladder Control Established?

Some children learn to use the toilet for urinating soon after they have achieved bowel control. (Some boys control urination first.) There are others who may continue wetting for several months. The large majority can learn control during the daytime at somewhere between the ages of one and a half and two and a half years.

It is better to put off any efforts to teach bladder control until a toddler can stay dry for at least two hours at a time. One mistake you can avoid is being so intensive in your teaching that your child spends half his time being taken to the toilet, resisting going to the toilet, or listening to you ask if he needs to go.

When you start teaching him to urinate in the toilet, you might also promote him from diapers to training pants. Training pants instead of diapers are a sign of your confidence in his ability to stay dry, and he is more aware of wetness and soiling. He may accomplish staying dry in a few weeks. It may take longer.

Little boys can more readily stand up to urinate if you provide a sturdy step for them to stand on at the toilet. Be sure the box, step, or whatever it may be is sufficiently solid, for a feeling of shakiness and insecurity may be frightening and discouraging.

Your child may tell you in some way —depending on how well he can use words—when he needs to go to the toilet. Answer this request promptly, but without fuss. If it is some time before he takes responsibility for telling you, ask him, or lead him to the toilet when it is clearly necessary. For a while you cannot expect consistent dryness. There may also be setbacks if he is ill or worried.

Toilet Seat or Potty?

The word "toilet" has been used here for convenience, but often the low chair made to fit over a small chamber pot is more comfortable for a small child. The wood or plastic seat with arms, that fastens on the toilet itself, may seem alarmingly high and unsteady to some children between the ages of one and two. The noise of the flushing of the toilet

A sturdy box as a step-up keeps a toilet seat from seeming alarmingly high.

Rae Russell

may be frightening. There is something frightening, too, in the finality of things being flushed away. The toddler may have the awful feeling that he might, without warning, be flushed away, too.

To other children, the toilet seat fastened onto the toilet has the advantage of seeming more like what other members of the household use, and therefore is preferable. You may need to experiment to see whether your youngster prefers the low nursery chair or the seat on the family toilet. If you have run into difficulty, a change from one to the other may help.

A Good Moment "Family-Wise"

Any new step requires a great deal of a toddler's energy. It is best to start toileting at a time when things are going smoothly. Of course, you will choose a time when the child's own health is good, to start this new kind of learning. There are a few crucial times to avoid. Just before or after a new baby arrives, or the family has moved, are clearly not good moments to start a new kind of learning. If there has been some special change in family ways, let well enough alone and avoid adding any strain.

Staying Dry at Night

Children usually wake up from their naps dry at about the time they begin to establish daytime control. Then comes the question, "Shall we pick her up during the night?" The goal in all your teaching about control of elimination is to have the child take the responsibility. Picking up a child at night does not seem to hasten the time he stays dry without being awakened.

Some parents wonder if rewards or stars on a chart would speed up or reinforce a youngster's nighttime control.

Rewards are always a two-edged sword, for they point up failures and may make a child anxious. Stars on a chart soon lose their meaning for a small child, and also emphasize failure in an unfortunate way.

Some children do not stay dry at night until the age of three or three and a half. For some, especially some boys, it may be even later. There may be occasional accidents for some time after that, especially at times of physical or emotional upset. The youngster who has learned to stay dry at night, and then lapses into frequent bed-wetting several months or years later, is another matter altogether. The chapter in this volume, on SOME CHILDREN RESIST THE TOILET, discusses this problem.

Confidence Is the Keynote

Some of your child's behavior as he learns to control elimination may puzzle you. Interest in looking at, talking about, and even handling the waste products of his own body is quite natural in a year-and-a-half or a two-year-old. If you understand what his behavior means to him, you will not find it upsetting. In the second year, children are extremely conscious of themselves as separate, independent beings, able to act on their own. They are proud of, and interested in, everything about themselves and everything they do. They will be less interested in body wastes when control is so easy that it no longer needs great concentration of effort.

During the weeks or the months that you are teaching your small child to use the toilet, you need to remember that the fact that he stays clean and dry is not nearly as important as the feelings that he acquires along the way about himself and about you.

HE DISCOVERS HIS OWN BODY

DONOVAN J. McCUNE, M.D.

Pediatrician, Permanente Hospital, Vallejo, Calif.

AS AN adult, you are aware of a large number of physical, emotional, and mental traits that, taken together, make up "yourself." Without this sense of self, you could hardly carry on the business of living, or establish relations with other persons. The unborn infant has no sense of self. He is in many respects simply a part of his mother. How does he gain this necessary sense of being an individual?

Although birth itself creates a certain amount of independence, the baby must have a great deal of experience before his distinctive personality is fully developed. During the first year of life, much of this experience comes to an infant from the discovery and exploration of his own body. Getting to know his own body plays an important part in the baby's mental and emotional development, and is absorbingly interesting to him.

How Do You Handle His Crying?

In all likelihood, the first thing that tells the infant that he has a body is the shock of being born. Thrust out from the warm, liquid environment of the uterus into the cold, dry air of the world is a shock. To this unpleasant news he responds by crying. This is a useful reaction, for it opens his lungs and ensures a supply of oxygen to the blood. The sensation of hunger, the next evidence

Combine

"My own foot is a wonderful toy! Always where I can reach it and Mother doesn't worry that I'll swallow it."

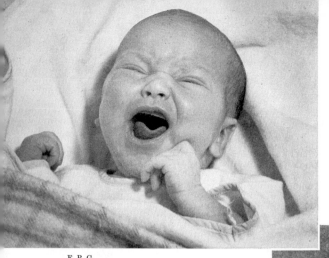

F. P. G.

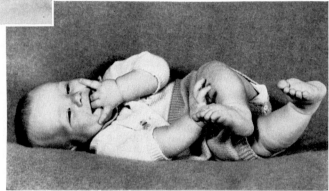

All babies live "from hand to mouth." It's a necessary step in growing up.

Elizabeth Hibbs

Crying is the only way a small baby can assert himself. It isn't misbehavior and it should not be ignored. He needs you!

he has that he is alone, is also unpleasant. This, too, he announces by crying. A little later comes the need to eliminate body waste. The attitude toward moving his bowels varies. Some infants apparently do not notice it. Others grunt, strain, or cry during the act. Still others give signs of dissatisfaction only after they have lain for some time in a soiled diaper.

The common response to these three types of stimulation is to cry. The way you answer this cry has an important bearing upon your baby's emotional development. Even during the first few days of life, your baby is amazingly sensitive to the moods of the persons around him. Babies sense tenseness, apprehension, insecurity, and anger, just as surely as they feel calmness and warmth.

Parents—particularly the parents of first children—should realize that the crying of newly-born and young infants is chiefly an automatic performance. It does not signify the conscious distress that it does later. It should be regarded as a signal for calmly-taken appropriate action, and need not cause you concern. But do not ignore it, for it does mean that a baby needs attention.

Hands Are a Great Discovery

One of the first things the baby discovers is his hands. Even before birth, he can get his fingers partly into his mouth.

It is instructive to watch the behavior of a newly-born infant. As he begins to feel hungry, he becomes increasingly wakeful and restless. After a time his hand is brought tentatively toward his mouth, but does not get there at once. He cries with annoyance. After several false tries, the hand enters his mouth. He sucks ravenously, and gives a series of contented grunts.

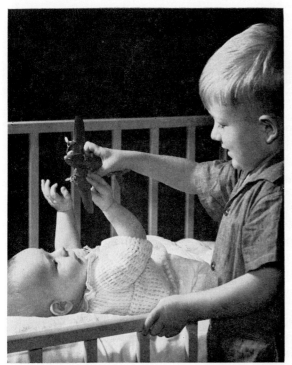
Century Photos

Why Does He Suck His Thumb?

Hand-sucking is a great solace to the baby's unappeased hunger. This is not hard to understand. But what about the infant who eats until he appears ready to burst, who may even spit up a little from his overstuffed stomach, and who then starts munching upon his hand?

This bit of behavior is the earliest inkling we have that the human being secures deep satisfaction from the use of his mouth. There is no fundamental difference between the baby who sucks his hand or thumb and the adult in whose mouth a cigarette, cigar, pipe, or chewing gum may often be found. The chapter YOUR CHILD'S TEETH in this volume discusses why babies suck their thumbs, why it should be permitted, and the effect on a child's teeth and jaws.

Thumb-sucking satisfies a real need in babies and should be allowed. Giving a baby over six months old some plaything

He has learned to use his hands to reach for something! How wide the world that opens up to him now!

that is more interesting than his thumb is always a sensible move. After the first few months, you can occasionally gently and casually remove a baby's hand from his mouth as you hand him a toy. If you do no more than that, no harm will be done. If the sucking is due only to habit, it will usually yield promptly.

What About Persistent Thumb-Sucking?

If thumb-sucking persists beyond the second year, it is evidently satisfying some unexplained need. In such cases, it is better to try to give a small child more affection and more satisfaction in his daily life. If sucking a thumb gives him the comfort he needs, matters will not be improved by attempting to take that comfort away, for the cause of his distress will not be removed.

Usually the demand to suck diminishes toward the middle of the second year. Sometimes it persists considerably longer. Until kindergarten days, many youngsters find a thumb in the mouth a comfortable way to go to sleep. Not a few first-graders under stress bolster their morale by this device. Persistent thumb-sucking frequently results from efforts to stop it when the baby actually needed the sucking experience, or when it served some other purpose.

In some children, a thumb in the mouth may be an instinctive gesture of protest against growing up. This reluctance to grow up is fairly easy to understand in some instances. When a new baby arrives in the family it is reasonably clear that the two-, three-, or four-year-old would like to be a baby, too. When

57

he sucks his thumb or fingers he lets us know how he feels, and he also attempts to solve his problems. Helping him over this difficulty is discussed in the chapter SOMETIMES RIVALS, SOMETIMES FRIENDS, in Volume 12.

There may be other and deeper reasons why a small child is not prepared to accept permanently the trials and tribulations of being a two- or three-year-old instead of a baby. The chapter WHEN CHILDREN ARE ANXIOUS, in this volume, considers cases of persistent thumb-sucking in two-, three-, and four-year-olds, and offers ways of handling them.

Is All Exploration Desirable?

Fingers and toes are not the only great discoveries. Sucking is so universal, regardless of age, that most parents, even though they may look at it askance, seem to appreciate its meaning. But parents are usually less understanding, and correspondingly less tolerant, of certain other kinds of exploration babies find absorbing. Adults often fail to realize that the baby cannot read, turn on the radio, or otherwise amuse himself as we do. He has only the exploration of the limited area of his own body as a means of entertainment much of the time.

Protruding parts that can be handled, and body cavities accessible to exploration with the fingers, are of particular interest to a baby. In addition to their preoccupation with fingers and toes, many infants will pull at their ears, handle their noses, or finger their genitals. All these activities have precisely the same meaning. They provide occupation for the hands and help satisfy legitimate curiosity. They help the child become aware of his own identity as a person. For reasons best known to themselves, some infants settle upon a favorite ear and pull at it so habitually as to lead to a suspicion of ear trouble.

Bearing in mind the inborn human fondness for hiding and rediscovery, it is not difficult to understand why infants, toddlers, and even older children hide small objects, such as peas, buttons, or crayons, in the ear canals, in their noses, and occasionally in openings more difficult of access. Psychologically, for the most part, these practices are above reproach. They are objectionable only because of the fact that these foreign bodies, once introduced, often cannot be withdrawn, and may cause hardness of hearing, or a discharge from the nose or other openings.

Graphic House

One-year-olds or four-year-olds may still be thumb-suckers in moments of discomfort or boredom, or if all Mother's attention goes to someone else.

Babies Discover Various Organs

In the course of their explorations, babies discover their external genital organs. It is generally believed that early approaches to the reproductive organs have not the meaning to a baby that they have to an older child. Sometimes they introduce the baby to the pleasurable sensation of handling the genitals, and may cause him to indulge in the activity for a short period of time. It is not necessary to take a baby's hands away from the reproductive organs when he touches them. In fact, doing so tends to fix his interest on those areas. In the infant and toddler, handling the genitals is merely a phase of self-exploration and need cause no concern. It will persist only in infants who suffer grave emotional starvation, such as those who are blind, or those who are confined to hospital beds or to institutions for long periods.

Occasionally, fingering the genitals continues after it has ceased to be a field of exploration or a source of pleasure, and has become largely a habit. In such cases you can provide new interests and toys to encourage a youngster in using his hands in other ways. Under no circumstances should a child be blamed or punished. Both serve only to give the activity undesirable prominence in the small child's mind and to arouse resistance. No harm can come from a baby or a small child's handling his genitals, but harm can come if he is made to feel this to be seriously wrong.

Experiments with Noise

The baby's discovery of his ability to make new noises opens another kind of exploration to him. This he frequently practices until you may begin to doubt that he is mentally sound (or that you can stay that way). There is also the

Rae Russell

He may try out his noise-making ability at the most inconvenient times. Let him know when and where it is all right to be as noisy as he pleases.

time when your baby, who previously slept through the night, finds that by one means or another he can create chaos in the household during the early morning hours, and tests this new ability until he has learned its limits. In this volume, the chapter Some Children Have Trouble Sleeping takes up this question.

You need not try to keep in mind a list of the activities the experts label "exploratory." All you need remember is that most of the things the baby does that you find a little hard to understand fall into this category. By a slight stretch of imagination, you will find it more possible to understand why babies act as they do. Then you can offer opportunities for them to go on to new steps in development.

59

HE FINDS OUT WHO IS IMPORTANT TO HIM

KATHERINE M. WOLF, Ph.D.

Associate Professor, Child Study Center,
Yale University, New Haven, Conn.

Suzanne Szasz

Recent studies have given us a clearer understanding of the vital part that recognition of the mother plays in a baby's development. Your baby's behavior will be more understandable, and you will be better able to co-operate with the forces of development, if you know how this recognition comes about and how it affects an infant.

The newborn feels best if he does not feel anything happening inside himself or in his surroundings. He seems quiet and peaceful if he is not tortured by hunger, thirst, or pain, if he is not disturbed by loud noise, glaring light, or a sudden draught of air.

The world, which later on will be the field of conquest, with its stimulation of joy, work, play, and love appears only as a threat to the newborn infant.

Mother—A Savior in Distress

In the life of even the most sheltered infant, disturbances cannot be avoided. Every baby experiences hunger and thirst. When he wets his diaper, he feels cold. These disturbances disappear when the infant is fed, when his diapers are changed.

No imagination can possibly transmit to us what it would feel like to live as a newborn baby does, in a world that is only a threat and a shock. But we are able—at least to a certain degree—to figure out what it means to be relieved of overwhelming disturbances when we are completely powerless. Every time the baby is fed, or his diapers are changed, he is saved from distress, his peace is restored.

However different these experiences may be for the infant, they have two things in common. He feels the disturbance disappearing, and his mother's face appears in his surrounding world.

At Whom Does a Baby Smile?

It is not mere speculation that the baby learns to associate relief from distress and tension with the sight of the human face. If you want proof, watch how his uncertain glance focuses on faces in his second month. The baby in his third month really smiles for the first time, and he smiles at the sight of the human face.

An infant smiles not just at his mother, but at everyone who speaks or nods or smiles at him for the first few months of his life. That does not mean he does not *recognize* his mother. It would be more accurate to say that in every face he sees he "recognizes" his mother.

This smiling response to any human being is more characteristic for some children than for others. Each baby observed at the Child Study Center at Yale University, where a careful study of this phase of development was made, had his own way of responding. Sammy smiled radiantly at everybody who approached him, for months and months. Alice's smile was first observed in relation to her mother, and only after that in relation to others. Barbara's smile never had quite the same vigor and intensity when it was directed toward strangers. But the first smile of all the babies was a smile at a person.

An Interesting World Dawns

When the sight of the human being has become a signal that satisfying events are to be expected, the world of the infant starts to transform itself gradually. It seems as if his trust in human beings had made his surroundings less threatening and more inviting. The baby becomes interested in what goes on around him. Usually he is interested first in how things sound and feel. Light and color are sought by the baby between his fourth and sixth month.

As Mother Is, So Is the World

A baby's relation to the world of objects is born out of his relation to his mother and shows the imprint of that relation. At an early age, each baby reacts to objects in much the same way as he reacts to his mother.

Dorothy, who had a strong and exclusive relation to her mother, became attached to any inanimate object and could not part from it. Silvia reacted as negatively to toys as she reacted to her mother and as her mother reacted to her. Sammy, who was surrounded by a happy, healthy, friendly family, welcomed any new toy with eagerness and joy.

"From where I sit, looks as if mighty queer characters hang around here."

Suzanne Szasz

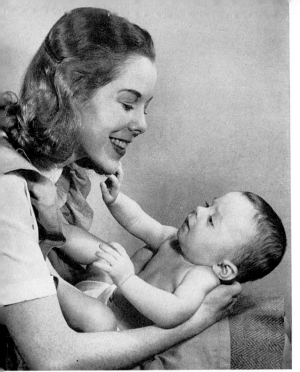

Elizabeth Hibbs

Mother's face is the light and the sunshine. When she is in sight, all's well with the world and comfort is at hand.

How Does He Learn to Accept or Reject?

As the interest of the child in his surrounding world grows, he practices seeing, hearing, and feeling, and learns to make distinctions. The majority of children, between their fifth and seventh months, are still ready to smile at every human face. But it would be wrong to assume that they have not yet started to react differently to outsiders from the way they react to their mothers.

If someone other than his mother feeds Tommy, for instance, this person looks clumsy, even though she is an expert baby nurse. It is quite obvious that Tommy expects the movements of his mother and is ready to respond to them. He feels the difference in handling, and has trouble in being comfortable with it. Mary has to stop any occupation if she looks at a stranger, but she can glance at her mother while she is playing with a toy. Sammy can stay lying on his back, even though he dislikes it thoroughly, only if his mother's hand touches him. While the baby is learning to differ-

entiate his mother's way of handling him from other ways, he is learning to accept some things and to reject others. He learns pleasure, discomfort, and anger. Through his mother's guidance, this discriminating attitude becomes more and more useful in dealing with his world. To a growing extent, the infant experiences pleasure when a situation leads to gratification. He is angry when he feels pain or when frustration is to be expected. The discrimination between mother and outsider enables the child to take the next step in his development —an active approach to the world.

Beginnings of Independence

At about six months, the baby's entire behavior seems changed. The child, who up to then was passively lying in his bed waiting for the adult to hand things to him, starts actively to get something for himself. His hand moves toward the toy, his fingers close around it, he grasps and manipulates it. He changes his position to see and hear better, or to get nearer to objects he wants. He also starts to move away from situations and things he finds displeasing. Sometimes he removes things with his hand if they become too disturbing. He puts himself into the position he prefers. No longer does he wait until the adult starts to speak to him. He babbles at him and pulls the adult's hair and nose.

How Does He Act on His Own?

The infant, who has been dependent on his mother to gratify his wishes and to relieve him from pain, has started, in

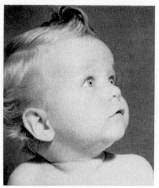

George Schaub, Cushing

"You don't say."

A new face brings out a different response from each baby . . .

Korling

"You never can tell."

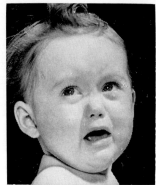

Korling

"Not on your life!"

slight but important ways, to master his own surroundings. He has learned from his mother how she provides pleasures, and he attempts—quite tentatively, of course—to provide them for himself. He has learned from his mother what situations are painful and, with many errors, begins to try to avoid them when they come. At the same time, he keeps and enforces the contact with his mother that has proved so valuable to him.

This first active approach toward the world is different in different children. Sammy learned first how to change into the position he preferred and how to move toward a toy that he wanted. Mary acquired her mother's attitude that it is dangerous to put things into the mouth, and hesitated every time she wanted to grasp something. Dorothy did not want to be separated from her mother if she was sitting on her lap. At the same time, she grew so independent that she walked at an age of hardly eight months. Sue, whose mother's approach to her child was merely through words, communicated with human beings and things by babbling.

He Becomes Aware of Himself

In the course of his active conquest of the world, the child becomes increasingly aware that he and his mother are two persons. He realizes that the world around him is a world independent and separate from him. This amazing discovery is based on, and also brings to the infant, greater independence and security. But it also leads to a partial loss of security, for the possibility of separation from his mother dawns on the baby.

Why His Anxiety Toward Strangers?

Somewhere between the fifth and the tenth month, children cry if Mother leaves them. Around the same time those children show a dislike of strangers.

Each child reacts in his own way toward strangers. A great number of children seem to smile when the stranger approaches. Then something "breaks" around their mouths and they start to cry. But there are also many children who turn their heads away if they see a stranger. Others hide under a blanket.

63

There are some who grow deadly serious, or even yell loudly, if an unfamiliar person picks them up or talks to them. Most children can be comforted if the stranger turns his back and waits until the child makes an overture.

This reaction to the approach of anyone who is strange can last for months, or only for a brief time. We have no evidence that it is not a normal part of development.

Unfriendliness May Be a Sign of Growth

In any case, anxiety in the presence of strangers should not embarrass you. You should not have the uncomfortable feeling that your friendly child has suddenly become shy or unfriendly. On the contrary, through his growing perception and discrimination the child has learned that mother is an individual who cannot be replaced by any other human being. One cannot react positively to an entire species. One can love only an individual, a person. The unfriendly reaction to the stranger is the birth of human attachment, of love.

What About the Ever-Friendly Baby?

This reasoning should not tempt us to assume that children who show no anxiety toward the stranger do not love their mothers. In these babies, development has taken a slightly different course. They were so successful in their active conquest of the world that they are not as afraid to be separated from their mothers as other children are. Therefore, they are not so disappointed if they see a stranger. They show their individual attachment in some other way.

Sammy, for instance, who was friendly toward strangers throughout his first year, singles out his mother by "speaking" exclusively to her. He looks at her while babbling, and adopts the loudness of his "conversation" to the distance she is away from him. George obeys only his mother, and turns to her at the sight of any danger.

Whether the recognition of the mother as a person takes the form of discrimination against the stranger, or of favoritism for the mother, at the end of his first year, the child has learned and realized who is most important to him. He has begun to learn to give affection.

Mothers Are Essential

During his first year, your baby has made a guided journey in development. Born into an unknown and threatening world, he discovers this world gradually at the hand of his mother. He learns first that the removal of discomfort is associated with his mother's face. This trust in one element of the outside world changes his attitude toward the world as a whole and awakens his interest in it.

When he dares to hear and to look at what is happening around him, he learns to distinguish between promise and threat, and gains enough security to act on his own.

His own action gives him the feeling that he is a person in his own right. He starts to experience himself as a "Self." The gap this awareness creates between him and his mother is bridged by the link she has forged by love during the preceding time.

Some unfortunate children have been forced to grow up in orphanages or institutions without this guiding love of a maternal figure. Their development was arrested or distorted, and they are tragic witnesses for our reasoning that mothers are, indeed, essential for the healthy and wholesome development of any child.

HE LEARNS THROUGH ACTIVITIES AND TOYS

LILI E. PELLER, M.S.

Lecturer, City College, New York, N. Y.

A BABY's understanding is far removed from ours, yet the great distance separating his intellectual world from ours will have shrunk by the time he enters school. How does he travel at such tremendous speed in his development?

How Does a Baby Learn?

A baby's capacity to learn must mature from within. It cannot be speeded up. The development of the child's muscles, his senses, his nervous system, and the sheath surrounding each nerve all play a part in his maturing.

So do the child's feelings. Love and trust, or fear and hatred, are the most powerful agents in shaping his happiness or unhappiness. They determine the use he will make of his intelligence. He absorbs and reflects the feelings of the people around him. He absorbs not only how they feel toward him, but also how they feel toward one another and toward the world outside their home.

He Learns Through Activity

Babies possess a strong urge to explore the world around them. A baby is compelled to look, touch, sniff, and poke at everything within his reach. There is a tremendous satisfaction for him in any step ahead in the mastery of his own body—a sweet satisfaction following any exertion he makes of his own accord. We can respect his interests, and not try to impose upon him our plan of getting ahead in the world.

65

A baby learns through play. He chooses his play activities spontaneously. They bring pleasure and lend themselves to innumerable variations and repetitions.

What Is a Good Toy?

A toy is good if it calls for muscular activity as well as activity of the mind. But, unfortunately, with certain kinds of equipment, the toy itself is the star performer. The child can only set things in motion, then be the passive onlooker. His muscular activity is limited, and, what is more important, his mind is idle. He cannot invent variations. Such toys are greatly admired in the show-windows of toy stores, and there they really belong. Do not bring them into the nursery!

In handling a toy, a child gets rid of surplus energy. Without this outlet, such energy might easily turn into anger or destructiveness. Channeling energy is but the first step in the toy's usefulness. While he plays, the baby is keenly aware of the toy's response to his efforts. A good toy responds to various degrees of skill. See how a young child uses building blocks. His co-ordination is necessarily poor. He will use just a few pieces, yet be pleased with his masterpiece. And indeed, the structure, even if a little lopsided, pays a compliment to his ability.

Good Toys Have Many Uses

Four or six months later, we find the same child using the same material in a different way. Now he is choosy about the pieces he employs—play ideas run ahead of his manual activity. He is either

"What new marvel is this?" Grandpa's watch is as exciting to the baby as a new continent would be to an explorer.

pleased, or so displeased, with his work that he kicks it down and starts all over again.

A few months have gone by, and now several children co-operate in carrying out a plan. Or the child asks to leave his structure up overnight, and the next morning he goes on from where he left off the evening before. He should be allowed to do so. His ideas and his ambition have grown and are bigger than what *one* person can do in *one* day.

The Simpler the Better

Simple toys are better than complicated ones. Toys where the small child understands (or can come to understand) what happens, are better than those with a complicated or concealed mechanism. With the simple toy, the child has the joy of inventing variations. A new twist that means nothing to us means a great deal to him. Also, the simple toy has the

H. Armstrong Roberts

greater life expectancy, as there are fewer parts to break or to lose.

What Are Safe Toys?

Young children always put things into their mouths. Make sure the paint on any plaything is harmless, and that there are no small parts to be swallowed. Metal toys are likely to have sharp points, and are therefore unfit for young children. Plastic comes in bright, attractive colors, but some types tend to splinter easily. Keep toys clean with water and soap.

A playing baby needs to be watched constantly, but you can cultivate the art of watching without hovering or interrupting unnecessarily.

Choose Toys That Last

Today we are keenly aware of the value of emotional ties, of human relationships lasting for many years. In a comparable way, it is well if some of a young child's toys are chosen so that they will remain his playmates for a long time. Most children get far too many flimsy toys. When toys are being sorted out to be given away, a child often shows an "unreasonable" attachment to some tattered and torn old-timer, or to some childish toy. Here is a feeling we would do well to respect.

The Toys and Play Materials chapter in this volume has many suggestions for safe and durable toys for the early years.

Everyday Things Make Good Toys

Often the best play values cannot be bought in stores. A baby starts exploring the things you use in taking care of him. There comes a day when he reaches for the box of absorbent cotton, and reaches again and again as you put it farther

A. Devaney

Flour and water paste to play with— that's fun, and can be permitted occasionally if you limit its use to a corner of the kitchen, and watch what is doing.

away. Or he gets hold of a near-by napkin, or puts his fist right into his cereal. He probably pokes a finger into his filled potty.

Once he begins to crawl, he may make straight for the kitchen. The pots and pans in lower cupboards are not safe any more. They make a satisfying sound when he bangs them with a spoon.

He Learns as He Explores

A collection of the best toys is no substitute for exploring and playing with things in his surroundings. Within the lines protecting his own safety and the possessions of others, a youngster should be able to handle everyday household objects. Examining the things that contribute to his well-being, his body care, the preparation of his meals, his clothing, is really his "educational activity."

67

Any toy made while the baby or toddler looks on, or helps, will be that much more appreciated. A simple wooden cart, or a doll made from a stocking, is more valued than one you buy. When you bring home bought toys, let the baby help with the unwrapping.

How Can You Use Waste Material?

The play value in many things that are considered "waste" in most households cannot be overrated. Empty boxes—especially with well-fitting lids—milk cartons, pieces of string, excelsior or shredded paper, and used envelopes are sources of endless pleasure to the child. Tissue paper is one of the play materials he can enjoy earliest. He pokes his fingers through it, tears it, packs it in balls, and is pleased with what he has accomplished. The extra bonus is the pleasant noise the tissue paper makes. Later on, tearing old magazines is a satisfying occupation. Do not worry that tearing, or, still later, cutting, old magazines will make your child less careful of books.

The kitchen holds good play material, too. A piece of dough for the baby to roll and pound can be made from flour and water. A piece of stale bread soaked in water is satisfying to shape and squeeze. There is nothing wrong with tea leaves or even coffee grounds. He enjoys shoveling these from one container to another with hands or spoon. No harm is done if a bit enters the child's mouth.

While a year- or year-and-a-half-old baby is playing with something like coffee grounds, he may suddenly show

What is more absorbing than experimenting with the drip and trickle of the cold water faucet, if Mother lets him take time for this in the tub?

disgust. That does not prove that your choice of material was wrong, but it does show that something in him is pushing him toward our adult values and discriminations. He is trying to imitate our feelings about anything messy.

Let him also help with the removal of things considered messy and undesirable. At two or three, he loves to dump wastebaskets, to dump and wipe ashtrays. Let him carry and empty his potty and flush the toilet or, if he uses a *toidyseat*, hand him the paper with which he was wiped and let him throw it into the toilet. (Such a trifle from our point of view —so important from his.)

Water Is a Priceless Plaything

Water play offers possibilities, too. There should be varieties of water play, in the kitchen sink or bathroom, or with a bowl of foaming soapsuds. A rubber tank with tepid water in the back yard on a warm day is the greatest of treats, but never leave a baby or a small child alone with a tub or tank of water. He needs cups, ladles, a sponge, boats, and other water toys for his play. Remember to change them from time to time.

E. J. Burgoyne from *Photography*

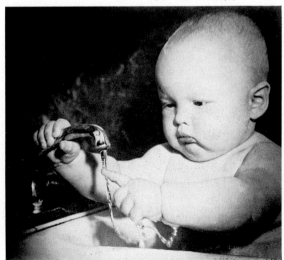

"The ball minds me"...

"I make it go away"...

"Now it is hitting the wall"...

"Wonder if it will come back"...

"Here it is. See!"

Every Baby Needs a Ball

The baby's first toy is usually a rattle. The infant shakes it, bites and sucks it, and may fling it far away. That's that.

The first *real* toy—the thing opening the door to the world of play—is a ball. A ball lends itself to varied and prolonged play activities. These seem to be accompanied by imagery and a playing-out of the child's wishes and feelings. At this early age, he does not distinguish clearly between things and living creatures. The ball moves; it scampers away. It may "hide" underneath the couch, or hit the leg of the table and return. Watching the playing child's expression, you can have little doubt but that he experiences the ball as alive.

What Does a Ball Mean to Him?

The earliest deprivation a baby must adjust to, and therefore a severe one, is the occasional disappearance of his mother. No matter how devoted a mother she is, at times she leaves the room and is out of sight. The infant overcomes this misery as he "learns" that she will be back *before* his hunger or his loneliness becomes unbearable. If he could be reached by words, we could save him many tears by telling him this, but it will be a long time before that will happen. He is too young to be taught, but not too young to learn through his own experience.

The only way of telescoping experience, of having a lot of it in a short time, is by *play*. In the game with the ball, the baby learns that something gone now is not necessarily gone forever. The ball rolled far away—all the way to the wall —but now it is coming back. In another second he will be able to grasp and hug it once more! If he is seated in such a way that the ball rolls back to him, there will be no end to this play.

Obviously, he is so tireless because he learns something, or, to put it differently, he gets even with us. Mother decides when to leave and when to return, but with the ball he's the boss! He sends it away and he makes it come back. The fact that he can be in active control in one segment of his daily living makes easier the acceptance of having other people in control so often.

You can easily make a baby's first ball at home, of soft material, loosely filled. It is difficult for the infant to catch hold of a ball by letting it roll into the hollow of his palm. He would have to rotate his wrists, and this he learns much later. Back and forth with the homemade ball can be enjoyed without this skill. He can grab the ball by digging his fingers into it, if it is filled loosely. This ball does not roll as well as a rubber ball, and it has no bounce. As soon as the baby learns the technique of catching it in the hollow of his hand, it should be replaced by a rubber ball.

The Importance of Dolls

In much of their play, small children often do to something else (or someone else) what has been done to them. In so doing, they are learning to overcome their fear, their resentment, their anxiety. A good plaything enables the child to reverse the tables: "I do to you what mummy did to me."

Think of all the times a child must hold still while Mother washes his face, pulls his arms in and out of armholes, or puts food on his plate. Dolls can, in turn, be treated in all these ways. There is no one type of doll that is preferable. Different children show different preferences at different times. Fancy dolls that speak and walk may cause breathless enthusiasm the first day, but they are soon forgotten in favor of their simpler sisters. Dolls which can be bathed, dolls whose skin feels like real, soft skin, are well liked.

Should Boys Play with Dolls?

Almost all young children like dolls, but they are considered girls' toys. The prejudice is so strong that a two-year-old boy walking out proudly with a doll-baby in his arms might be ridiculed. You can avoid this if you give him a teddy bear whose shirt and cap can be put on and off, and whom he can pretend to feed. Fortunately there is nothing unmanly about a teddy bear! There are also dolls dressed like boys, or like sailors.

Play Is a Serious Business

Toys are the child's tools for learning. Whenever a small child is fully absorbed, unaware of what goes on around him, we should not interrupt him. We should see to it that he is not interrupted by others. His attention may shift shortly, but while he is absorbed, let him alone.

Some parents are afraid their child will "wear himself out" concentrating so long on one thing, and they try to divert his attention. Yet the ability to concentrate is a gift comparable to any other talent. And this is as true for the eight-month-old child as it is for the eight-year-old. Hard play, play which is deeply satisfying, is the best preparation for hard, fully gratifying work.

THE TODDLER

Rus Arnold

Once your baby has become a toddler, able to get around under his own power, his most important job is to achieve a feeling of being an individual capable of acting on his own.

He wants to do things himself. Sometimes what he wants to do will fill you with delight, and sometimes with dismay.

The toddler is constantly making remarkable discoveries as he explores the world of things. Gaining an understanding of the objects around him in this way is another one of his important tasks. He is testing and experimenting with relationships, too. He is finding out that refusal as well as consent is a possible response.

Tactful handling can often cope with refusals and make consenting easier for the toddler. Tact is your best tool. It can frequently be the bridge between what the toddler wants to do and what he needs to do in order to become a member of a family and get along with other persons in our kind of world.

Glen Fishback

THE AGE OF "ME-CAN-DO"

FRANCES L. ILG, M.D.

Director, Gesell Institute of Child
Development, New Haven, Conn.

THE third year of a child's life is a year of vital, rapid growth and marked extremes. The year begins so gently that one is not at first aware of the hidden sources of dominating power that will be unleashed in its midstream, or the period of exhaustion that will invade its last quarter. When we say the third year, we do not mean a period beginning abruptly at one birthday and lasting until the next. These stages occur *somewhere around* the third year.

Two-Year-Olds Have Come Far

In many families, TWO is the favored of all ages. TWO has come out of his impulsive, thrusting, bumbling eighteen-month-old ways, when he saw nothing to the right of him or to the left of him. At that age, he went straight to his goal and plowed through anything in his way. He needed the protective, restraining help of a parent to break his fall, to teach him danger.

TWO has also come out of his twenty-one-month-old ways, when he tried to be his own protector, when he froze in his own tracks, often from fear. Then, he needed the reassuring help of his parents. He unfroze, and grew warm in their loving, understanding care for him. Soon he clung less and grew more independent. Above all, he grew in love for his parents, who became "my Mommy" and "my Daddy," in the most endearing terms.

They Are Pleasant to Have Around

TWO can express his affections both by the sound of his voice and by his

Maybe he is not much actual help, but he is learning what grown-ups do and how they feel. How important that is for him!

cozy, snuggling ways. There is an easy give-and-take between parent and child. He is more himself, and speaks of himself by his given name, usually coupled with some demand. "Johnny wants a cookie." "Mary wants to go outside." He not only expresses his desires but he wishes to have things all his own. The air rings with the oft-repeated refrain, "It's mine, it's mine." He must first learn "mine," before he knows "thine."

What a delightful companion he can be in the home! He moves around the house with greater ease. He goes on little errands. His favorite one is to fetch Daddy's slippers. He loves to go out for a walk, to walk on low, wide fences and walls, but he always loves to come "home" again.

The world around him is pouring through his eyes and he remembers what he sees. He knows where things go. He dotes upon putting away the canned goods. He loves to watch all the household activities. The vacuuming of the floor, the making of beds, the beating of eggs, and, especially, the scrubbing of the bathroom fascinate him. He is beginning to take a hand in all these activities himself. He delights in imitating. He enjoys working with his own miniature equipment, side by side with his mother.

He cannot yet be given the run of the house, for he still produces havoc in his own way. He gets into Mother's powder and creams. He strews and smears. Doors need to be equipped with high hooks, now that he can turn knobs so deftly.

The Same Thing, in the Same Way

TWO likes the feeling of the same things happening day after day. Routines suit him. "Again" is an oft-repeated demand. In the morning—bedroom slippers, bathrobe, toileting, watching Daddy shave. The sequence is inevitable. The evening has its special sequence, too, including "bookie." The favorite one might be the *Golden Dictionary* by Ellen Walpole, or *Goodnight Moon* by M. W. Brown and C. Hurd.

Even in eating he likes repetition, but that eternal dessert of apricots every night for supper will not go on forever. By his own choice, his diet may be quite

Everything is a source of fun. Even pudding on his face produces hilarity.

Rae Russell

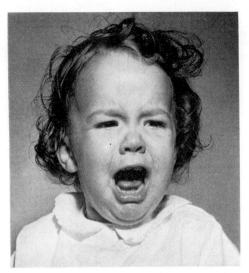

Glen Fishback

Sudden showers and fleeting storms are characteristic of two-year-olds. Sunniness is restored more quickly if you can keep reasonably calm yourself.

restricted, though adequate. Green vegetables are more commonly refused. He feeds himself the things he likes best, but still with considerable spilling. Often he eats best alone and calls his mother when he is "ready" for the next course. One really good meal a day is all that can be expected of him. He is likely to eat less well at the other two.

When Contrariness Sets in

Life can be quite smooth and delightful with the two-year-old. That is why it is such a jolt when, several months later, he becomes tense, explosive, and rigid. His routines are tight and overritualized. Thumb-sucking usually increases. Stuttering may appear temporarily. He screams and produces temper tantrums on the tiniest provocations. This once-enchanting youngster has now become a

demon, or, better said, a despot. He has discovered the pronouns "I" and "me," and he uses each with the lack of moderation of the beginner. He proclaims "I need," "I must have," "me can do!" If requests are not granted he flies into temper tantrums in a truly regal way. Royalty should be respected, and especially this little royal highness, but not to his own downfall and the consternation of the entire household. He should certainly be listened to. In all probability he will be given in to more than at succeeding ages, just to keep peace in the family.

Why Is This an Age of Extremes?

It is important to understand what is happening within the two-and-one-half-year-old. He is made up of extremes. He cannot soften his responses or curb his behavior. This is part and parcel of the growth process. He is exuberant one minute, shy the next. He says "me do it myself" when he cannot do it, and "you do it" when he can. He clamors for

In his own little way he can be a conspirator too, for he sets Daddy and Mother against each other when it serves his own purposes.

a special food one minute, rejects it the next. He insists on feeding himself one meal, then often, when his mother is busiest, demands complete help. He is keen to possess a certain object. He snatches it from another child, but he is indifferent to it when he has it. Grass is always greener in someone else's pasture. He acts with sudden speed or he dawdles endlessly. He disrupts parent harmony by pitting Mother against Father.

These characteristics are not easy to live with. The child who is growing through this stage, as well as the parent who is subjected to these sudden changes, has troubles. A certain amount of swing needs to be allowed, even as a pendulum swings. But too often a parent unknowingly pushes the child into further extremes, until a blow-up is inevitable. Parents need to be helped to avoid the direct clashes leading to these blow-ups.

What Shall We Do About His Rituals?

The child himself solves his own problem, in part, by setting up elaborate, sometimes humorous, rituals to keep himself on the right track The ritual helps him to avoid the conflict of choice.

He may have a dressing ritual, and Father had better learn about it before he tries to take over! Putting on a shirt before pants may be an adequate reason for a temper tantrum, if the usual procedure is pants first. Some of these rituals take a long time and, if not adhered to correctly, have to be gone through all over again.

Rituals can be a tyranny. One little girl insisted upon putting her thirty-seven dolls to bed each night. The error was not so much in the ritual as in the possession of so many dolls. Three or four are quite enough. Two would be better.

Shall We Let Him Choose?

This is probably the worst age for choices. Two-and-a-half wavers back and forth, and, if he finally settles for one, is bound to go against his own choice in the next few minutes. The simple choice between chocolate or vanilla cookies may ruin an excursion to the store. This can be by-passed by telling him in advance exactly what is going to happen. "We are going to the store. You may ask the man for chocolate cookies. He's going to put them in the bag for you to carry. Then we're coming home, and you

Korling

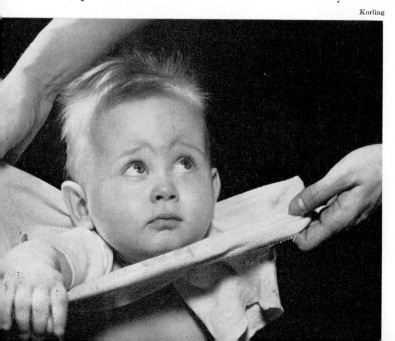

Here is a doubting Thomas! Even father's style of putting on a shirt is eyed with suspicion if it differs from the way mother does it.

may eat one on the way." His repetition of this sequence of events will show that he assents, and he will generally carry it through. Parents need to know when they should pull up on the reins and take over.

Avoiding Trouble Spots

There are some techniques of handling difficult situations that frequently make life smoother. Naps are often a storm center. First, a youngster will not settle down to sleep, and then he sleeps too long if he is not wakened. Part of his delay in settling down is due to the fact that he wants to sleep any place except in his crib. On the radiator, under his bed, or in a block-enclosed area on the rug might be his choice. Sometimes the best solution is to skip naps for the time being.

If the child tends to sleep too long, wake him after an hour, so that the night sleep will not be delayed so long. Often your youngster may wake up cross, and grow worse if you try to comfort him. If you putter around his room, and pay no attention to him, you may bring him round most readily.

There may be difficulty with elimination. Girls, especially, have long spans of five to even ten hours between urinations. Three or more days may elapse between bowel movements. These children need to be helped, so that they do not put off elimination too long. Play with water, their favorite pastime, may help them to urinate. Being read to as they are seated on the toilet may produce the needed atmosphere for them to release their bowel movements. Sometimes laxative fruit juices may be needed. Consult your doctor before you decide to give any other laxatives, for otherwise you may do more harm than good.

The Charms of Music

Perhaps most conducive to a relaxed atmosphere is the use of music. Mothers can profit by singing the whole day through. A chanted request, such as

Rae Russell

Favorite records often tide two-year-olds over those times when everyone is tired and tantrums threaten.

"Time to come to breakfast," is not only acted upon by the child, but is even answered in a chant of "all right." Records, records, records—nursery rhymes especially—are just the things for those low periods at the end of the morning, or at the end of the afternoon, when tantrums frequently occur. Some children, especially boys, prefer to have their own machines and play their records for hours. You will find a list of records for younger children in Volume 11.

How Much Can He Do Alone?

Dressing is an especially prickly problem. Simple clothing with zippers, large buttons, or elastic belts will help. Place

"Well, did you three have a nice walk?"

your youngster's shirt on the bed with the back uppermost, or spread out his pants ready to slip into, so that he can more easily dress himself. He will accept suggestions if he is not helped physically, or touched.

Some day the child may go to the other extreme of demanding to be dressed, and go limp like a doll or a baby. Or he may run away when it comes time to dress. Chasing him for fun is one thing. Chasing him in order to dress him is often an unsuccessful pursuit! Better that he be told to come to the bathroom when he is ready. If he is excluded, especially by a closed door, he usually comes. Then stand him on a hamper or a chair, and conclude the matter of dressing with dispatch. He may be much more proficient at undressing than dressing, and may delight in removing his shoes hourly.

Two-and-one-half-year-olds often use the word "no." An inevitable "no" follows the question, "Do you want to eat lunch?" A positive statement, "It's time to eat lunch," or "You need to eat lunch," allows less chance for a royal rebellion. The chapter WHAT DOES HIS "NO, NO" REALLY MEAN? in this volume has more to say on this subject.

One More Fling at Babyhood

It is no wonder that a period of exhaustion follows this highly-demanding, royal period. Somewhere around the age of three, children usually complain of being tired. They often ask to be carried. Never go on a walk without a stroller, or something your child can sit on, even though he is apt to refuse it at the beginning of the walk. You may end up carrying a tired, heavy child, if you leave the stroller or the little red wagon at home. Whining is a part of this fatigue.

The child not only feels like a baby but also wants to be one. He is apt to hold on to certain phases of his present age, however. As one girl of about three put it, "I'm a little baby. I can't walk. I drink my bottle in my carriage, but I can talk." And this she did from morning till night.

There is no more-favored bedtime story for this age child than hearing about his babyhood. He wants to know what clothes he wore. He wants to know where he slept and what people said about him. It is like music to his ears to hear that someone said, "You are the best baby in the whole town."

Two-year-olds, with great individual variations, traverse quite a circuit in the third year of their lives. If you grow discouraged, remember that some day you will look back on this period with humor, and even with wistfulness.

78

Elizabeth Hibbs

CAUTION—
TODDLER AT WORK HERE

MARY ELIZABETH KEISTER, Ph.D.

Head, Department of Child Development and Family
Relations, University of Tennessee, Knoxville.

W HEN you travel unfamiliar high-
ways, you watch out for warning
signs, such as "Men at Work";
"Proceed with Caution—Construction
Under Way"; "Slow—Loose Gravel."
Such signs make travel safer.

How helpful it would be if similar
caution signs were posted along the
highway of the toddler's development!
We cannot post such signs for the eyes
to read, but we should "write them
on the tablets of our hearts" and keep
them steadily in mind.

Growing Out of Babyhood

Growing out of babyhood must be
something of a disappointment and a
letdown to the one-and-a-half- or two-
year-old. Imagine what it would be like
to go from babyhood, where the grown-
ups think everything you do is just too
cute for words, to that period where
grown-ups seem to put a stop to everything you want to do.

The life that grown-ups lead must
seem like paradise to the two-year-old.
If he could put his feelings into words,
he might say,

"Look at those lucky people! They
come and go as they please. They put
dishes on the table and carry them off.
Nobody stops them when they take
things out of drawers and cupboards and
sewing-boxes."

TODDLER
EXPLORING
AND
LEARNING

"Here's something pretty! Feels nice and smooth. Smells good. Doesn't make a noise. Wonder how it tastes?" Finding the answers is a liberal education to a small person.

Suzanne Szasz

Your two-year-old tries to imitate you and the other people in his life. Half of his troubles come from a misinterpretation of what you want him to do, or a misinterpretation of what you are doing.

He Learns Through His Senses

The toddler is, first and foremost, an explorer. Even those individuals who discovered the Pacific Ocean experienced nothing like the heady excitement the two-year-old knows when he has at last mastered the task of propelling himself on a tricycle. The deep satisfaction the one-year-old has when she touches a flower and a baked potato, Mommy's velvet collar and Daddy's silky tie, mud and soap flakes, sandpaper and the shiny magazine cover, is greater than the satisfaction of famous inventors.

The toddler learns through *all* his senses. Handling, smelling, and tasting give the toddler vivid impressions. Tod-

dlers seem at times to be driven to try out every new experience with every one of their five senses. They have a strong drive to learn about their world and about the people in it. Their only way of learning is to try out everything, be it animal, vegetable, or mineral. They are constantly touching, tasting, smelling, looking, and listening.

This spells almost constant activity for the toddler himself, and for the sometimes weary adult who must serve as combination bodyguard and teacher. This "into and onto" behavior is not naughtiness or wilfulness. It is, rather, the toddler's business. It is as necessary to his future development as is the food he eats.

Does Everything Become a Habit?

You fear that all this mouthing and handling, this enthusiastic taking-apart and putting-together will go on forever

80

and (oh, hideous thought!) "become a habit."

You do not need to be too worried about "habit." For you know now that the child who has been allowed to explore will have *less* need for it later than will the child who has been balked at every turn in his active wish to find out.

"Bad Habits" no longer loom as the fearsome giants of child training. You realize that, at different ages, behavior necessary and appropriate to each age will show up. If the stage is lived through fully and in a satisfying manner, the youngster will go on to the next stage. You do not need to be eagerly insistent that every youngster "learn the right way from the start."

Safety for Toddlers and for Breakables

If you have had more than one child, you realize that the toddler will not get into things forever. Because you know this, you can more cheerfully arrange your home life so that wear and tear on adults and bric-a-brac is reduced.

Matches, ash trays, scissors need not be placed out of reach for the rest of the family's natural life, but they must be out of reach right now. When you find yourself too busy to give the toddler the almost constant supervision he needs when at large among family possessions, it is better to remove anything that will harm, or be harmed by, small children.

If your little girl does get hold of something she should not have, it is less likely to be broken if you do not swoop down on her and grab it instantly away. The toddler's parent who does not "swoop" deserves, at the end of each day, "Honorable Mention" for steady nerves and fast thinking. Substitute something else for the forbidden object and you will probably get the precious or dangerous object back safely. But there is going to be some breakage, no matter how clever and quick you are.

Living with Grownups

Perhaps the most important lesson the toddler learns is that grown ups are patient friends and teachers, and are not really out to stop him at any cost.

FAMOUS LAST WORDS

"We're not going to quit living just because we have children. They'll have to learn to leave things alone."

TODDLER LIVING WITH GROWNUPS

Your toddler wants to please you. We all wish to please those we love and those whom we want to love us. Have you ever stopped to think what an ally this wish to please is? The fact that your toddler does not always please you, that often his efforts create inconvenience and trouble, is not proof that the *desire* to please is not there.

The toddler's strong drive to imitate you gets him and you into a lot of trouble. Yet it is your best guarantee that, as he grows up, the good qualities in his parents will be found in *his* make-up, too.

How Do You Make Rules Clear?

The wish to please, which makes for good relationships with people all through life, is kept alive in children by affectionate care and patient teaching. Children like rules when they are lovingly enforced. Rules make it clear what may not be done and what should be kept in mind in this game of living. To teach even the simplest rules, you will have to say "no" and *mean* it, many times. Do not be afraid to say "no." Being a definite sort of word, it clears up many confusions.

You can be careful not to say "no" constantly. Save it for the things that you really want to teach, for the things that really matter. "No" can become a habit with you as well as with the toddler. If you say "yes" more often than you say "no," it is quite likely you will be imitated in that, too.

The "noes" can be applied firmly and affectionately. Attractive suggestions can be offered for diverting a youngster from the less desirable activity. Satisfactory channels for exploration and play can be provided. Eventually, all this will help your toddler learn to understand and abide by your "no." He will do it cheerfully because he wants your approval and he likes the way it feels to be looked on as a law-abiding member of the household.

Can a House Be Toddler-Proof?

The formula for a toddler-proof household is not simple, but these precautions may help. Remove as many dangers and temptations as possible from the toddler's reach. Provide as many materials as possible that are safe and that satisfy his need to explore, to take apart and put together, to push and pull, to run with, and to bang around.

In addition to whatever measures are taken to make the household safe for any of its members, a few extras may be necessary in a home where a toddler resides. Accident Prevention Is Your Responsibility, in Volume 15, tells about safety in your home. A hook similar to that used on screen doors may be placed high up on the kitchen door to keep the small child out when Mother is not in the kitchen. The hot water can be regulated so that it does not come from the faucet scalding hot. The lock on the bathroom door may need to be removed or "immobilized" for a time. Electrical appliances and lamps can have their dangling cords pinned up out of reach. Hooks on window screens can be checked frequently. Porch railings can be built high and kept in good condition. Precious breakables can be put out of reach.

Your child needs a space to play where everything is safe to handle and

Publix

Right now, emptying a drawer is this toddler's only ambition. If he does it to his heart's content, he will be ready to go on to the next stage.

This young lady finds the soft, slippery feel of creams and pastes irresistible. Give her acceptable ways of feeling such textures, and then she will grow into new interests.

A. Devaney

everything is there to be enjoyed. It need not be equipped with expensive toys, for the toddler has simple tastes and is delighted with the most ordinary household objects. An ancient egg beater, a pack of old playing cards, a tin cup and a set of measuring spoons, a discarded coffee can (if the rim is not sharp) full of clothes pins and empty spools, will keep him happy for some time. More suggestions for playthings can be found in Toys and Play Materials, in this volume.

Dealing with Overactivity

Keeping a two-year-old safe and happy is easier said than done. But if your two-year-old seems restless or unhappy, or is steadily in difficulties due to his over-activity, you might ask yourself some questions. Are you meeting his needs? Or are you perhaps expecting too much of him?

Does he have satisfying play materials of his own that he is allowed to use as he likes? Is he sometimes given a chance to play, run, and let off steam in a place bigger than his own room or his own yard? If the answer to these two questions is really "yes," then you are probably on the right track. The restless, overactive youngster may be suffering

from too much pent-up energy.

Is he under pressure to "be good," to "stay dry," or to "keep clean"? Is he punished severely when he "forgets" or disobeys? If the answer to these two questions is "no," you are probably moving in the right direction.

Perhaps you will decide to revise some of your ways of handling your small child if, when you check on your attitudes and your routines, you find that you are not taking your toddler's needs

83

TODDLER GROWING OUT OF BABYHOOD

into consideration, or expect too much.

There is one other question to ask yourself. Are some things worrying you or your husband to an unusual degree? Worry, anger, dissatisfaction, boredom are all catching. If either or both of you is under great strain, even your smallest children feel vaguely uneasy. Under these circumstances, toddlers sometimes try to get rid of their uncomfortable, worried feelings by ceaseless efforts to get at things they cannot reach. It is almost as if they were literally trying to reach for or come to grips with the intangible cause of the worry; as if the thing out of reach contained the answer to the puzzle of life.

If you understand that the toddler's extreme overactivity is a reflection of your own troubles, you will be more patient and more careful in giving him supervision. A little more affectionate attention from you lets him know that the bottom has not really dropped out of the world. He may be calmer if he can count on more time alone to enjoy your company.

Sometimes small children who have not had firm enough guidance, or who have not had consistent, friendly training, are more overactive than those who have known gentle, affectionate treatment, with limits and "rules" clearly established.

What Do They Need Most?

As you live with your two-year-old, there are a few points to keep in mind that may make it easier for you to understand and guide him. Perhaps these points, too, should be signs that are figuratively in front of you much of the time.

Exploration and its natural consequence, inconvenience for the grown-ups, are the toddler's stock in trade. The age of intensive exploration is temporary. If it can be lived through cheerfully, it is the toddler's best guarantee of a bright and lively future.

Kind words and gentle, loving gestures make a deeper impression on toddlers than do crossness and angry grabbing and shaking. They need an extra supply of loving and cuddling in these months when there is so much for them to learn about how people expect them to behave.

You will have to say "no" many times, and it will be about the *same* things over and over again. Make the "noes" firm but loving, and offer a substitute for the fruit that is forbidden.

The toddler's memory is short, especially when it comes to matters that hold some particular fascination for him. It is not "meanness" or "willfull forgetting" that makes him go again and again to dump the wastebasket's contents or to open the door to the basement. It is his need to explore and to learn by trying out everything. He needs a bodyguard or a fence if he is to be expected to stay out of trouble for long at a stretch.

Mothers and fathers have rights, too, and mothers and fathers with toddlers have more need than most for periods of relaxation and time for themselves. It is all right to "blow your top" now and then, just so all that wrath does not descend upon your toddler's bewildered head.

Taking time now to *teach* what is expected, and to understand *why* your child finds it so hard to learn what you have to teach, will yield rich rewards in a year or two. Gentle, patient, firm teaching usually produces a "reasonable" little boy or girl of whom you will be proud.

WHAT DOES HIS "NO, NO" REALLY MEAN?

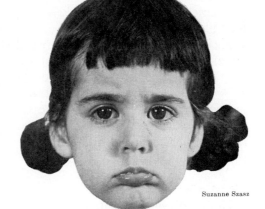

GERTRUDE E. CHITTENDEN, Ph.D.

Author of "Living With Children"; Formerly
Head, Child Development Department, Iowa State
College, Ames

Suzanne Szasz

CONSCIENTIOUS parents who have taken pride in the rearing of their baby are often shocked to find that, at about the age of two or two and a half, he is becoming contrary and self-assertive. They wonder if they are to blame for this behavior. They wonder if it means they will have a stubborn, hard-to-get-along-with son or daughter for the rest of their lives. They wonder what other people will think.

Self-assertion at this age is as normal for children as walking or learning to talk. Nobody is to blame. Some children show more of it than others, but all children go through a contrary stage. In spite of their behavior as two-year-olds, children develop into fairly easy-to-live-with individuals. You naturally think about what your two-year-old will be like when he grows up. His present contrariness does not foreshadow willfulness at three or stubbornness at fifteen. His contrariness is a sign of growth. If you understand what this phase of develop-

ment means, you will realize why you can let him be his age. Contrariness is one of the many kinds of behavior that is appropriate in a two- or two-and-a-half-year-old, even if it might need more serious consideration in a much older child.

He Wants to Be Independent

At this stage in development, a child makes some interesting discoveries about himself and his relationship to other people and to the things around him. He is finding out that he is an individual separate from other individuals, with abilities of his own. He is learning that he can operate "under his own steam" in many situations. He experiments to find out how capable he is. No longer must he wait upon an adult to take him to the many fascinating things he wants to touch and taste and lift and squeeze. He can get to them by creeping or walking or climbing. He does not welcome adult interference when he can do for

85

himself. He has an urge to grow up, to become a self-reliant, independent individual. Whenever that urge is denied, and sometimes we do have to deny it, he feels like saying "No."

He is learning the nature of the world around him through his explorations. He tastes, he touches, he pokes, he hits, he squeezes, he lifts. Such exploration is important to him. He will feel like saying "No" whenever he is curbed in his freedom to explore. And, remember, some curbing is necessary at times.

Choosing Is a New Power

He has discovered that in almost any situation there are two possible responses, "Yes" and "No." When Mother calls him to come to her, he can run the other way or he can run toward her. When bedtime is announced, he can say "Yes" or he can say "No." Either is possible for him. He experiments to find out what the alternative results are. Perhaps he says "No" in an attempt to clarify just what response saying "No" brings. He has to learn by trying the various possibilities.

Do We Work Against His Nature?

Perhaps our way of bringing up children creates pressures that make a little child feel like saying "No." Perhaps our emphasis on "right" ways of feeding and toilet training and disciplining builds up antagonistic feelings toward adults which come out in the form of "No" at an early age.

To understand what "No, No" from a particular child means, one should be well acquainted with him and with his parents. But probably some general statements can be made about what children are trying to tell us when they are contrary and non-co-operative.

Such pronouncements as *You don't need to help me, I can do it myself, I am getting big,* are frequently made through a "No." Sometimes a firm setting of the feet and jaw by the two-year-old speaks louder than words. A group of ten two-year-olds were climbing the stairs to the second-floor sleeping-room for their afternoon nap. Jean's feet lagged a bit and her eyelids were beginning to droop, so Teacher carried her up the last five or six steps.

Jean stiffened in the teacher's arms the moment that she was picked up, and a sharp "No" accompanied the stiffening. When the teacher put Jean down at the head of the stairs, the child immediately walked down the five or six steps, turned around, and walked up to the top in stony silence. She had said, "I can do it myself," as plainly as if she had talked. Fortunately, the teacher un-

"Oh boy! What a discovery!" But there may be trouble ahead for this explorer, for even the most thrilling discoveries are not always permissible.

Edith Loder

"Here's that nice big pail.

derstood, and accepted Jean's behavior without comment.

Do We Expect Too Much?

You are pushing me too hard. Give me a little more time and I might say "yes." Ask me to do only those things that I can do at two years. All this may be conveyed in that one word, "No." We forget that the child cannot be neat in his eating because his muscle co-ordination will not allow it. He cannot sit still, because the urge to be physically active is so powerful at this age. He cannot control his elimination perfectly.

I am learning so many new things right now. When you ask one more thing of me, I say "No" in self-defense, hoping you will reduce the pressures of things I have to do. When a child is between two and three, he is learning at a tremendous rate. He is learning to control muscles, to talk, to get along with adults and other children. He is building up a great store of information about the world around him. It is no wonder that he may say "No" when adults ask him to do so many things.

I have trouble making up my mind. When you give me a chance to say either "Yes" or "No" I cannot decide quickly. I'm likely to say the word that is easiest and that word often is "No." Frequently a child will say "No" to a request, and then do exactly what you asked of him. He is not unintelligent; he simply has

. . . Goody! Water in it too.

. . . Can't quite get my feet in, but that water sure feels cool and wet on my hands and on my hair."

All photos by Rae Russell

Plenty of chances to follow their own whims in harmless ways like this, tends to cut down the number of "noes" you will hear in a day.

87

When "no" is your toddler's only response, listen to the distribution of "no" and "yes," "you may" and "you mustn't" in your own conversations. Noes are highly contagious.

not had enough experience in making decisions and putting his responses into words to be quite sure of the meanings of "Yes" and "No." He is experimenting with them.

If the two- or two-and-a-half-year-old could put his feelings into words, he might say to his parents, "You are saying 'No, No' so much that I am absorbing the 'No, No' approach to things, too." Children are great imitators. If they were not, they never would learn the ways of behaving that are expected of them. If they are constantly surrounded with "No, don't touch that," and "No, you'll get hurt doing that," and "No, Mother doesn't want you to do that," they are almost certain to try the same technique on us and even on themselves. You have probably seen a child get near a forbidden object, slap his own hand, and say "No, No." As long as you are keeping a desirable balance between the "No, No" and the "Yes," yourself, your child's "No" probably does not have this meaning.

Is His "No, No" Testing Us?

I am having fun experimenting with you. A "No, No" from me ties you up in knots. *I can tell by the way you behave. It's more fun to say "No" than "Yes." I really don't mean half the "Noes" I say. I just want to see what will happen when I do say them."* Finding out what effect he can have on another person's behavior is important to the toddler. If he can produce concern in his parents, if he can become the center of their attention by saying "No," he probably will say it. Wanting to find out how he affects others is a normal part of his growing interest in people. If he derives a feeling of power by saying "No," he feels he commands a highly desirable and useful way of influencing people.

Occasionally a child really means "I won't" when he says, "No," but a "No" based on unfriendly feelings toward the adult who has made the request is relatively rare. All the other meanings of "No, No" appear far more frequently.

Avoiding the "Noes"

When a child's "No" is taken for its real worth, ways of avoiding some of the "noes" immediately come to mind. Perhaps the best thing to do is to receive the "noes" good-humoredly. They are not a personal insult. A child who says "No" is not trying to deny your authority, now or forever. He just wants to make a few decisions himself. He is not striking out maliciously at anyone. He simply is showing you that he is growing up, and that he knows it. If you are not disturbed by a child's contrariness, he stands a good chance of dealing with it effectively now, and of overcoming it before long.

If requests can be stated positively, not in the form of a question, there is less opportunity for a child to say "No." If a request is stated or a direction given positively, the child hears less of the "mustn't," "don't," restricting kind of language that brings resistance.

Requests that give a child time to change from one activity to another are more likely to bring a "Yes" response than are those that demand that he stop what he is doing, immediately. He needs time to make the change at his own pace. Better still are the chances that a request accompanied by action on your part will bring a positive response. A little child does better if you take his hand and lead him to the next activity than if you just tell him what to do.

How Can You Get Co-operation?

Requests that allow for some leeway in both time of response and manner of responding are likely to be effective. "Pick up your toys now" for the two-year-old should mean: "Within the next little while let's work together on getting your toys picked up and put back into the places they belong. They don't need to be arranged neatly, just so they are back in the box where they belong." He cannot be expected to remember a direction long enough to carry it out alone. He needs an adult to help him.

Making a game out of his "No, No," by responding good-humoredly with "Yes, Yes," and leading him expectantly to the next activity, can relieve much tension and prevent balkiness on his part, too.

A toddler is ready to make only the simplest decisions. Avoid offering choices that might be too hard for him. Don't insist that he make up his mind and stick to his decisions, for he is not capable of such strong-mindedness. He cannot decide when it is cold enough to wear a cap. But he can decide whether to put his cap on backward or forward, and his decision need not affect anyone

but himself. He cannot decide when to go to bed. That decision rests with you. But he can decide *how* he wants to go to bed. He may crawl like a bear, or ride piggy-back on a good-natured daddy's back, or go up the stairs on his knees. How he goes to bed can be his own decision, as long as the method he chooses gets him there in a reasonable length of time. In ways such as these, he can feel independent and still not be asked to make decisions that are beyond his ability.

A child's "No" usually means that he is asserting his right to be an individual, a right that is precious to everyone. To whatever extent his parents can find ways to help him preserve this right, while conforming to necessary rules, he will be more successful in becoming a co-operative, well-adjusted, friendly individual and group member.

Your youngster should know you mean what you say. When you announce bedtime, never mind how he goes to bed, as long as he goes happily.

Elizabeth Hibbs

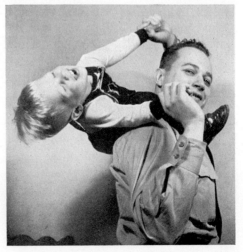

Korling

GUIDING HIM TACTFULLY

ARNOLD GESELL, M.D., Ph.D.

Research Consultant, Gesell Institute of
Child Development, New Haven, Conn.

Tact is the watchword. That seems fair. Tact implies a certain considerateness befitting the parent and benefiting the child. Tact with children is a form of sympathetic understanding, doubly useful when the toddler becomes a bit too turbulent. Tact is closely allied to courtesy, and for this very reason it has a special value in the day-to-day management of the preschool child. Tact is discernment.

How a Young Mind Grows

Now there cannot be discernment without some knowledge of how the young mind grows. The child's mind grows with dramatic speed and intensity during the toddler period, even though the daily gains are not always apparent. It grows with a sureness calling for optimism rather than discouragement.

To appreciate this basic sureness, one needs only to look at the remarkable mental growth a baby accomplishes in the first fifteen months of his life. In the early weeks after birth, he can scarcely balance his head upon his shoulders. When he opens his eyes, they seem to move rather aimlessly. His hands remain closed in tight fists. But, under the irresistible pressures of innate growth, he gains progressive command of his head posture, of shoulder, trunk, arms, and legs. The tide of development moves from head to foot.

In the course of a year the baby rises to his feet. By fifteen months he generally takes steps by himself. He can creep if need be; but usually he prefers to toddle. He is not often in a mood for sitting still. His whole action system strains at the leash. He wriggles and squirms while he is being dressed. He pulls from his mooring to get under way. He feels an urgency in hands as well as feet. He reaches out for objects. He likes to carry something in each hand; he also likes to cast objects. For good measure he babbles jargon at the same time, heedless of any voice other than his own.

What Is a Pattern of Growth?

Who can deny that these are important undertakings! In all this abandon, a child is not simply giving vent to raw energy. His activities are governed by deep-seated growth forces. His energies are organized into patterns of behavior. These patterns are the outward evidences of his growing mind. New patterns emerge as the child advances from stage to stage and from age to age—from fifteen months to eighteen months, from two to two and a half and three years. When we perceive the direction and the drift of this developmental process, we also begin to see the everyday problems of child management in true perspective. A detailed survey of the psychological growth of the preschool child is presented in *Infant and Child in the Culture of Today* by Arnold Gesell and Frances Ilg.

Even young children are sometimes dimly aware of the growth process. When two preschool children, differing several months in age, chance to meet, the older child is likely to assume a senior relation to the junior. When a three-year-old child declares, "I don't do that any more," he speaks in tones which indicate a sense of growth. The six-year-old begins to think about what growing up means. One seven-year-old

Maybe you don't think this jumble of blocks is a neat job, but it's a triumph in building for a toddler.

even wrote and illustrated a small wrapping-paper volume, bravely titled *Handbook: A Child from Two to Five by T. J.* The book begins: "A child of two, at least some, is a good eater but he is a poor sleeper," and concludes, "At five they are very nice. He is a fairly good sleeper and a good eater. The End."

Why Should We Understand Growth?

The process of psychological growth continues into the teens and the twenties. When the young child is viewed as part of the total continuing cycle of growth, the behavior events of the preschool period take on new interest and significance. The heightened interest such a view brings, plus a reasonable degree of acceptance, makes for improved parent-child relationships.

Tact Co-operates with Growth

Tactful guidance in the day's routine depends first of all upon an awareness of the child's maturity as shown by the patterns and the intensity of his behavior traits. The typical fifteen-month-old infant, as we have seen, has already come a long way. He is something more than a

Philip Gendreau

"mere" infant. The nature of his self-assertiveness certifies to that. To some extent we must "go along with him" in his burst of self-assertion. It certainly is neither wise nor tactful to combat his demands, for the sheer sake of teaching him to mind. To "go along with him" does not lead to aimless indulgence, but to constructive guidance.

Why Does He Like to Throw Things?

Why does he make a business of casting or throwing everything down? It is because he is impelled by inner growth forces to exercise and to improve his growing ability to release, to hold on, to let go. This is a new kind of voluntary behavior. When he was a mere baby in arms he could grasp an object, but he could not release it when he wanted to. His everlasting casting and throwing may look like uncontrolled behavior, but it is really an exercise in elementary self-control. It involves eyes as well as arms and hands.

Note how intently he looks at what he is doing when he casts from the perch of his highchair, or through the railings of his pen. He is suiting eye movements to hand and arm movements. He is co-ordinating important patterns of be-havior. He places one block upon a second block, the first step in tower building. He can release a bit of toast into a cup. A child often appears over-demanding when, in fact, he is not so much demanding things of us, as he is demanding things of himself. He is asserting a growing measure of self-dependence.

How He Learns to Feed Himself

At feeding time the fifteen-month-old insists on having a try at that difficult implement, a spoon. Now his ability to see and understand relations in space and to command control of his small muscles is rudimentary. He seizes the spoon with a crude grasp near the handle, dips rather than scoops, brings it upside down to his mouth or its vicinity, and gives the spoon a final twist if its contents reach their destination. His enthusiasm outruns his neatness! Vigorous boys, in particular, are eager to feed themselves, but they adjust to tactful assistance. A child, for example, accepts a measure of help if the mother fills his spoon from a spoon of her own, and then assists by supporting the handle of his spoon as he lifts it to his mouth.

Spilled morsels are skillfully recovered by refined pincer motions of grabbing.

"I think he went that way."

IRWIN

Whether it goes in right-side-up or up-side-down, getting spoon to mouth is a major achievement, and a praise-worthy one, too.

Philip Gendreau

Finger-feeding is definitely the preferred method at this age! For several reasons, this method is natural and beneficial to the child. It would be unwise to interfere unduly simply for the sake of tidiness, manners, or routine. It is, of course, unwise to push routines for their own sake.

Why Does Interest in Self-Feeding Vary?

Routines are always subject to variation from child to child and from day to day in the same child. The desire to feed himself is characteristic of what, for convenience, we call the fifteen-months' maturity level, but not all children are equally interested in doing so at that age. Inborn temperaments vary and some children do not show such a strong interest as others. There are variations within the day. Fatigue reduces the desire for independence. Breakfast often is accepted without his trying to feed himself. At supper the child may insist on taking over, unless, perhaps, the father claims the privilege of feeding him and is rewarded with co-operation. Indeed, it is reported that the fifteen-monther

But fingers are more reliable for getting a good meal. Being independent and enjoying eating are more important at this age than manners.

Suzanne Szasz

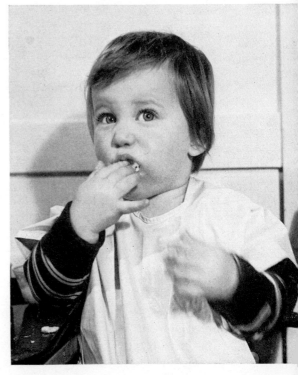

93

sometimes turns the tables and takes delight in feeding both Father and Mother.

What Kind of Routines?

Rigid routines are clearly out of the question. Common sense requires that some kind of working plan be set up each day. But matters tend to progress more smoothly if we take what cues we can from the child's ways of behavior and his ways of growth. There are daily behavior variations that may need to be dealt with in the usual routine. But there are also the deep changes that subtly come with increasing maturity.

In a dozen weeks, by the age of eighteen months, new cues and characteristics emerge. The eighteen-monther is so charged with energy that he may not take as readily to a carriage as he did at fifteen months. He prefers instead to push the carriage himself. He has a great fund of new ways to use his muscles and he wants to try them out. They are so interesting that he is rather heedless of restraining instructions. It is almost necessary to go along with him; and that means a runabout stage for mother as well as for child!

How Do You Enlist His Co-operation?

Yet there are pauses, when he completes a situation in a burst of conclusive satisfaction with an "Oh my!" or "All gone." He is a man of few words. In general, it is well to use language sparingly to guide him. He responds better to a single, duly inflected word (for example, "Hat?" or "Walk?") than to an elaborate sentence. Addressing him by name is more effective than using a pronoun. "Jimmy come here," is a sentence he can understand.

But for the eighteen-monther every street is figuratively a one-way street. He is not good at altering, abandoning, or reversing a course of action. To avoid resistance one must resort to gradual change-overs, luring him with a toy to get him from one room to another. Much depends upon accurate timing. If there is real resistance and all the usual techniques fail, pick him up, like a bag of rags, in a gale of laughter.

Some of his resistances need to be fully respected. He may object strenuously to the play pen he accepted a month or two earlier. He probably needs a wider and rangier area for play, and for exercising his growing understanding of space and distance.

There is some increase in night waking, but, after a drink or a cracker, the child usually quiets down. In the following months, the going to sleep may become less smooth and easy. There is an increase of tension in the way he stands, sits, and walks, and in his play activities. The child may tend to cling to his mother as he is put to bed. He needs time to make the change-over from daytime activity to nighttime repose. A few extra moments devoted to bedding him down for the night affectionately may stave off storms and protests.

Two-Year-Olds Have Limitations

The third year, that is, the period from two to three years of age, presents many problems both for the child and for those who live with him. It is especially a time of change. The last milk teeth are cutting. Jargon is dropping out to give way to sentences. Complex controls are demanded of larynx, tongue, and jaws; of body posture and the way he uses his hands. Control of bladder and bowel is being acquired or perfected. Self-help, obedience, and household deportment require much of him, too. And all these controls must be brought into co-ordination more or less at the same time. There is truly a danger that we expect too much too suddenly of the two-year-old. He is, after all, an infant-child.

For these reasons, routines frequently need to be simplified in behalf of the two-year-old child. An interesting instance is the temporary difficulty the toddler has in adjusting to two parents at one time. The child is fond of both his mother and his father. The father, indeed, may be a favorite, and yet the child clings to his mother. This constitutes a genuine behavior difficulty, based on a sheer though passing immaturity. Accordingly he adjusts better to a single adult at a time, whether it be Mother, Father, nursery-school teacher, or baby sitter. The routines set up at meals and bedtime can take this circumstance into account.

Matching Your Pace to Theirs

The two-year-old is also given to slow and gradual waking up. He does not like to be rushed through the routines of rising and dressing.

Routines should be consistent and considerate; but parents can avoid solicitous hovering or constantly talking at a child. There can be a detached enjoyment of the valiant independence the two-year-olds display on occasion. Some children insist on feeding themselves entirely—and messily. Others accept being fed, but insist on tidiness in a manner worthy of the most particular housekeeper.

Some wish to be left distinctly alone when seated on the toilet. Others for a time refuse the bath. But characteristically the two-year-olds display a marked interest in washing and drying their own hands. Naturally routines should relax sufficiently to give fair scope to such efforts at independence.

Why Do Choices Bewilder Them?

Self-dependence is a complex quality. It is determined not only by the spirit of the child, but also by his capacity to make choices. These choices grow in number and variety as he himself grows older. At about the age of two and a half

Rae Russell

The best moments of his day may look like mere dawdling to a busy mother. Give a toddler time to enjoy life, and he will be easier to live with.

years, there seem to be almost too many choices to make. At any rate, this is another period of change when life is especially charged with double alternatives. At eighteen months, all streets were one-way; now they are two-way.

In countless situations, the child is called upon to make prompt choices in word or action. Such distinctions as those between *yes* and *no*; *come* and *go*; *fast* and *slow*; *now* and *wait*; and *give*

So many possibilities set small heads awhirl. Wise mothers make positive suggestions and offer occasional choices that will not be confusing.

and *take*, are a real hurdle to the two-year-old. He is too inexperienced and too immature to handle all the dilemmas with skillful ease and amiable compliance, so he reacts in various ways. Some of his reactions disturb routine and reflect his limited capacity to make a straightforward choice. He "disobeys." He does the opposite of what he is asked to do. He does nothing. He flares up with a tantrum. He dawdles and delays. He resorts to a familiar routine of his own with determined ritualism.

Clearly, these varied symptoms must be managed in relation to the situation where they occur, and with common sense. They should be regarded as signs of the child's immaturity rather than as "naughtiness." They do not necessarily indicate that the child has not been "reared properly." Sharp punishment tends to aggravate the symptoms. Avoid issues. Use dramatic humor and by-play in which the child participates. Patience is needed with long-drawn-out dawdling. In fact, dawdling may prove to be an interesting, instructive, and even relaxing incident for a parent to observe. It affords, as all behavior does, glimpses into how the child's mind operates and grows. Dawdling in the two-year-old has not the same meaning that it would have in a child four or five years older. Nor does it require the same handling.

They Do Grow Up!

If it happens that the two-and-a-half-year period is trying, both for child and parent, there remains at least one reassurance. Some day this child will be three years old. He will reach that next higher level of maturity, and a stage of relative equilibrium. Alternatives will no longer bewilder him. He will actually like to make choices of action (and obedience), for he will then be competent to make them. With your help, he will even shed the rituals that he held with such firmness a few months ago.

Tact, again, is your watchword. Tact in child care is a form of understanding that discerns the potentials of growth in the ever-changing patterns of immaturity. No two children show these patterns in precisely the same form. No two parents see these patterns precisely alike. But wisdom in child care begins with an acknowledgment that there is a patterned process of growing. The pattern and the process are profoundly governed by natural law.

WHAT DOES HE LIKE TO DO BEST?

TERRY SPITALNY, B.S.

Former Director, Nursery School, Sarah Lawrence College, Bronxville, N. Y.

LIFE is thrilling for the toddler. He can do things on his own and he is eager to try his hand at everything. He loves play so dearly that he turns each event in the day into play. The more good ways we can find to let him enjoy his new achievements, the easier he will be to live with. He wants reassurance from us over and over again that we are on hand and that we approve of him. He counts on us to be there every morning of his life, and to welcome the new day with him. He doesn't understand that sometimes we are too sleepy to find the day as glorious as he finds it.

He Likes to Be Near Mother

As soon as his day begins, he wants to follow us to the kitchen and help us get breakfast. We might just as well be gracious and invite him to come along. Although we may not find the kitchen a fascinating place, it's just possible that Johnny thinks we do. We spend a fair amount of time there doing things that require our undivided attention.

97

F. P. G.

Watching Daddy shave is always an exciting affair. There is no better way to start the day for this youngster.

How Can You Keep Him Out of Trouble?

We long ago discovered that there is little use in trying to divide our attention between Johnny and the toast. Neither co-operates. Johnny is far more reasonable than the toast. If we have set aside a shelf just for him, with his pots, covers, plastic cups, wooden spoons, discarded cans with edges smoothed, he will give them his undivided attention. Watch his absorption as he tries to fit small covers on large pots, and his glee when he finds the right size. Watch him

when he tries to fit a large can into a small cup and note his smug satisfaction when he discovers the right formula. In the not-far-distant future, his arithmetic teacher will work hard to invent ways of showing him the relation of small numbers to large ones. The feeling he is getting for sizes and shapes now will be valuable in later years.

Johnny likes the importance and satisfaction of managing things and imitating that remarkable person, his mother. A bit of conversation and admiration from us is not only appreciated but rewarded. The more Johnny finds that he can command our attention, the less need there is going to be for him to demand it.

Mother's Approval Puts Him at Ease

That special shelf for Johnny's own kitchen utensils may seem to be a simple matter. It is one of those simple investments that pays large dividends. When we provide ways Johnny can safely use the things around him, we further his emotional growth as well as his educational development. Small children are entirely dependent on us. They know deep inside themselves that we are necessary for their preservation. They become amazingly sensitive to our feelings and behavior. Their greatest fear is that we might desert them. They do not know that no matter how displeased we may be, we are not going to abandon them.

What might the course of events have been had we not provided anything to keep Johnny happily occupied in the kitchen this morning? First, we might have had to stop what we were doing to snatch a sharp knife from Johnny. Then he might have opened the refrigerator door, before going to the stove to turn on the gas jets. Each time we had to interfere with what he was doing, we would have become more exasperated. Naturally, Johnny would have thought we were angry at him. This is the very risk Johnny could not afford to take.

According to his two-and-one-half-year-old reasoning, these *things* he played with got him into trouble. If this same pattern were repeated day after day, Johnny would turn his back on all things. He doesn't want them. Having a good time isn't important. The only thing that matters is winning Mommy back. It looks to him as if independence and accomplishment bring about Mommy's disapproval. It's safer to be dependent. If he is afraid to use the things around him to learn and grow and play happily, there's not much left for Johnny to do but whine and cling to mother.

When Routines Are a Lark

The kitchen is not the only alluring place for Johnny in the morning. There is the bathroom and Daddy. Quite unlike Daddy, Johnny thinks shaving is pure joy. He will watch for a while, but he would rather be useful. He loves doing the same thing over and over again. Putting a toothbrush back in its holder,

or the soap in the soap dish, is a satisfying accomplishment for a two-and-a-half-year-old. Let him put the razor-blade wrapper in the wastepaper basket and Daddy's slippers in the closet, and he will be ever so pleased with himself. He will do these chores methodically day after day. He will scold if the order is reversed. He will remind us when we forget, and even Daddy will enjoy Johnny's busy housekeeping.

We may loathe washing dishes, but Johnny likes to do it. Put a rubber apron on him, like your own if possible, and rubbers on his feet. Give him a large basin filled with water and soap-flakes, an easy-to-manage egg beater and his own dishes, and let him "go to town." He will beat until the suds stand up like whites of egg. He will pour and scrub, and squeal with pure joy. He will get wet, but he is protected. The floor will get wet, too, but a mop takes care of that. Johnny feels good if we are unconcerned about his clothes or the floor. It is good for him to see that our interest in him includes the things that are fun for him. Too often our interest is only aroused when he finishes his food, goes to sleep, or has a bowel movement.

How Much Shall He Play Alone?

"Is he never by himself?" "Must he always be under foot or within earshot?" It's those words "never" and "always" that are such troublemakers. We say "Johnny never leaves my side." Yet if we go over the events of the day, we will find that Johnny was on his own a good

Protect his clothes and the floor with something waterproof. Then let him go to it with foamy soap bubbles and some plastic dishes which are his own.

part of the time. He doesn't like aloneness as such, but who does? Neither would he like to think he was alone because we thought it good for him. He will play by himself if we thoughtfully plan "by-himself times."

If Johnny doesn't have a room of his own, we can fix up a corner of a room just for him and his belongings. We won't leave him alone to roam around the house. He is too young to under-

F. P. G.

Teddy bears make no protest if they are squeezed or pushed. They may seem far easier to get along with than other children at this tender age.

stand either his own limitations or the strains and stresses furniture and bric-a-brac can take.

What Does He Like to Play?

We will not give Johnny too many toys at once. We know he enjoys his own power of making and unmaking, so we will give him blocks and push-toys. He'll push over his blocktowers and be proud of his strength. Gradually we'll help him be as proud of putting them together again. He loves to act out the familiar. A doll to dress and undress, to feed, to cuddle, to put to bed, and to spank will keep him busy and happy. We need not feel uneasy about the spanking. Around the age of three he often punishes his dolls, even though he himself has never been punished. He may be spanking those dolls for his own misdeeds, real or fancied. It is his way of teaching himself "right" and "wrong." Sometimes this is called the beginning of conscience.

When the world is so full of a number of things, he has to try them *all*. In time he will select favorites. Some children become selective sooner than others. They cherish certain toys and ignore others. They enjoy some activities and turn their backs on others, but as long as there are "others" to choose from we certainly won't interfere. We just want to be sure that what we call *choice* is not boredom or lack of interest.

He Enjoys Other Children

Watch a two-year-old when he catches sight of another child or a group of children. He can hardly contain himself. They are a miracle to him. Although his unbounded joy would indicate that he senses that they are quite different from the other toys in his life, he may at first treat them as he would treat a toy. His teddy bear didn't care how hard he was squeezed. This new "toy" does not like being poked or squeezed, and says so in no uncertain terms. For this reason, although he begs to be with other children, he needs our help. He needs time

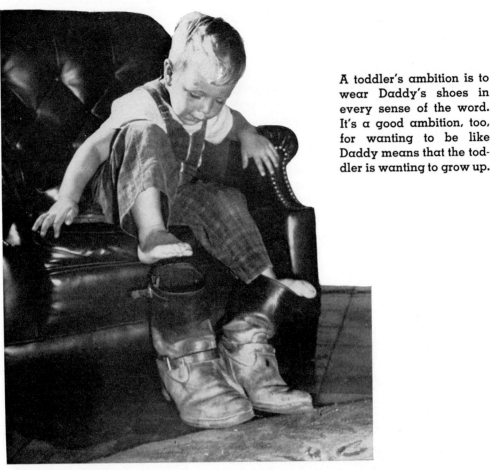

A toddler's ambition is to wear Daddy's shoes in every sense of the word. It's a good ambition, too, for wanting to be like Daddy means that the toddler is wanting to grow up.

Vivienne Lapham

to learn to play *with* other children. We can't let him experiment as he does with his toys or with the grown-ups. We don't want him to be discouraged by continuous rebuffs.

When families were large, Johnnies and Marys seemed to learn to get on together naturally. Perhaps they learned because there was always a group of children around. Perhaps because mothers were so occupied, the children found ways to work things out for themselves. Today few children live in such households. Mothers must find other children for their youngsters under school age. Sometimes they can be found in neighboring back yards, sometimes in the parks or playgrounds near home.

What Can You Do When They Hit and Grab?

Mothers might as well agree that at two or three years of age children will show their interest in one another in strange ways. Unnecessary embarrassment could be avoided if nobody expected sociability or politeness of the usual sort. Two-year-olds and even two-and-a-half-year-olds are pleased to be together, yet they pay little attention to one another. Was it worth walking six blocks to the park so Johnny could play with Mary Ann? Johnny is putting stones in a pail and Mary Ann is sitting near him talking to her teddy bear and paying scant attention to Johnny. Children of this age play side by side rather than actually co-operating in an undertaking. Playing together will come in a year or two. The children are becoming accustomed to one another, and it is therefore definitely worth the effort to bring them together. They take so little notice of one another some days that you are tempted to leave them on the porch or in the yard with no grown-up. They are not ready for that much responsibility yet. Someone must keep an eye on them.

When they do take notice of one another, there is likely to be a fair amount of pushing, hitting, grabbing, and even knocking-down or pinching. Such behavior is no reflection on anyone's *bringing* up. It is a necessary part of *growing* up. The children are too young to share, but they are not too young to want what the other fellow has. Sharing comes *after* owning. Try to forget all about "selfishness," "greediness," and "unfriendliness." These words cannot be applied to two-year-olds.

How Can You Keep the Peace?

Try to find a small group of children. Mothers can bring similar toys to the park or back yard where the children play, but leave the most treasured toys at home. That stuffed animal that goes to bed with Johnny, sits at the supper table, and comforts him when he is hurt, and cannot be shared any more readily than you would share your toothbrush.

A day may come when there is no harmony at all, when everyone wants what the other one has. Then it is wiser to pack up and go home before the grown-ups' emotions become involved. Come back another day, and you will be surprised to find that what seemed like an impossible situation on Tuesday is all sweetness and light on Thursday. How often it turns out that, if you leave a difficult problem *before* you get into a temper, you can go back to it later and find an easy solution. Wise mothers try not to get themselves out on a limb.

You Must Believe in Them

Growing up takes time. The most important part of growing up is the day-to-day growing. The child's horizon has widened tremendously. Because he can now do so many things, he wants to do everything. It is fortunate that so many of the things he likes to do best are the very things that further his development. He does not know his limitations; he cannot foresee consequences. He does not even know when he is tired, but he needs us to set limits for him. He needs our encouragement. He needs above all to know that we are on his side.

A five-year-old revealed how much being "on his side" means. He had been upset because his baby brother had swallowed a nail. He had witnessed the resulting anxiety, the comings and goings of doctors, and the X rays. When he finally could talk about it to the other children, they laughed at him. They said it was impossible, no one could swallow a nail. "We don't believe you." He was crushed. It had been so hard for him to talk about it and now he was not believed. He burst into tears. His best friend put his arm around him and said, "I believe you, Tommy. I just don't believe it was a nail." Tommy dried his tears. He was satisfied. His friend believed *him*. The nail? That was just a detail.

Feeling that they are trusted is important for even the smallest members of the family. With such trust they can enjoy the events of each day. There will be many different kinds of things they like to do. Perhaps what they really like best is the business of living!

THE NURSERY YEARS

Frederic Lewis

Three- and four-year-olds are interesting, delightful persons even though sometimes they are somewhat tiring to have around. They are more fun if you understand them. They like to be busy. They want to act on their own initiative and try out their powers in many directions.

As they advance in their own ability to use languages, they are better able to get along with other children, and playmates become increasingly fascinating. Through their play and their imagination they grow in an understanding of the world, of the different kinds of people in it, and of their relationships to them and to each other.

For the development of healthy personality, it is important that children in these years form a picture of themselves as boys or as girls who are "all right." Children who are lively, ready for new experiences, who like other people and feel they in turn are liked, are not apt to be "spoiled," even though they will sometimes be mischievous, angry, and troublesome.

Elizabeth Hibbs

HE LIKES TO BE BUSY

MOLLIE S. SMART, M.A.

Co-author with Russell Smart of "It's a Wise Parent," Kingston, R. I.

A TRAINED athlete once attempted to spend a whole day doing exactly what one preschool child did. Any parent of a three- or four-year-old can guess what happened to this vigorous, healthy young man. He ran, climbed, squatted, swung, rode, built—and gave up from exhaustion. His little model continued to be busy, and fresh as a daisy. A three- or four-year-old is a bundle of energy. There seems to be no end to his desire for action and more action.

Three-Year-Olds Are Steadier

Compared with the effort it takes to care for a child between the ages of one and three, the lot of parents of a three- to four-year-old is easy. A two-family picnic provided a nice example of a toddler's dependency and a young child's capability. Three-and-a-half-year-old Jane Spangler undressed herself and got into her swimming trunks, while Mrs. Cushman undressed twenty-two-months-old Danny and put on his trunks. Jane played in the shallow water except when Mr. Spangler took her for rides in the deep. Mr. and Mrs. Cushman took turns watching Danny, taking stones out of

his mouth, and bringing him back when he went out too far. Jane helped to dress herself. Danny had to be dressed. Jane sat at the table between her parents, with a pillow on her chair, and fed herself the adult food. Mrs. Cushman held Danny on her lap and fed him from a jar of baby food.

How Much Can They Do Alone?

Jane got down from the table, played in the sand, and threw stones in the water. Mr. and Mrs. Spangler knew where she was and what she was doing, and they both sat at the table through the whole meal, while Mr. or Mrs. Cushman ran after Danny periodically.

"You're lucky to have such an independent child," said Mrs. Cushman.

"Jane used to be just like Danny, but now she is three. She has herself well in hand," Mr. Spangler answered.

Jane, like other children her age, is pleased with the many things she can do for herself, and she is eager to use her abilities to please her parents. She is willing to work at dressing, washing, eating, and managing her own playthings. She needs help at times with all these

105

It is a rude awakening for Dad, but you cannot persuade a four-year-old to waste the best part of the day.

activities, and her parents are there when she needs them.

It's a Busy Day!

Three- and four-year-olds like to get up early. There are so many fascinating things to do! A favorite way to start the day is with a romp in Daddy's and Mother's bed. If a child wakens too early to be welcome in his parents' room, he can go to the toilet, provided his pajamas are easy to manage, put on slippers and bathrobe, and play quietly with books and toys.

How Much Freedom to Roam?

Outdoors is the best place to spend most of playtime. Most Threes and Fours cannot cross streets alone. But a few, especially those who live on quiet streets, can be trusted to observe safety rules. The art of parenthood includes figuring out just how much responsibility your Billie or Sally can take at the moment. A child needs limits that are right for him, but the limits vary from child to child. A fence around the yard is right for one. Perhaps a rule that he must not go off the block is good for another. Limits should change as youngsters develop, and youngsters develop fast at this age. Billie may appear to be ready for a new responsibility suddenly, but actually he has been growing up all along.

What Equipment Do They Need?

Outdoors is the favorite place to play, because Threes and Fours need long periods of the kind of play that uses the whole body. They also like short periods of quiet play, using the indoor playthings such as books, paper, crayons, paints, scissors, paste, puzzles, peg boards, dolls, and animals.

Young children cannot sit still and work quietly for many minutes. Their bodies demand activity. These children have come a long way in learning to manage their bodies. They can run fast without bumping into things. They can climb, swing, and jump. They love to ride tricycles and to haul toys, blocks, and children in wagons.

This wisdom of the body seems like magic, for it tells children to do the very things their minds and muscles must feed upon. Now they are perfecting the skills that distinguish them from babies. They are adding new skills, and laying the groundwork for what they will learn as kindergartners.

Children need space and equipment for play. Almost any yard is big enough for a packing box, plank, ladder, and perhaps a swing. One family fixed a tiny yard, with a ladder attached to the back porch. A wide plank sloped from the porch landing and served as a slide. A homemade easel was attached to the wall of the near-by garage. And of course there was a sandbox. Toys and Play

106

If you are looking for perpetual motion . . . you will find it . . . in any three- or four-year-old.

MATERIALS, in this volume, and MAKING THE MOST OF YOUR HOME, in Volume 8, have more suggestions. If children do not have space to run, climb, jump, and shout at home, they should go to parks as often as their parents can manage the trip.

Supermarket Manners

The simplest trip or expedition delights a young child. It is fun to walk to a neighbor's house, to go to the store or post office, or almost any place with Mother, Father, or an older child. Threes and Fours are good companions on a walk. Whereas Two wants to explore every sidewalk and bush along the way, Three walks right along at a slow but steady pace, enlivened by occasional running. Or he may ride his tricycle, so that an adult can walk smartly.

At the grocery store, Three or Four is interested in buying, and is likely to demand gum, candy, ice cream, and books. Faced with this situation, you can do two things. First, take a firm stand about what he may buy, and lay down a policy that the child can understand. One purchase on each trip is a helpful rule. Second, let him play a part in buying. He can select the brands of cereal he knows, count three or four cans of soup into the basket, and push the cart. He can hand over the nickel or dime for his own purchase, and maybe even hand the price of your order to the clerk. He likes to feel that he is helping.

Outlets for Energy Indoors

Children are sure to run, climb, jump, and shout, indoors as well as out. It is easiest on everybody to make some provisions for vigorous play indoors. A playroom is fine, but a living room also can be adapted to preschool play for a few years.

For many parents, the sacrifice involved in putting away precious, breakable objects is amply rewarded by the resulting peace of mind. A rather expensive set of rings, a swing, and a trapeze

107

can be fastened in a doorway without marring the wood, and it can be taken down in a few seconds. Less-costly equipment for three-year-old acrobats can be screwed into the ceiling, if you know where the beams are. Then, when David and Dorothy follow their natural impulse to jump and climb on the furniture, you can say, "Not here. Those tricks belong on the swing and trapeze," and there are no hard feelings.

Dancing is a wonderful way to let off steam indoors, and it can be done with no equipment at all. You can sing songs like "Hop, Little Bunny," and, of course, you can use records. If someone can play nursery rhythms on a musical instrument it is even better than records. Children enjoy having parents, brothers, and sisters join in the dancing sometimes, and they may get new ideas about what to do, from them. YOUNG CHILDREN AND MUSIC, in this volume, and Volume 11, MUSIC FOR THE FAMILY, have more helpful suggestions.

Three- and four-year-olds need companionship of those of their own age. OTHER CHILDREN BECOME MORE IMPORTANT and WHAT NURSERY GROUPS OFFER, in this volume, discuss this question.

What About Rest and Naps?

Children need rest as much as they need vigorous activity. Many young children naturally balance periods of activity with periods of rest. Peter and Margy build a big house with a box, plank, and blocks. Then they sit down inside to

Her helpfulness can be encouraged, though it may need to be directed toward something she can manage better than a vacuum cleaner twice her size.

play house. Freddie rushes around with his wagon, putting out a fire, and then goes to bed in the fire station. Peggy comes in from outdoors and works on a puzzle. Sometimes a suggestion changes the pace of play and gives a child a chance to relax. Midmorning drink of juice, paper and scissors and paste to play with, a story, or records can do the trick without ever a word about resting or being tired.

A real afternoon rest is a good idea throughout the preschool years. Many children refuse to go to sleep, at three or four years, but will stay in bed with books and toys. Some children will stay quietly in their own rooms if a "play-rest" or "play-nap" is part of the routine.

Learning Through Helping

Parents are big, wonderful, and practically perfect people to Threes and Fours. They want to please their parents, help them, and imitate them. Since a little child spends a large share of his

Suzanne Szasz

Lucien Aigner

What's up so early in the morning? The early bird catches the worm, but she may catch a scolding, too, when Mother finds her outdoors at this early hour.

day with Mother, housekeeping activities are important in his play. Children pretend to cook, wash, and clean, but they want actually to do these things, too. Making a cake in the sandbox is fun, but it is not a substitute for making a real cake with Mother. What a thrill for a youngster to stand on a sturdy stool and dump in the sugar and eggs between whirs of the mixer! Or if he is not quite steady enough to do that, he can unwrap squares of chocolate and put them in the pan for melting, put cupcake papers in the muffin tins, and sift the flour.

A young child can wash potatoes moderately clean, shell a few peas, wash and dry a few pieces of silver, or wipe up a puddle or spot from the floor. He can put down the dog's or cat's dinner and pick up the dish when it is empty. What fun he has helping to set and clear the table, scrubbing the sink with cleansing powder, and trying to run the vacuum cleaner for a little while!

How About Putting Away Toys?

There are many more such jobs. They vary from one family to another. The important thing is to give the child a chance to feel and be useful. But remember that he will be satisfied with a few minutes of helping, and that you can be satisfied with that, too. His contributions to the family will not be of any great assistance. It is the helping spirit that counts. He will not do a big job like picking up a roomful of toys. The best he is capable of doing here is picking up a few things, while you do the main part of the work.

They Learn from Father

Children want to imitate and help their fathers as well as their mothers. It is easy to imitate a farmer, carpenter, or doctor, but many fathers do work that young children cannot understand. Luckily, though, fathers have homemaking activities and outside interests. It means a great deal to both sons and daughters to share in what Father does. If he is an amateur carpenter, painter, or plumber; a gardener, bird-lover, or ballplayer, his children will profit from helping and learning. And Father will be rewarded with love, admiration, and companionship.

Preschool children are forming ideas of what is right for a man to do and what is right for a woman. Father is the ideal man, Mother the ideal woman. If Father lends a hand with the dishes, diapers, and bottles, then Jimmy knows that it is all right, even desirable, for men to help their wives with these jobs. Betsy learns to expect this kind of help from a man. THE FATHER IN THE FAMILY, in Volume 12, discusses relationships with Father in detail.

Feelings Are Contagious

Children are quick to catch feeling tones. They sense how their parents feel about doing their work, about being men and women, about being parents. Jimmy or Betsy could not tell you in so many words how Daddy feels about giving the baby his bottle, but they know! Some of their own feelings about babies, bottles, and fathers giving bottles grow up in response to the feelings they sense in their father.

A child develops important feelings about himself, too. When you provide outlets for his tremendous energy and initiative, his body and mind are satisfied. He feels that he is good because he can do the things he feels impelled to do, with the full approval of his parents.

HIS LANGUAGE IS RICH AND FLUENT

EVELYN M. BEYER, M.A.

Director of Nursery School, Sarah Lawrence
College, Bronxville, N. Y.

GROWN-UPS, particularly parents, are the most important influence on children's language during the first few years of life. Our idea of what is important in teaching language to small children has changed over the years. We are less concerned with the actual number of words that children acquire than we are with their enjoyment of words and their delight in their use.

How Is Language Acquired?

We know that vocabularies grow rather slowly at first, and then increase quite rapidly throughout the preschool period. There are great individual differences in the range of vocabulary.

We all know some three-year-olds whose vocabularies are meager, but who easily communicate ideas through gestures, signs, and sounds. By five or six years of age, these same three-year-olds may have acquired sizable vocabularies.

How Can Speech Be Improved?

Some children will speak in brief, but complete, sentences, clearly and correctly, from the beginning. Some will be slower in speaking, and may retain babyish language forms until nearly school age. Parents need not be too concerned with such language behavior. It is usually wiser not to focus attention on incorrect or baby talk, or to work hard at correcting it. The youngster who stutters or stammers will not be helped by calling attention to his difficulty. You can read about the reasons for stuttering in

the chapter WHEN CHILDREN ARE ANX-
IOUS, in this volume.

By five or six, word games emphasiz-
ing beginning or terminal sounds can be
played. These are fun for children, especially if they are done in a spirit of discovery, rather than drill.

How Do Children Use Language?

Young children use language to make
known their needs and desires and feelings. They also use it creatively, for fun
and play. Adults tend to be more interested in the communication aspect of
language, for most have long since forgotten that language may be a tool for
art and play.

We tend to put our teaching emphasis on correct speech rather than on joyous expression. Too often we miss the
fun that young children bring to the discovery of sound and rhythm.

Listen to the language of preschool
children. They have learned to use a
great many words because these words
have meaning to them. They know
about many *things* and they know the
words that describe these things. They
are also learning about what *happens* to
things, and they are learning the names
of these happenings. The preschooler's
world is rapidly expanding, and so is his
language.

Most preschoolers are expressing
themselves fairly clearly. Occasional
ones surprise us with the extent of their
understanding and use of words. A four-
year-old, new to nursery school, was exploring. He spied the jungle gym and
asked, "And what is that contraption?"

**At this age, youngsters really have an
ear to the ground. They like to imitate
the sounds around them.**

A long stretch from the two-year-old's
"Wha's 'at?"

Language Furthers Friendliness

The preschool child whose language
has developed normally is capable of
conveying his needs, of reporting his
observations and interests, and of expressing his feelings. He can make himself understood to the grown-ups in his
life as well as to children his own age.
To the extent that he is able to make
himself understood will he be able to
have successful and satisfying relationships with both children and adults. The
child who is not able to make himself
understood sometimes has difficulty
with other children. He has to resort to
more primitive forms of communication
and expression, such as biting and
snatching and hitting. Frequently these
children are able to make themselves

Suzanne Szasz

clear to grown-ups with little, or unclear, language. They have, apparently, not needed words in order to get their ideas and feelings across.

Language Enriches Play

The preschool child's language tends to accompany every activity. When you are three, you can't play train without being a train and making train noises.

The two-year-old will push a train across the floor with a "choo-choo-choo" accompaniment. Three-year-olds will add "chuff-chuff" and "ding-a-ling." Four-year-olds will elaborate with "puff-ity-pum" and "chug-a-ling along." Five-year-olds will chant "all aboard."

This imitative quality is highly characteristic of preschool language, in both content and form. Preschoolers speak the language they hear, and it will be as dull and proper, as cut-and-dried, or as poetic, shining, and colorful as the language of the grown-ups they are imitating. In addition to this imitativeness, it has freshness, naturalness, and vividness. A child is so close to the ground and to the excitement of discovering the world of sound and smell and texture, that he seems to draw a freshness and vividness of speech from that thrilling contact.

How Does Language Expand?

The quality of the imagery of young children's language will depend on the richness or the poorness of the child's experiences. A child who has watched trains, trucks, and steamshovels will describe them with the vivid language of experience. He will recall the sounds and sights, the movements, the feelings of these experiences, and his language will be enriched by them.

Young children are constantly experimenting with sounds and words and word patterns. They will chant a seemingly meaningless phrase over and over again as they play, apparently for the pure pleasure of the sound it makes. Often this is harmless enough, but sometimes it becomes annoying to adults who prefer to have language make more sense. The fact that our preference makes little sense to young children apparently never occurs to us.

The Case for "Silly Talk"

When children first find out that different words sound alike, they are hilariously excited by the discovery. A whole new world of rhyme is opened to them, and frequently it becomes a silly one. Four-year-olds can become infected with the intoxicating delights of silly rhyming. "Boo boo, poo poo, moo moo" can throw a group of four-year-olds into stitches of laughter. This is the age when "bathroom" talk reaches its height.

This stage of language development is likely to be somewhat painful to adults. It may be an appropriate time to supply the children with the adult terms for elimination. "Pee pee," "wee wee," and some of the other terms grown-ups offer children seem to invite nonsense use. "Urinate" is a grown-up word, and a "B.M." is a "B.M.," and there isn't much you can do about it.

Parents may try to offer substitutes for terms that are socially unacceptable, but they need to realize that the urge to play with words is good. It should not be entirely squelched, just because it may be annoying to the adults. This may be the time to introduce legitimate nonsense rhymes—the Edward Lear kind of thing. Make a game of silly rhyming and contribute to it. It is a stage that does not last forever!

New sounds to hear, new sights to see, new textures to feel on farm visits bring out new words to describe these wonders fittingly.

Century Photos

Interest in Meaning Grows

Silly talk soon passes into an interesting and challenging stage. Most five-year-olds discover that words which sound alike have different meanings. This is usually exciting to them, and can be fun for the grown-up who cares to participate in the game. A group of five-year-olds called it "Those Words." "Bill" of a bird, and "Bill," our Bill; "cent" that your daddy gives you, and "sent"—when you sent a letter. There is the "jam" that traffic gets into, and "jam" that strawberries get into. One five-year-old excitedly offered "lie" when you tell a lie, "lie" when you lie down, and "July"! And thoughtful Peter suggested "night that comes after the day," and the "knight on a horse."

How "Bad" Is "Bad Language"?

Four and five are also the ages when what some people call "soap words" flourish. "Soap words" is a term that describes slang, profanity, vulgarity, or whatever the adult in question "cannot take." Painful as these words are for grown-ups to hear, adults often are the unwitting teachers of the offending phrases. Daddy may make use of some expressive words when he hammers his thumb by accident. Even Mother may express her feelings forcefully when she drops a piece of her best china. These words are heard and readily imitated by the young children, who get into trouble for saying what they have heard their parents say.

Soap to wash out the bad words is not effective. When the child uses such words with the obvious purpose of trying out their effect on the adults, it is generally better to ignore them. If the adult responds with a bang, verbal or otherwise, the words are automatically enhanced in value, and are more likely to stick.

Young children will also pick up from

All the astonishing expressions your four-year-old may use are not learned on the street. In the best homes, too, this may happen sometimes.

older children some of the harmless, objectionable terms that are characteristic of this stage of language development. "You dummy dope" is the flower of them all. If you hear your four-year-old addressing his grandmother with this term, it does not mean that he will become a delinquent. You can try to help him use the terms somewhat discriminately. You can tell him that you know that the other children say these words and that sometimes he feels like saying them, but that some people get tired of hearing them. You can also plant the seed of the idea that after a while he won't need to say them any more. Beware of labeling them "wicked." It is the best way of making them seem worth cherishing.

Keeping the Vividness

There are many things that we might

The sparkling language of poems that fairly sing and of well-told stories add to the vivid speech of a small person who will be quick to pick up new expressions.

do to preserve and stimulate the naturally fresh and vivid quality of young children's language. Certainly reading stories and poetry of good quality is important in encouraging shining, lively language. Parents need to become good critics of children's literature, to be able to select the things that will be meaningful and enriching. BUILDING A HOME LIBRARY, in Volume 12, and STORIES FOR YOUNG CHILDREN, in this volume, will have helpful suggestions.

Telling as well as reading stories helps children become acquainted with the joys of good language experiences. It also stimulates children to enjoy the truly creative experience of making their own stories.

If adults would listen to the language of young children, they would learn how prosaic and colorless our language has become. We say "as quiet as a mouse," "as flat as a pancake," "as easy as pie," "as quick as a wink," and we keep on saying these things. If you listen to a group of five-year-olds—or even to one at a time—and help them to think of the quietest things in the world, or the easiest or the deepest or the slowest, you will hear vivid, beautiful things. "As quiet as cutting cotton"; "as quiet as a splinter comes in"; "as slow as one man building a bridge"; "as deep as a giant." These are the things that children will say if they are encouraged and listened to.

Experiences in Their Own Words

Adults can also help children to develop colorful language by encouraging them to translate vivid sights, sounds, tasks, feelings, and smells into language. Children who were taken to a farm for the first time were full of excitement at what they had seen and heard and smelled. The teacher was able to help them to express some of these experiences in words by asking, "What did it feel like?" "What did it sound like?" David was telling about the cow, "She licked my hand. Her tongue felt rough and prickly with suds. Her eyes were like wet lollipops, and she looked at me with her lollipop eyes."

A walk in the woods offers countless opportunities for discovery. Expression of the discoveries in language clarifies and deepens the experience.

A group of preschoolers came upon a worm one day. The teacher guided and challenged their observations by suggesting that they watch carefully to see how the worm moved. "Does he walk?" she asked. The children watched intently, then Peter delivered this description of worm locomotion. "A worm has a way of walking . . . he wiggles into himself . . . then stretches out . . . and flats himself along . . . in a jiggering kind of way . . . I think his head goes first."

When Silence Is Golden

Such encouragement of vivid language is fine, but what about the child who never stops talking? What about curtailing some of this language? Is it ever legitimate to suggest that there be a little *less* talking? The answer is yes! Quiet times are as essential as talking times. "Whispering times" or "listening times" may be suggested when things get too noisy. No child suffers from such occasional curtailment, especially if the grown-up shares it with him.

Adults influence the vocabulary of the preschooler by listening to, encouraging, and approving the natural vivid quality of his language. Let us not make it poor, skinny, and halting like ours, for his language is indeed rich, fluent, and his own.

HE'S A GREAT PRETENDER

ROBERTA COLLARD, B.S.

Former Nursery School Teacher,
University of Chicago Nursery School

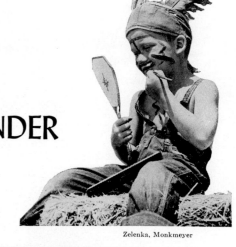

Zelenka, Monkmeyer

Your child's imagination is one of his most valuable possessions. Through his imagination, he is able to play constructively and creatively. He is able to enjoy stories, poems, and forms of art such as painting and modeling with clay. All scientific discoveries and inventions, and the great works of engineering and architecture, as well as art and literature, grow out of man's imagination.

As a parent you are the one who has the most influence on your child's development. You need to understand how imagination grows, the purposes it serves, and your part as a parent in encouraging or discouraging its expression.

Imagination and Learning

Before a little child has had a chance to have much experience, he sees the world the way he feels it is, or wishes it to be, rather than the way it really is. His imagination helps him to understand and express his feelings and wishes, and to seek fulfillment in the real world.

A child's imaginative play builds a bridge between his inner needs and feelings and the external world of reality. In acting out his wishes and fantasies in

Peter Gowland

make-believe play, a child may become interested in asking questions about the real world. Pretending that a stick is a boat in the water may lead to questions like: "Why does wood float and a stone sink?" Make-believe play often leads to greater bodily skill. For instance, as children play that the top of the jungle gym

117

Rae Russell

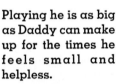
Small boys, like their fathers, find that bathing a baby occasionally is a satisfying occupation.

Philip Gendreau

is an airplane, and climb up and down to reach it, they are learning balance and muscular co-ordination.

How Imagination Grows

The chief pleasures of the child between one and two years lie in learning to walk and run, and in exploring and handling new objects. A child of fifteen months is able to imitate some actions he sees, such as making a sand cake or pouring water into a toy cup. He often pretends that a toy can do the same things he can do, such as eating or sleeping.

A two-year-old still gains great pleasure out of learning to use his body. He is still interested in exploring and handling objects. When he builds with blocks, most of his fun lies in handling them.

In his make-believe play, the two-year-old expresses the feelings that are of most importance to him. He is still greatly concerned with eating, and much of his play is pretending to eat things or feed someone else. In his play with sand and water, he is able to express some of

Playing he is as big as Daddy can make up for the times he feels small and helpless.

the pleasure in being "messy" which, to a great extent, he has given up to please his mother.

A two-year-old may care for his doll as he has been cared for, feeding or bathing it or putting it to bed. He likes to imitate the things grown-ups do, such as cooking a meal or driving a car, and he is a great mimic.

Three-Year-Olds Play House

A three-year-old has begun to combine toys, and plays with them in a

118

more imaginative way. For instance, he may build a road of blocks to run his toy car on, in contrast to the two-year-old, who just runs his car about on the floor. A three-year-old builds more complicated structures with blocks, and usually gives names to them. He may say, "I'm making a barn," or "This is a bridge."

Marvin Koner, Black Star

"Tch, tch, it's nothing serious. Just keep her quiet." Tone and expression imitate the doctor's exactly, as this young physician treats her patients.

All aboard the Packing-Box Express! When imagination has free rein, this train may take its passengers around the world and out to the farthest points in space.

A three-year-old is more aware of being a member of a whole family, for his father and his brothers and sisters have become relatively more important to him. When he is three and a half he often plays "house" with one other child. Boys, as well as girls, like to play house at this age. One child pretends to be the mother and one the daddy, or one may be the mother and the other the child.

In this family play, a child may act out his rivalry to his brothers and sisters, and his jealousy and love toward his parents. A little boy pretending to be a daddy is playing out his wish to be like his father, and in his play he is learning to be like him.

How Four-Year-Olds' Play Widens

Four-year-olds use toys in a more elaborate and realistic way than three-year-olds. One child at nursery school built a large round house of blocks with

Edwin G. Weidlich

Behold the happy warrior as he prepares to face the fiery dragon!

many train tracks going in and out. Three of the children played at "bringing in broken trains to be fixed."

A four-year-old usually likes to dress up and play out dramatic stories, or act out dramatic things he has seen. He likes to play heroic roles such as fireman, engineer, doctor, or cowboy. He is a great hand at making up stories and "tall tales."

As four-year-olds want to seem big and impressive, they are given to exaggeration. They are also developing a sense of humor and a sense of the ridiculous. This shows that they are well on the way toward distinguishing fact from fantasy.

How a Child Uses Play

In all imaginative play, a child is able to express his feelings, his wishes, and his fears. He may express his feelings of love by pretending to feed his mother or others he loves, or by caring for his dolls. He may also express some feelings and wishes he cannot be allowed to express in reality. He may hit his doll instead of his new baby brother.

Through his play, a child may fulfill some of his wishes not granted in reality. One little boy who could not go on a fishing trip with his daddy, comforted himself by pretending to go. A little child wants to be big and strong like his parents, and pretending in his play that he is the mother or the daddy makes him feel that he is.

In his imaginative play, a child is able to work out some of his conflicts, and master some of his fears. This lessening of conflict and fear makes it easier for the child to control himself in the real world. After a frightening visit to the doctor, a child often pretends in his play to be the doctor himself, and this helps him master his fear.

Through his imagination a child may deny unpleasant facts. A little girl whose kitten has been lost may pretend, "My kitten came back; it didn't run away." In the same way, a child's play at being an adult is a denial of his helplessness.

Some of a child's imagination is used for the pure pleasure of playing or creating. After a child is four, "making things" from clay gives him pleasure in addition to the fun of handling the clay.

Imaginary Companions

Children sometimes pretend to have imaginary playmates such as imagined children, animals, or creatures like fairies or elves. These imaginary playmates serve many purposes to the child. They may have constructive value in the child's personality development, for they often make up for lacks he feels himself to have.

Barbara, a lonely child of five, had two imaginary playmates (aged two and three) who were her "little girls." These children had golden curls (in contrast to Barbara's straight hair) and were beautifully dressed. They were always good, and were well fed and taken care of by Barbara. Due to her mother's long illness, Barbara did not receive as much care as she wanted, and she was able to gain some satisfaction by pretending to care for the two imaginary little girls. These children had all the characteristics she herself wanted. They satisfied her wish to be pretty and well-dressed, and her wish to have children of her own. They also kept her from being lonely.

Imaginary Companions Play Many Parts

Some children may blame an imaginary creature for the things they themselves have done. Linda (four years old) always blamed her misbehavior on "Little-Linda-in-the-Closet" who represented her bad self. A child may pretend his imaginary companion does things he is not allowed to do or is not able to do. A girl who feels her parents would have preferred a boy, may have an imaginary companion who is a boy. A little boy who feels he needs protection may have a strong imaginary companion who fights for him. A child may also give his imaginary companion all the bad traits that another child or a parent has, and then imagine them to be punished. He may use his imaginary companion to scold himself or to threaten others.

A child may find his imaginary creature remarkably useful in controlling his parents. Rosemary, a little girl of three, had an imaginary companion called "Mousie." One night Rosemary wanted to keep her mother with her longer than usual after she had been told it was time to go to sleep. She said to her mother: "But I can't go to sleep yet, because Mousie isn't in bed yet." Her mother said: "Can I get her for you?" Rosemary pointed to the ceiling and said: "Yes, she's up there." Her mother held her hand up to the ceiling and called: "Here Mousie, come on, Mousie; hop into my hand, Mousie," and she pretended to hand Mousie to Rosemary. Rosemary

The magic carpet-sweeper carries them to a land far removed from humdrum insistence on hand-washing and hot cereal.

said: "Oh, Mama, you got the wrong Mousie!"

Shall Imaginary Companions Be Encouraged?

You must remember that the imaginary companion is needed by the child who creates it. But you need not let yourself be controlled by your child's imaginary companion (except unwittingly!). You can treat it with consideration of your child's need for it, but never pretend to destroy it. When his need for it passes, your child will give it up of his own accord. If he seems too preoccupied with his imaginary companion, try to understand why he needs it and to correct the cause if possible. If he is lonely for companions, perhaps he could be entered in a kindergarten or play group, or be taken to a playground where other children play.

Your Part in His Pretending

Until a child is three years old, he may often confuse what he imagines with what is real. He may not only feel he *wants* to do something, but that he *has done* it. It is hard for him to distinguish the wish from the deed, because his wishes may be so intense that they fill his whole world when they are felt. After three or four, he is almost always aware of the difference between make-believe play and reality. He may create a make-

believe boat, but he knows it is make-believe.

It is your job as a parent to help your child gradually to distinguish what is real from what he feels or wishes were true. A little child tends to see reality in the light of his own needs and wishes and fears. Because of this, adults should usually be on the side of reality to help the child correct his self-centered thinking.

You may enter your child's make-believe play in the spirit of a joke, but let him know it is a joke and that you really do not believe it. If you enter your child's make-believe play, it is usually best to do so at his request. When your child tells "tall tales," go along with him in a joking way and then tell him it is fun to pretend things like that sometimes. If it is about something a child wishes were true, you might say: "I know you *wish* this were true" or "I know you'd really like to do things like that."

What Are the Danger Signals?

If you feel your child prefers daydreaming or pure fantasy play to the exclusion of more realistic, constructive play, try to find out why this is true. In trying to decide if this is so, take the child's stage of development into consideration. Remember that play becomes more rational as children grow older.

Too little imagination may indicate that a child is afraid to express his feelings in play, one of his important safety valves. His fears may interfere with his pleasure in play and with his creativity. Sometimes a small amount of imagination may be a sign that the child receives enough satisfaction in reality, and is able to resolve his conflicts sufficiently without using a great deal of imaginative play.

Imagination varies greatly in different children and at different ages. It is only in extreme cases of too much or too little imagination, when the child is unhappy or makes others unhappy, that you need feel concern.

Furthering Creative Imagination

Children need to be given an opportunity for free imaginative play, because their interest in the real world and their creativity grow out of it. You can see to it that your child has the opportunity to play with toys or materials that can be used imaginatively. Simple toys with many uses, instead of just one use, stimulate imagination. Indoor toys of this nature include blocks, boxes, toy cars, planes, boats, toy animals, dolls, and housekeeping toys. Old clothes or costumes and bright strips of material for "dressing up," art materials (clay, crayons, paints, colored paper, scissors, paste), string, carpenter tools, and scraps of lumber also suggest many kinds of play. Outdoor playthings that encourage imagination are sand, dirt, sand toys, water, large boxes, barrels, boards, wagons, and lengths of rope and rubber hose.

A child's imagination may be encouraged by reading or telling stories to him (appropriate to his age) and by encouraging him to make up stories.

You can encourage your child's creative imagination by showing an interest and pleasure in his creation, even if it be a two-year-old's first mud pie or a three-year-old's first house of blocks. The small child's creative efforts are worthy of respect, for out of this early imaginative play grows much of the constructive, creative behavior of men and women.

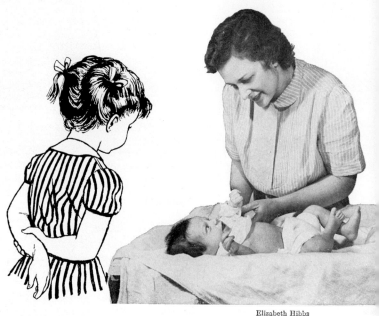

Elizabeth Hibbs

HE LEARNS
ABOUT DIFFERENCES
BETWEEN BOYS AND GIRLS

MILTON I. LEVINE, M.D.

Associate Professor of Pediatrics, New York Hospital, Cornell Medical Center, New York, N. Y. Co-author with Jean H. Seligmann of "A Baby Is Born" and "The Wonder of Life"

and

JEAN H. SELIGMANN

Formerly Assistant Teacher, Bank Street Nursery School, New York City

A CHILD is alive with curiosity. He asks all sorts of questions about the things he sees around him; about the trees, the stars, automobiles, water, the sun, people. Parents, to the best of their ability, try to answer these thousands of questions because they know that this is the way that children learn.

One day, along with all the why's and where's and how's, the question "Where did I come from?" is going to arise.

To the little child, the questions that he has about the human body, the differences between boys and girls, or men and women, the how and why of birth, are just as natural as "Where does the wind come from?" or "Why do the stars come out at night?"

Some parents, it is true, can give a calm, simple, and correct response. Others of us may find that this is not easy. We often become embarrassed and emotionally upset. This reaction is due, most likely, to the kind of thing that we ourselves were taught to believe when we were young. Perhaps we were told, "It isn't nice to discuss such things." We may have been warned that the parts of the body and the facts related to sex were vulgar. Sometimes we may feel confused just because we do not know exactly what to tell a young child.

Ewing Galloway

Children are curious about all forms of life. Here is a fine opportunity for a clear and simple explanation.

What Is Our Goal?

Many parents think it would be easier to avoid, to put off, or to foist onto somebody else the job of telling about the "facts of life." But remember this: Sex education does not begin or end at the moment that the child asks about the origin of babies. Like all education, it begins when your youngster is still a tiny infant, and it goes right on through childhood and adolescence. You cannot give sex education in a single dose any more than you can teach a child to read in one session.

You, as a parent, want your children to have wholesome and properly balanced attitudes toward sex. You want to help them become happy and fulfilled husbands and wives. You want them to be warm and loving fathers and mothers. Guiding their development toward manhood and womanhood is just as much a part of your job as is feeding, dressing, caring for, and loving your children. Your attitude and relationship toward your children when they are little helps

to build the groundwork for achieving these goals. Accept your children's curiosity about the parts of the body, about the differences between boys and girls, and about the birth of babies as utterly normal and natural curiosity. Then you will have laid the cornerstone for their own satisfactory marriages in later years.

Why a Correct Vocabulary?

You may have been brought up to think that the organs of the body which have to do with body eliminations and sex belong in a special department. Many people invent nicknames for these parts and their functions. Perhaps you sometimes call the sex organs "privates." You say "wee-wee," "tinkle," "number one," and "number two." But you call the mouth and nose and eyes by their correct names. It is difficult for many of us to use words like "penis" and "vagina." You may not believe in baby talk, and yet you actually encourage it when it is used in connection with these parts of the body.

No matter how young your child is

when he asks about the parts of the body, always give him the correct names. There is no need for manufactured terms. The use of the real terms helps to keep the child from thinking that certain parts of the body, and the things they do, cannot be discussed. It helps to build a vocabulary for your talks with your children about sex. It keeps the children from having to learn twice.

Answer When They Ask

The first time that your two- or three-year-old comes to you with the question, "Mommy, where did I come from?" you may find yourself covered with confusion. You may think, "she's not old enough to know about these things." Or you may feel like putting him off with, "I'm too busy now."

But the best time to answer a child is when he asks. If you keep putting him off, he will go elsewhere for his answers. That is when he probably gets the half-true or completely false information that confuses him still further. He will think to himself, "Mommy doesn't want to tell me. There must be something pretty special about this."

This is exactly what you should avoid. There should be as little special mystery as possible about these questions. For your child's sake, for his future well-being, then, make a valiant effort to be calm and collected, even if you do not feel that way! Answer him in as easy and natural a tone of voice as you can—but don't put him off!

Why Do the Smallest Ones Need the Facts?

Parents' confusion is not due entirely to embarrassment. Knowing exactly what to tell the youngster is often a stumbling block. Some parents still tell him that the stork brought him, or that

he came from the doctor's bag, or that an angel flew down and left him. Any of these stories will most likely satisfy the young child. Perhaps you do not see why it is storing up trouble to put him off with such statements. Put yourself in the child's position. Suppose that you asked information from a great professor, and later discovered that he had invented a completely untrue explanation for you because he did not feel you would understand the real one. You would not go to him again for information, would you?

Children are like that, too. Some time or other, the child will discover that you were not telling him the truth. He will have lost a great deal of his feeling of trust and confidence in you as a parent. He may seek his information outside the home, and you will wonder why he never asks you questions. What is more, you will not know what information he has, or how he acquired it.

How Much Shall We Tell?

"Well then," you ask, "what do I tell my little three-year-old?" The answer to that is, *tell him the truth.* Answer only what he asks, simply and accurately. Don't go into elaborate details. As the child gets older, his questions will naturally become more detailed, and the story is built up little by little. But remember, it is *his* questions that you are answering, not *your* information that you are giving.

Let us take a sample dialogue between a three-year-old and his mother.

CHILD: Where did I come from, Mommy?

MOTHER: From your mommy.

CHILD: But where?

MOTHER (placing her hand on her abdomen): From a place inside here, not too far from Mommy's stomach.

Usually, the child at this age will be satisfied with this much. You have purposely said in a place near the stomach, because of the confusion so many children have when told that the baby is in the stomach. One child, for instance, said, "What! With all the carrots and beans down there?"

Parents should not be surprised if the child asks the same questions over and over again. Many times he is satisfied with the same answers that were given before. If this is so, do not volunteer any further information. But you should listen to the meaning of the question. The same question may need a different answer for the six-year-old from what it did for the three-year-old. If a good relationship has been built up between the youngster and the parent, if he knows that asking is permissible, he will usually ask for more information as he needs it. He may not refer to the subject for several months or more. But he may ask the same question over and over just to test you. Will you still give the same answer? He may have forgotten or he may only want to assure himself that it is all right to ask.

Later on, the child will suddenly wonder, "But how did I get there?" Here again he should receive a simple, direct, truthful answer. A baby begins as a tiny egg, no bigger than a dot made with a pencil. It grows and grows in its special place inside the mother until it becomes a baby.

Eventually the thought will occur to the child, "Well, how did I get out?" He may then be told with utter simplicity about the birth process. There is a special opening between the legs, called the *vagina*, through which the baby comes out when it is time for it to be born. Do not describe labor, or labor pains, at this age, unless the child specifically asks about such things. When he is older, he is more likely to wonder whether or not it hurts when the baby comes out. He can be told then that there may be some pain, but that it is worth it to be able to have a lovely baby.

What About the Father's Part?

Most children, during their early months, or sometimes even years, of sex questioning ask little or nothing concerning the father's part in reproduction. The fact that a baby grew from an egg in the mother's body seems to satisfy them. Sooner or later, the child will start wondering just why he has Daddy's eyes, or why they say he looks like Daddy.

Then he should be told about the sperm from the father which must join with the egg, to make it the kind of egg which will develop into a baby. This sperm is so tiny that even the sharpest eyes are not able to see it. It can only be seen through the strongest magnifying glass, called a *microscope*. "But how does the little sperm go from the father to the egg inside the body of the mother?" is frequently asked.

The reply should not be complicated or detailed. Usually the answer that the sperm goes out of the father's body through the penis and into the mother's body through the vagina is sufficient and satisfying.

This sounds easy, written on paper. Actually, we all know that it is not easy to talk about this casually. Most of us do not have the same calm manner in speaking on this subject that we have when we are talking about airplanes, boats, or cabbages. Many of us were brought up in homes where we could not speak freely or openly about sex.

Do not worry if you make some mistakes in talking to your child. The important thing is for your youngster to feel free to talk to you and to come to you with all his questions. If he has the feeling of confidence in you, there will be many opportunities for you to make up for past mistakes.

Will the Children Be Discreet?

One question that always occurs to parents is, "What will the neighbors think if my child tells their children about where babies come from before they have given their children this information?" You cannot be perfectly sure this will not happen, but you can say to your own child, "These are things we talk about at home together. We don't talk about them with everybody." Usually, such an attitude, together with the assurance that he can always talk to Mother and Father about these matters, goes a long way toward giving even the chatterbox a sense of discretion.

The Child Who Never Asks

But what about the child who asks no questions? Is this unusual? Should efforts be made to arouse his interest and bring out such questions?

It is not always easy to determine why certain children hold off their inquiries concerning sex and reproduction. They may have been made to feel by various members of the household, or even by outsiders, that this is a subject not to be discussed. Some children are just a little slow in entering this developmental stage of curiosity.

Newly-hatched chicks bring home again the wonder of life, and the helplessness and appeal of small creatures.

It is a good idea to offer the child an opportunity to ask questions of this kind. You can read one of the excellent books about babies, specially written for young children, to your four- or five-year-old, as well as to your older children. All boys and girls love to hear about the days when they were infants. Seeing a mother cat with her kittens, or a dog with her puppies, or, better still, having a pregnant animal in the home can be the starting point for conversation about babies and how they are born. A trip to the zoo or a farm will also present opportunities to talk about birth. The way life begins is explained in Volume 9 of Childcraft. It cannot be repeated too often that your children should feel entirely free to come to you with their questions, and should receive prompt, truthful, and satisfying answers.

Both Sexes Are Important

There is much more to sex education than explaining where babies come from, how they got out of their mothers, and how they got started. What you tell and how you tell it is, of course, a vital influence on your children's future attitudes toward sex. But there is something more

that you can do. You must give your children the deep-down sense of being loved and wanted. You need to give your children the firm conviction that boys and girls are equally valued. You should emphasize that both boys and girls, both men and women, are important.

You want your children to grow up to be human beings capable of giving and receiving affection. Then they, in turn, can be good husbands, wives, fathers, and mothers. Boys must like the idea of being boys. Girls should be proud of being girls. At the same time, each can like the members of the opposite sex, too.

You help your children to reach these goals through your own attitudes, your example, and your feelings and beliefs.

It is often difficult for a child to realize that, once a boy, he will always remain a boy and grow to be a man, and once a girl, always a girl. This fact needs emphasis even though all adults take it for granted. A small child's confusion on that point can be truly worrisome.

How About Their Curiosity?

Every child, along with his other curiosities, is normally curious about the differences between boys and girls. He wants to know if all children of his own sex are built the same way. That is why children peek, pull up skirts, or undress other children and make comparisons.

In all kinds of behavior you need to make a distinction between what is to be expected and permitted in a small child and what might be unacceptable in an older child. The preschool child's natural curiosity about how other people are made is a different matter from some of the sex play of the eight-, nine-, and ten-year-olds. The small child who is permitted to find out what other chil-

dren of his own and the opposite sex look like is far less likely to engage in unfortunate and unacceptable activities later on. He will probably not be worried about or preoccupied with sex matters, for he has the information he needs. What is more important, he has a wholesome attitude toward the whole question.

It is normal for small children to attempt to satisfy their curiosity by observing other children's bodies. Many of us, when we observe this "peeking" activity, scold the child, call him "naughty," and immediately make efforts to separate him from children of the opposite sex. It is far better to let children of both sexes play together. You can arrange that they see children of their own and the opposite sex nude, at least until the age of five or six.

If you feel a child is preoccupied with questions of sex, you should keep an eye on him in his play.

How Can They Learn About Sex Differences?

Giving small children an opportunity to see other children of both sexes nude serves two important purposes. They will see that there is a decided difference between boys and girls. They will also gain a great deal of reassurance as they find out that all boys are built alike and all girls are alike. This knowledge is of particular importance to little girls, for many of them, after seeing boys, wonder if they once had similar external organs which were lost or taken from them.

A simple explanation that boys and girls are different because girls grow up to be women, and to be mothers, and boys grow up to be men, and to be fathers, is in order. Such an explanation is usually satisfying to a child whose other questions about sex have been answered.

It is comparatively easy for children to learn the differences between boys and girls in homes where there are a number of children of both sexes. Here the children dress and undress together, and even bathe together. The whole relationship is casual and avoids any special emphasis.

But what should be done in homes where a little boy has no sister, or where a little girl has no brother? How can these children be offered the opportunity to observe for themselves the difference between the sexes?

This is not as difficult as it may seem —but it usually does take planning. Do any of your friends or neighbors have infants? If so, arrange to pay them a visit with your child. He will certainly have the opportunity of watching while a diaper is being changed or while the baby is given a bath. Let him make his own observations.

You might invite some playmates of the opposite sex to stay overnight or to spend the weekend. You might enter your child in nursery school. Most nursery schools and groups for two-, three-, and four-year-olds understand the needs of young children. They have toilet rooms where youngsters will have the opportunity to observe one another. In nursery schools there is an adult present in the toilet rooms with the children, to answer their questions as they arise.

This Is a Two-Sexed World

You want your children to know that this is a world of boys and girls and men and women, and that this division into two sexes is a wonderful arrangement. You want them to know that both sexes are equally valuable and equally important. You want them to know, too, that you are happy that they are just what

Suzanne Szasz

When you make it clear that boys and girls are equally loved, equally important, you are giving your children good preparation for happy adulthood.

they are, that your girls are girls and your boys are boys. Both boys and girls need to feel loved and wanted. Children should be impressed with the importance of growing up to be fathers or to be mothers. Little boys can look forward to their future masculinity. Little girls can thrill with the thought of being able to have babies when they are grown up. Children should, by observing their own parents, gain the realization that both father and mother have equally important and desirable roles in home life.

It should be your goal to give to your children a wholesome and balanced attitude toward sex. All that you can do to help them grow up accepting themselves as boys or girls, and liking and accepting the opposite sex, will make them better able eventually to find satisfaction and happiness in marriage and parenthood.

OTHER CHILDREN
BECOME MORE IMPORTANT

CORNELIA GOLDSMITH, B.S.

Chief, Division of Day Care and Foster Homes,
New York City Department of Health, New York, N. Y.

A BABY whose first concern is with himself has a long road to travel before he becomes a sociable four-year-old. A good relationship between the infant and his mother starts him on that road. When this relationship is warm and sure, other relationships are more apt to be affectionate and reliable. Gradually the world of people expands from parents to other members of the family, from neighbors to policemen and bus drivers. From playing with one other child, he graduates to playing with the group in the back yard or nursery school. When a youngster is sure he is a worthwhile person in his mother's eyes, these steps will be made more readily. Such a child will be accepted more easily by his playmates, too, for he will have the capacity for friendliness.

He Is Hungry for Companionship

Signs of readiness to play with other children may appear before a girl or boy is two years old, or somewhat later.

When a youngster has a compelling urge to be with other children of about his own age, when he is drawn to them as though by a powerful, irresistible magnet, he is letting you know he needs companionship. But being ready to get acquainted does not mean that he has acquired the skills necessary for the give and take of play with other children.

It does mean that you can provide opportunities for your small boy or girl to explore and investigate what other children are like. They are different from the adults he has known. They make no allowances for him. They are not solicitous for his welfare. They do not cater to him. Fortunately he has acquired a certain amount of skill in walking and talking, and can make himself understood. He can run toward another child, but, when necessary, he can also run away from him. He can express approval, but he can also express disapproval in clear and certain words.

Just as learning to walk meant many tumbles, bumps, and bruises, so the first experiences in playing with other children mean countless tugs-of-war over possessions. Slowly but surely, the words "I" and "mine" give way to "we" and "ours." You begin to hear "give it to us" instead of "give it to *me*," or "may we have some ice cream" instead of "may *I* have it." The real meaning of "we" and "ours" must be experienced before the vocabulary change occurs. But the hunger for companionship with his own age group is as real as the hunger for food.

Why Don't They Play Together?

When young children seek each other's company, each plays alone in solitary, but parallel, play. This type of play is legitimate and should not be disturbed.

When two- or three-year-olds have just begun to come together, there are frequent conflicts over possessions. Each wants precisely the same toy that the other one wants, and at the same moment. Each child is equally convinced that it is his inalienable right to have and to hold the toy, and both will do battle then and there. Offering a duplicate or a substitute toy may or may not solve the problem, and often the going is rough indeed.

What Practice in Sharing?

The thing each holds so tightly in his own grasp is what he wants so desperately to possess. To discover that someone else wants what you want at the same time and with equal intensity, doubles and redoubles one's determination. Sharing is still an unknown idea. Logically, too, it seems one must truly *possess* something before one can share it. One must be sure of one's turn, before one is willing to risk taking turns.

You need not be embarrassed over your three-year-old's grabbing, and hanging on to what he grabs. His behavior is not a reflection on your own politeness. It is an unavoidable stage in learning to play with other children.

You can help children over these hurdles by being patient and understanding through these battles. You can help each child understand better how the other child feels. They know only too well how they feel themselves. It

A. Devaney

One digs a hole, another makes a sand cake, while a third builds a track for his train. Yet these youngsters take real pleasure in being together.

When young playmates see eye to eye on how to use sand and water or how to build a block house, what they look like or where they live are unimportant at the age of three or four.

is also helpful whenever possible to provide some duplicate toys so that a child can share without suffering deprivation. When a child is willing to relinquish a favorite toy to another child, it should be returned to him within a reasonable interval so that he will feel more ready to run the risk of sharing next time.

Sharing Ideas Is More Fun

Other children become still more important when the discovery is made that it is more fun, more interesting, more challenging, and more stimulating to play with other children than to play alone. By the time children are four, and far more when they are five, imaginations are soaring. Zest is added to dramatic play when several children take part. Ideas bounce back and forth like popcorn in a popper, and each is more savory than the last. In the rich play life of the nursery school and the kindergarten, and sometimes in the playground or on the street, children learn not only the give and take of their possessions but the give and take of ideas as well.

What Does Group Play Teach?

The shift from family life to the play-life of a group of age-mates is a dramatic and fundamental change. But just because children are lumped together does not necessarily mean that they are having a satisfactory or beneficial group experience. Unless relationships between the children themselves are real and have

meaning to them, the children will be like bunches of grapes on a vine—clustered together but not important to one another.

Children playing together may be a "group" in fact as well as in name, whether they are in a nursery school, in an informal play group, or in the back yard. Whatever the setting, the youngster finds himself more of an independent person taken at his face value. At home he may have been the most tender little one, entitled to special protection. He is now one of several, a member of a group. He must take his chances along with everyone else. As an independent human being, he becomes a part of something bigger than himself. He discovers a situation probably more challenging than anything he has met before.

He has moved from individual play, through parallel play, to group play. This play becomes his very life. Here is the give and take of companionship, the movement of ideas and of imagination. Here is exploration and experimentation, the basis for learning. Here are fun and gaiety, absorption, adventure, and creative expression, trying and failing and trying again. The way may be hard, but satisfactions are great.

Letting off Steam

More and more we recognize group play for four- and five-year-olds as essential. It provides release from nervous tension and pressures. It acts as a safety-valve to let off emotional steam. Inner tightness, fears, and uncertainties can be expressed through play, and often lessened.

Mastering New Situations

As they play together, children explore and understand their surroundings, both the physical world around them and the human world. They become acquainted with things and people. They increase their knowledge and their skills, and feel more and more adequate. Playing in a group develops initiative, ingenuity, and judgment. All kinds of situations, both real and imaginary, are met. They are tested, tried out, and solved one way or another. New experiences become familiar experiences. All kinds of ideas are

Rae Russell

given consideration, weighed, accepted, or rejected. Mistakes are evaluated and, when possible, remedied. All this is learning.

Understanding People

In dramatic play, children pretend to play grown-up parts and have dress-rehearsals for growing up themselves. "You be the father and I'll be the mother." "You be the engineer and I'll be the conductor." So they learn about many different roles in life. They learn to understand themselves and each other better. They find playing together more fun than playing alone.

The opportunity to establish a place for themselves among their own friends comes about as they play together, too. They learn to value and appreciate each other and to be valued and appreciated themselves. Sharing ideas and experiences may lead to conflict from time to time, and to misunderstandings. Resolving quarrels and remedying mistakes are often also a part of learning to understand others as well as ourselves. Given time, encouragement, and equipment adapted to their interests, it is surprising how often the four-year-olds and even the three-year-olds can work out solutions to their disputes. The kind of equipment that makes a good setting for their play is described in the chapter TOYS AND PLAY MATERIALS, in this volume.

How Do They Choose Friends?

Companionship is a necessary ingre-

**"You can be nurse and I'll be doctor."
The fun is doubled when two play together, and they grow in understanding of each other and of themselves.**

dient in children's lives. Friendship develops inside as well as outside the nursery school or the kindergarten, or, for that matter, the grade school.

But friendship does not come in a ready-made package, done up neatly just as parents might prefer or visualize it. Each child seeks another child because of his own particular and peculiar inner need for companionship. He does not choose his friends because they are particularly well-mannered or particularly clean. The particular race, color, creed, or economic level of his family has no significance for a youngster in most cases.

Can Young Children Be Loyal?

Young children do not feel any obligation to sustain friendship because it is the right and the kindly thing to do. At three or four, they often try out the varying responses. They want to discover the advantages or disadvantages of having friendships with different kinds of youngsters. They will drop one person and take on another. They feel free to change their loyalties without preliminary notice, explanation, or apology.

How Can You Handle "Swapping?"

"I'll give you my bicycle if you'll be my best friend" sets parents back on their heels. Not only does the four- or five-year-old seem totally unaware of the monetary value of the bicycle, but he seems to be descending to highly questionable behavior in an attempt at bribery. Actually, he is testing, perhaps a bit rashly but perhaps also quite desperately, his power to win over a challenging and highly desirable friend. And, for the moment, the bicycle is purely incidental. Likely as not he would win the bicycle back another day. But it is a risk hard for a prudent parent to take. More than one

explanation is necessary to prove the point that such trades are impractical and unwise.

He Wants "to Be Like Everybody Else"

To have the friends you want on your side, to know the ways of pulling them over when they are hard to persuade, to belong to the group, to be considered "in" and not "out," becomes a matter of tremendous importance at four and five. If the group has decided that "we like turnips," a child will like turnips though they may have been abhorrent to him until that moment.

A child whose mother has always dressed him with care and in good taste suddenly finds that he cannot wear the kind of suit she has bought him. It must be of another style, even though it be unbecoming and inappropriate. To belong, you wear what the others do. This is even more vital than parental approval, important though that be. At such times, giving in and recognizing the powerful new impetus of group approval is wiser than attempting to do battle for style or good taste.

Friendship Grows from Within

If you attempt to dominate and control these matters arbitrarily, and without recognizing the strong social forces awakening in young children, the children tend to become like puppets. They become set in a rigid pattern, unable to be real or important to one another.

Teachers, particularly, need to keep in mind how important for the growth of healthy personality are the spontaneous relationships between children. Through the give and take of ideas, the sharing of thoughts and experiences, the testing and retesting of friendship, young children create a true group life.

A. Devaney

WHEN ARE CHILDREN SPOILED?

MARJORIE MOMYER, M.A.

Chairman, Child Study Department, Stephens College, Columbia, Missouri

IT IS a great temptation, every time a child does something unpleasant or annoying, to say "that child is spoiled," and to assume that he has been overindulged. All children, even those who are usually the happiest and most radiant, occasionally cry, whine, or nag, or get into trouble and behave in ways that we might describe as "spoiled." Actually, some behavior that is perfectly normal at one-and-a-half or two years might be considered a sign of spoiling in a three- or four-year-old. We need to remember that a great deal of behavior that is to be expected occasionally of a three- or four-year-old might be a sign of spoiling in a six- or eight-year-old.

What Is a Spoiled Child?

It is not a particular incident, but the consistent pattern of behavior from day to day that marks the unhappy, restless, spoiled child. A spoiled child is one who is insistent, willful, and dissatisfied. He has really had his capacity to enjoy life, to have confidence in himself and others, spoiled. It is clear that spoiled children are not happy. They lack the inner security that is so necessary for a joyous, confident, wholehearted approach to play, to work, or to relationships with other people. A spoiled child is really suffering from a kind of emotional malnutrition.

Overindulgence and Spoiling

Most people feel that overindulgence is sure to spoil a child. It is certainly true that even a three- or four-year-old who invariably has things all his own way is not likely to be happy, or easy to live with, no matter what means he uses to achieve his ends. Children need opportunities to practice consideration and co-operation in small doses.

Frequently parents who have had a child late in life seem almost to be afraid to stand up for their own rights or to set sensible limits on their child's behavior. The child who is never told in a firm but friendly way, "This is as far as you may go," or "Now this must stop" begins to be afraid of what he *might* do if nobody controlled him. The "wheedler" is another familiar result of a lack of friendly firmness. Wheedlers, too, may

well be said to be spoiled children.

It is a curious thing that parents who really love and enjoy their children seldom hesitate to be firm and consistent with them. If parents can be firm when the occasion demands it, their children are not likely to be spoiled, even though there may be days when they are cross, and times when they get angry or whine.

Do Material Possessions Spoil a Child?

You have probably often heard the comment, "She's spoiled. She has too many toys." Yet equally often you may hear, or say yourself, "In spite of all the playthings that youngster has, he isn't one bit spoiled." Is it possible that in the first case the surfeit of playthings is a symptom of some deeper grievance? In the second, the toys did no harm because the youngster had real security.

You can probably call to mind instances of parents who have showered their children with elaborate toys, but who have not seemed to enjoy spending time with the children themselves. It is not the toys that spoiled the child. It is the lack of the feeling of being a person who is truly valued that makes a youngster disagreeable. Of course, overwhelmingly many toys or poorly selected ones may result in confusion for a child.

How About the Child Who Never Is Satisfied?

"Daddy, buy me that train. Daddy, I want another candy bar. Daddy, why can't I have that ball?" You have proba-

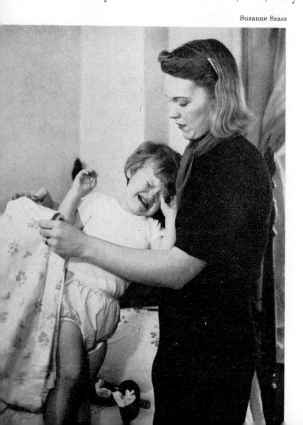

Suzanne Szasz

Maybe you can dress her faster than she can dress herself, but give her time to practice. You don't want to spoil the desire to "do myself," for that is at the root of all learning.

It's a major tragedy to have the balloon break! Disappointments and failures are more easily borne when they come in small doses, when they are balanced by successes, and if adults encouragingly suggest ways to do better next time.

bly seen children who are constantly asking for something, but who never seem to be satisfied even if they get it. These demanding children want something, but they themselves do not know what. If they could put their deeper feelings into words they might say, "I'm not sure I'm all right. I'm not sure you love me. If you buy me this train, this candy bar, this ball, then perhaps I will be sure." Of course, no toy or sweet will satisfy their longing to be loved, to be valued, to be approved.

Some parents, out of fear of spoiling a child, say "No" more often than is necessary. But flat denials are not the answer. It takes a readjustment of relationships, a change of attitude, before the insistent demands grow less. The child who is finding satisfaction in life and is sure of himself enjoys the things he is given. He is also able to accept a "no" from Mother or Father, when that is necessary, without unbearable disappointment. We make a mistake in feeling that the demanding child is the child who has been spoiled by having every wish granted. He is more likely to be the one whose deeper needs for affection and status have been overlooked.

137

What About Spoiling and Selfishness?

Parents are likely to be embarrassed if Tommy insists on playing with his own truck and is unwilling to let his guests, Ned and Don, have it. Three-year-old Tommy is not capable of much unselfishness. If too much is not expected of him too soon, he will gradually be able to do a better job of sharing. With practice, he will learn to share, but the practice can be in appropriate small doses. The chapter, OTHER CHILDREN BECOME MORE IMPORTANT, in this volume, discusses the question of sharing in more detail.

Can They Take the Consequences?

Sometimes you may feel a child is spoiled if he makes a great fuss when something goes wrong because of his own failure to conform. You may say, "He's never learned to take the consequences." This matter of taking the consequences is an extremely delicate affair. Often there are no "consequences" that make any difference to the small child when he has failed to do what you have asked. Equally often, the consequences would be too heavy. "If you aren't ready, you can't come to the picnic," would be treatment far too severe for a little girl who is exasperatingly slow in getting dressed. Her very excitement on the day of a long-awaited excursion may keep her from concentrating on dressing.

Perhaps the best we can do in this matter of taking the consequences is to see that the consequences of heedless or selfish behavior come in small and bearable doses. The goal may be to help a child learn that you cannot have everything your own way all the time.

Routines Can Be too Rigid

In a misguided effort not to let their children "get away with anything," some parents enforce rigid routines right from the start. Even as babies, some children's need for affection has not been adequately met. They never have had the opportunity to develop that sense of basic trust in their parents that is the foundation for a happy, confident personality. The chapters WHAT CHILDREN NEED FROM LIFE, in Volume 12, and FEEDING HAS MANY MEANINGS, in this volume, explain in detail how a baby develops trust in his mother.

Susan was a four-year-old. Her mother claimed it had become impossible to live with her. She brought Susan to the psychologist's office and explained that she had never been any trouble until recently. Sue had been weaned by six months, toilet-trained at eighteen

He's not necessarily spoiled because he hangs on to his toys. Willingness to share will come gradually if what he shares comes back to him promptly.

Some children need more affectionate attention than others, just as some need more bread and butter. The right kind of love never spoiled anyone.

Korling

months. She had eaten what was put before her, and gone to bed without any objections. But now Susan's mother had the long and all-too-familiar list of complaints about an "impossible" four-year-old!

When the psychologist asked, "Do you love Susan?" her mother replied, "I used to love her, but she is so naughty now I don't really know how I feel about her lots of times."

The psychologist explained to Susan's mother that the little girl was rebelling against those early years of unnecessarily severe schedules and training. She had been deprived of the comfort and the affection she needed then. If she had been deprived of milk or other essential foods, her bones and muscles would have shown the results. Deprived of emotional nourishment, her personality was showing the results.

How Can You Make up for Deprivation?

The psychologist went on to explain that Susan could not be made over in a day, or even in weeks. It had taken her four years to get this way, and it might take many months for her to become more agreeable and sure of herself. Children like Susan need an extra measure of affectionate attention. Time alone with Mother or with Father is one of the best healers of their hurts. Encouragement and a chance to gain self-confidence through success are good medicine, too. At the same time, it should calmly be made clear that there are better ways than bullying, throwing a temper tantrum, or whining to get something you want.

It is not always easy for parents who have felt they were doing just the right thing in enforcing strict routines to become more relaxed. For instance, Susan's parents found it difficult to realize that they were not "spoiling" her when they let her stay up half an hour later the night her nursery-school teacher came for dinner. Yet the feeling she gained of belonging in the family circle did more for her than a half-hour's sleep could have done. Certainly it did her more good than being sent to bed to cry with disappointment for an hour because she had not been allowed to have dinner with the family when her own special friend, her teacher, was the guest.

Overprotection Is Spoiling

During the nursery-school years children need to experiment, to try out their powers. Sometimes it may look to you as if your child had no sensible regard for danger. If you watch carefully, you may discover he is more cautious than you give him credit for being.

The first time Mary climbed down from the jungle gym, she grew frightened on the last step, for she did not realize how near the ground she was. The nursery-school teacher gently took hold of one of Mary's legs and guided her foot to the ground. Mary was pleased and surprised to see that she had almost climbed down alone. Her ability to be independent had been reinforced, not spoiled.

In the same way, you can avoid "spoiling" your youngster's ability to entertain himself, or to work out his own problems. When a three- or four-year-old is pulling his wagon and gets it stuck as he rounds the corner of the house, he probably will have to try several methods before he frees the wheels. Here is a real mechanical problem! If he seems to be floored by it, you might ask him, before he loses patience, "How do you think you could get the back wheels free?" or even, "Try moving the back end out a little." A suggestion, if he needs it, may give him a chance to solve the difficulty himself. If you lift the wagon clear for him before he has a chance to figure out what to do, you may "spoil" his ability to be independent.

There is a nice balance to be maintained between interfering when a youngster is managing for himself, and letting him become completely defeated by a situation that he is not able to handle.

How Close to Mother?

Many parents are afraid that if a small child stays near Mother most of the time, he or she will be spoiled. Nursery-age children need a chance to follow their mothers around. To be near Mother, and to imitate what she does much of the time, usually spell contentment for the three- and four-year-old. The child who knows Mother is available and willing to have him around is not likely to be as whiny, clinging, or demanding as the child who is always kept on short rations as far as Mother's company and attention are concerned.

When your three-and-a-half-year-old daughter is happy taking care of her doll family, it is only good sense to let her play uninterruptedly by herself. That is not the moment to suggest she come and sit on your lap, or that she help you set the table for supper. You can spoil a small child's ability to play independently if you interfere with what she is doing. Her ability to use her own resources grows stronger if she knows that Mother will be around for friendly conversation when the doll family fails to be responsive.

There was a time when parents were told that children must be treated severely and "put in their place" lest they become willful and demanding—"spoiled." Fortunately, we know now that the way to avoid unfriendly or nagging, spoiled behavior, is to give a child a chance to feel he is pleasing his parents, to let him like himself, act independently, and use his powers within sensible, clear, and consistent limits.

THE KINDERGARTNER

23. HE IS READY FOR NEW EXPERIENCES

24. HE ASKS ENDLESS QUESTIONS

25. HE STILL LEARNS THROUGH HIS PLAY

26. HE HAS A CONSCIENCE

27. HE GETS ALONG BETTER WITH HIS PLAYMATES

The kindergartner has come a long way on the road to being an independent, sociable individual. Now he is ready for new ventures. He is full of questions about everything and everybody in the world around him.

He does better at holding his own with other children and at playing co-operatively with them. Mother and father are still the last word, but what his playmates say and do is becoming more important. Play is still his chief way of learning and of working out feelings and ideas that trouble him.

The kindergartner has developed a conscience. While it is by no means an entirely reliable guide for him, it is a force in influencing behavior and in shaping personality.

If you understand what makes your kindergartner tick, you will be able to guide him more easily. You will be able to live with him more happily through the ups and downs that are always a part of growing.

HE IS READY FOR NEW EXPERIENCES

LYNETTE M. MESSER, B.S.

Former Assistant Professor of Education, San Francisco State College, Calif.

You have come a long way with your five-year-old. You have lived through the early preschool years and have probably done a good job. Now he is ready for new experiences.

Some of the experiences for which he seems ready may puzzle you. You may ask yourself how you can provide the kind of experiences that will help him grow still further.

The Fives Are Independent

Mrs. Brown had laid out Jim's clothes, but this morning Jim refused to dress. He did not want to wear what she had chosen. He wanted to wear the orange-colored socks with the red T shirt. Her responsibility was to see that he was dressed properly. After a battle, Jim was finally dressed "properly" for the day. Mrs. Brown was worn out and unhappy. And Jim himself was angry, frustrated, and in tears. At kindergarten he simply sat down on the floor and kicked at anyone who came near him. Jim was in no mood to profit from kindergarten.

The same thing happened the next day, and the next. Mrs. Brown discussed it with the teacher and found that such behavior was characteristic of many five-year-olds. It was decided to allow Jim to choose the clothes he wished to wear each morning, for here was an experience a five-year-old was ready to cope with and enjoy. It made no real difference if his choice of color combinations was unharmonious.

The first morning Mrs. Brown allowed Jim to choose the clothes he was to wear, he went through the whole drawer before finding what he wanted. There was no immediate change in Jim's behavior, but within a week he was coming to school in a happier, more relaxed mood. He alternated between a demand for independence and a demand for a good deal of help. The teacher had told the Browns this was to be expected, so they were ready with "Let me know if you want help," or "I'll start your breakfast while you start dressing."

Jim was asserting himself in other ways, too, as five-year-olds do. More good ways of being independent were found for him, for, really, only matters affecting health and safety needed adult control.

How Does It Look to the Child?

Many times, uncovering the underlying need at the root of a problem takes careful observation and understanding, as in Joan's case.

Joan came to kindergarten happily. The first two or three days went well. Then Joan protested against going to school. When asked why, she gave no reason, but accepted a day in bed in preference to school. This went on for three days.

The teacher could offer no explanation from what had happened at school. The supervisor suggested that Joan come to her office and play there. A friendly relationship had been established earlier between Joan and the supervisor, so Joan was happy with this arrangement.

Joan and the supervisor visited for quite a while and no questions were asked about school. Joan talked constantly about how big she was.

Look beneath the surface to find the cause when a happy youngster takes a sudden dislike to kindergarten, or to any other situation. Remedying that cause may be surprisingly easy.

Rae Russell

Never mind if socks and sweater don't match! Let your kindergartner decide which suit he will wear, for here is a good place for him to exercise choice.

"I am big now. I am so big I can reach my own toothbrush. I am so big I can reach my daddy's toothbrush."

The supervisor felt that Joan's bigness and reaching must play a part in her problem and she asked the teacher in Joan's room, "What is it Joan cannot reach?"

Out of this questioning, it developed that on the third day of school the teacher had placed all lunch boxes on a high shelf, out of reach of the children. At the supervisor's suggestion, the lunch box was placed where Joan could reach it, and the supervisor asked Joan to visit in the kindergarten with her. Joan never again protested against going to school. For this particular child, security was established by having her things where she could get them easily and readily.

Causes cannot always be discovered, but frequently they are comparatively simple ones. Listen to your child and try to understand the meaning back of what he says. Then you may be able to help him.

Independence Must Be Real

We glory in the child's growing sense of independence. But we often fail to remember that, to develop independent thinking, a youngster must have repeated and appropriate experiences in choosing and in working out problems.

In one kindergarten, the teacher called the group together, saying it was building time. One child wanted to work on the house of blocks that the children were building. "You know it is only on Thursdays that we can choose what we want to do," replied the teacher. "Today we are going to make a house of paper."

"You may choose the color you wish, Susie," said the teacher, holding out a package of multicolored paper.

Susie, a pale, colorless child in drab clothes, chose, "Purple."

Said the astonished Mrs. X, "You don't want purple. You never saw a purple house. What color do you want?"

Again came the answer, more quiet but just as sure, "Purple."

The question and answer were repeated three times. Mrs. X finally said in an exasperated tone, "Well, you may have purple this time, but I am sure you never saw a purple house."

Possibly having a purple house was immensely important to this colorless little girl. In a world where there are many limits for the growing child, it would seem the part of wisdom to plan ways to increase the range of choices. The teacher could have arranged each day a variety of activities, such as building on the house, cutting and pasting, painting and block building, to give the children experiences in choosing.

The Fives Enjoy a Group

Acceptance by his friends is becoming so important for the five-year-old that he wants to copy what the other children do. His interest in small groups for short periods of the day plays an important part in his life.

When Earl responded to a suggested activity with, "Says who?" he was reprimanded by his father. He replied, "All the kids say it. It's all right." How wise of his mother to help him see that there was a place and time for such a remark!

As parents and teachers, we need to be ready to have our ways questioned.

clothes she wore, said, "I can't go to school. I have no clothes to wear."

Mother said, "You have lots of dresses."

Mary's response was, "None of mine is as pretty as those the other children wear."

Mary's clothes were made as miniatures of her mother's. Children are likely to be unhappy even in kindergarten if their appearance is conspicuously different from others in their group.

In the space of a few hours, blocks will be homes or signal towers, doll families will encounter trials and joys, for variety is the life and breath of the five-year-old's play.

Ellis O. Hinsey

We can guide the child as he makes choices and compares authorities. We can remember how much he wants to be like the others. We can be sure it is necessary before we insist, "I told you to do it, and I know best."

Mary, who was unhappy about the

This situation was solved satisfactorily when Mother took Mary downtown to choose a pattern and material to make a dress like those of the other girls in her class.

Her mother's understanding made Mary happy, for she now "belonged" with her new friends. It also convinced Mary that her mother could be relied upon to help.

Five-Year-Olds Need Activity

One of the chief causes of irritation to the parent and teacher is the five-year-old's boisterousness and noisiness. You may be one of the few who have houses where noise does not present too many difficulties. Apartment dwellers know only too well the problem it creates.

Teachers can usually arrange programs that give opportunities for good noisemaking. Jane's teacher asked her what was the first thing she wanted to do when she went to her grandmother's farm in the country. Jane exclaimed, "Holler!"

Imagine waiting ten months to do something that your whole nature was pushing you to do! Jane's teacher suggested some games on the playground that helped Jane satisfy her "hollering" need.

A child who sits quietly all afternoon is not always the "best" child. The young child needs movement in order to grow. His large muscles are more developed than his small ones and he needs more activity involving the large muscles.

Can We Let Them Be Daring?

Sitting still for too long is not only hard to do but may actually be harmful. Can we arrange times during the apartment-house day when a youngster can be very active? Perhaps we can find a park or even a street where he can play, although he requires special supervision there. Schools can try to give a program so flexible that the five-year-olds can choose the activity that meets their individual requirements from day to day.

Vivienne Lapham

Kindergartners are beginning to see the advantages of working things out together. A small group can co-operate in building or constructing or in imitating some grown-up activity.

Then the need to be lively will be better satisfied.

As five-year-olds use their large muscles, they are likely to be daring.

There is a difference between "daring" and actually dangerous play. Teachers are sometimes fearful that young children will attempt too much. In one school the children were not allowed to use the beautiful play equipment unless they held the teacher's hand. Of course that was unnecessary and spoiled all the fun. We must protect the child from hazardous places, and dangers for which he is not ready, but we must be careful not to clip his wings.

We need to strike a balance, for we must both give directions and set limits sometimes. Children welcome direction. One youngster was asked, "What will you do when you go to kindergarten?"

He replied, "They will tell me the rules so I'll know what to do."

A child is as fearful of a world with no limits as we would be were we to cross a high bridge with no side rails.

Are Five-Year-Olds Honest?

We agree that we want our children to be honest, but often we misunderstand when a child takes something that does not belong to him, or tells tall tales. We can help children distinguish be-

H. D. Barlow, F. P. G.

Head first or feet first, up and down they go! They climb, they swing, they jump, they shout as pent-up steam is run off in happy, active play.

tween what is honest or dishonest, what is true or false.

Three kindergarten children found en route to the Sweet Shop were questioned, "Where are you going?"

"We are going to get popsicles."

When asked, "Where did you get the money?," they replied quite honestly, "Out of the jar in the kindergarten. There is lots there."

Let us contrast this with Susan, who had been playing with her mother's face powder and whose cheeks revealed it.

When her mother, in a reproving voice, asked, "Did you use my face powder?," Susan replied defensively, "No, I didn't."

Her mother could have achieved a more satisfactory result by saying, "Susan, when you want some powder, I'd like you to ask so that I can give you some in a box."

We can try to find ways of helping children be truthful instead of using ill-timed questions that invite a seemingly "dishonest" reply. Five-year-olds are still not always clear as to the difference between what happened and what they wish had happened.

One little boy told beautiful, fantastic tales. His father was distressed for he thought of them as lies. Gradually both the father and the little boy were helped to think of them as enjoyable make-believe. In this way they both saw the real situation more clearly.

In order to grow and work out the problems involved in their growing, five-year-olds need more independence, plenty of activity, and a chance to be part of a group of children. As they grow they reach out in new, and what seem to be daring, directions. Parents and teachers can take care not to stamp some of their experiments in words and actions as "dangerous" or "dishonest." Rather should we guide them into constructive ways of using their growing powers in new experiences that they can handle.

HE ASKS ENDLESS QUESTIONS

NINA RIDENOUR, Ph.D.

Secretary, Ittleson
Family Foundation

THE questions a small child asks are often astonishing. Frequently they are baffling. Remembering that the question does not always have the same meaning to the child that it has to you may serve as a good emotional shock absorber when you find yourself completely taken aback. That shock absorber may even be useful as you read this chapter, for all the questions dis-

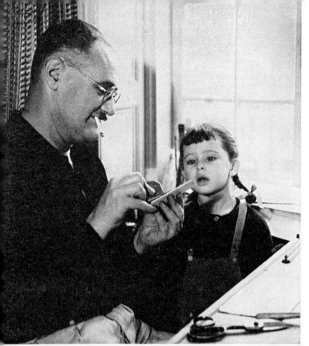

F. P. G.

She finds out how a craftsman uses his tools. As her questions are answered, she is learning something even more important: "It is all right to ask. It is safe to try to find out."

cussed here are real questions of everyday children.

Why Do They Ask Questions?

"How does spit come in your mouth?" "Where was I before I was a seed?" "What makes snow snow?" "Can God stop the days?" To a child, each question is a potential adventure, an exploration into the fascinating world. But children also ask questions for many other reasons than the desire to acquire information. From the way you treat their questions, they often learn far more than mere answers.

Nobody could attempt to give you the exact facts and phrases to use in answering the countless questions a young child asks. Your answers will depend on his age, his understanding, and, most of all, on the meaning of his question and the need behind it. The questions an older child asks purely for information are a slightly different story and are discussed in the chapters DISCOVERING THE WORLD OF SCIENCE, in Volume 14, and INTERPRETING THE NEWS, in Volume 15.

The Question Behind the Question

When Johnnie, age two and a quarter, sidles up to one of the adults in his family and asks conversationally, "Whatcha doin'?" he is learning several different things. He is learning about grownups. Do they like little boys and enjoy answering their questions? Or are their thoughts elsewhere and would they rather not be bothered? He is learning that asking a question is one legitimate way of obtaining some of the attention all children must have in order to thrive. He is also learning how to establish a social relation, for this is Johnnie's way of being sociable. After all, when you are only two, it is quite a new experience to discover that by putting together the words "Whatcha doin'?" you can get adults to notice you, to show you things, and to treat you as a person.

What Do Our Answers Tell?

Johnny is lucky. For, along with the names of things, he is learning that adults are friendly and helpful. He is learning that it is fun to find out, and that it is all right to ask any question that comes into his mind.

These are the ideas we wish children could absorb as they ask their questions. But, unfortunately, there are many things that interfere. Sometimes it is as simple a matter as the grownup's failure to recognize the importance of the question to the child. Sometimes adults an-

swer questions in a way that is too involved or not full enough. Neither way
gives satisfaction. Sometimes adults are
tired, preoccupied, or annoyed with a
child's incessant demands. Or perhaps
they are embarrassed because they do
not know the answer, or regard the question as improper. And sometimes they
fail to hear the question behind the
question, the one that is there but does
not come out in words.

Small wonder that adults so often feel
stumped by children's questions. Why
is the sky blue, and not green or purple
or yellow? It is quite natural to feel embarrassed or annoyed if you think that
you ought to know the explanation of
commonplace occurrences. When you
do not know, you may suddenly seem
to be otherwise occupied! "Don't ask
foolish questions," or "Run along now,
I'm busy." And yet, such a response
misses a good opportunity to keep the
child's curiosity alive.

Actually, it is no disgrace to admit
your ignorance to a child. "I should
know, but I don't," you say, "let's look
it up." Then the child gets his answer,
and, more important, he learns that
adults are people you do things with,
and that looking up things is fun.

Different Ages Need Different Answers

Perhaps you know the answer but do
not know just how much the youngster
can grasp. "What is Easter?" "How do
we think?" "What does a germ look
like?" The same question asked at different ages will require entirely different
answers. The three-year-old, comment-
ing lightly "How did the sky get 'way
up there?" requires only a brief reply.
The five-year-old, gazing pensively at the
sky and then inquiring thoughtfully
"Where does the sky end?" is ready for

**Knowing where to look for the answer
is the beginning of wisdom, and the
"Let's look it up" habit will remain a
useful approach for a lifetime.**

some solid explanations. SCIENCE AND
INDUSTRY, Volume 9, has the answers
to many of these questions.

Questions Reveal Growth

It is wonderful to watch a child's
steadily-growing ideas. Children wonder
about time, space, and numbers at surprisingly early ages. If you are five and
have learned to count to ten not so long
ago, and to 100 even more recently, then
you may conclude that "tenhundred" is
a vast number. But soon you learn there
are still bigger numbers, and so you ask,
"What's the biggest number in the
world?" Then you begin to wonder
about numbers that go on and on and
never end at all. And presently you are
puzzling about other endings and beginnings. "When did the days start?"
"Does the air end?" "Who made God?"

This is the way creative thinking starts.

Through their questions, children give us glimpses of their efforts at sorting out right and wrong, and show us where they need help. "Eating carrots makes your cheeks rosy, but isn't putting on rouge like doing a lie?" asks six-year-old Ann. "Did Jesus play marbles for keeps?" queries another six.

Adult-made differences come in for questions. "Why is Patsy's father richer when Daddy works harder?" A thoughtful question deserves a thoughtful answer. Most of all, it is important that children know that any question is all right at any time. Basic attitudes are sometimes determined by the way such questions are answered. The answer may establish the first feelings of the differences between "us" and "other kinds of people." The first notions of whether such differences are looked at askance or are acceptable can grow out of the answer. Your answer can let a young child know a great deal about the worth and dignity of all human beings. CHILDREN LEARN ABOUT OTHER PEOPLE, in Volume 15, can help you here.

Can They Understand Our Customs?

Through their questions, children also show us how they are groping to understand people and classifications of people. What do teachers do, and what do parents do? How are animals the same as children, and how are they different from them? Questions of nursery-school children remind us how much there is that is puzzling when you are two or three or four. "Do the turtles worry when we go home?" "Do cooks sleep?" And there was the little girl who, seeing her teacher for the first time in street clothes, asked in astonishment, "What's your name with your hat on?"

As they begin to notice what adults do, you can see their little minds working, making their own judgments. "Mommies have to do their work whether they want to or not, don't they?" You sense that the little girl who made that remark was acquiring some basic attitudes toward work and motherhood that might run something like this: "Little girls become mommies. I'm a little girl. I'll become a mommie. Mommies have to work whether they like to or not. How will I like being a mommie?"

If we are alert, we will occasionally be startled at the difference between what we assume a child understands and what he really understands. We will see that further explanations on our part are in order. This is especially likely to be true of children's ideas about religion and death. LOSSES THROUGH DEATH, in Volume 12, may help you here. Perhaps, too, your religious adviser can guide you.

Mary Lou, aged three, began her prayers, "God, can you hear me? I can't hear you." A little later she asked "Is God in Hartford, too?" Now and then it is well for you to reverse the questioning process. You ask the questions for a change. What does your prayer mean, for instance, or what does a song or a story tell you? You may be in for some surprises.

The Need Behind the Question

There is a curious notion prevalent that a child who does something "just to get attention" is committing an offense, and that he must be punished by being denied the attention he seeks. This is attacking the problem backwards. If he does things to get attention, then that is proof that he needs attention. The important point is that he be

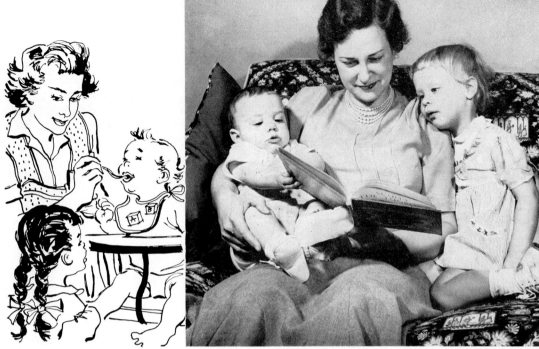

Elizabeth Hibbs

A continual flood of questions may be a way of asking, "Do you love me?" Reassure her on that point with affectionate attention, and questions may become less persistent and annoying, for she will be asking to learn, not to test you.

given the *kind* of attention he really needs.

Asking questions is a sure-fire method of getting attention. Children resort to it frequently when they are feeling deprived. Yet, in these instances, no amount of full and complete answering will satisfy the basic need. It is important to recognize the real need and satisfy it as directly as possible. It would be a mistake to continue answering endless questions because you had failed to recognize an unsatisfied need.

Suppose, for instance, that a child of four or five has a new baby brother or sister. He is feeling displaced, unloved, frightened. He resorts to scores and scores of questions, many of them meaningless. But they serve to hold the adult for a few fleeting seconds. His *basic* need is to be assured by word and action that

he is loved and wanted, that he belongs, that he has not been displaced. Children who have this assurance will be less likely to need to resort to other devices for getting attention.

Can Questions Be a Sign of Boredom?

Excessive questions are often a sign of plain boredom or other minor dissatisfactions. Here again the solution lies in fulfilling the basic needs. You can supply more physical activity, more outlets for creativeness, more companionship, or whatever may be lacking.

One cue to boredom questions is the steady flow of questions tumbling after each other without any sign of thoughtfulness, or perhaps without pauses for answers. "Why does the oil man come? Why does he take the hose away? Why do people want oil? Does he have a

153

apt to fall into this trap. The child learns at an early age that one sure way of holding a parent is to ask involved questions. Suddenly, just at bedtime, Richard develops an eager interest in seashells or electricity or stars, hoping that some sharp questions may stave off the distasteful moment. Most parents will be taken in by this now and then—but not indefinitely.

Questions That Point up Worries

Sometimes a child asks certain questions in order to avoid asking others that are bothering him. Children who have had a disturbing experience, or who are going through a period of confusion about where babies come from, or masturbation, will sometimes ask questions about everything they can think of except the one question uppermost in their minds. It may be a great relief to them if you cut through and show that you are ready to listen. It may help younger children if you give them some mild reassurance: "I'm going to be here all day. You may talk about anything you want to." With older ones, a question or two from the adult, skirting the edges of the subject, may serve to open up the floodgates. In answering indirect or direct questions of this kind, the chapter in this volume, He Learns About Differences Between Boys and Girls, will be helpful.

What Bothers the Worrier?

Children's questions frequently indicate a worry, and that worry, more of-

name? Where does he live?"

Another question that is not for the purpose of acquiring information is the nagging "Why?" which is really more of a complaint than a question: "Why do I have to brush my teeth?" The answer to this may be "Why not?" or perhaps, with little children, "You tell me why." The busy mother who is about to go crazy with her five-year-old's ceaseless flow of apparently inane questions may save time and temper by stopping to think, "What on earth is the matter with this child that he asks so many questions?" The solution may prove to be a needed change of scene, reassurance, more attention, or a new challenge in play.

Must We Always Answer?

Without doubt, some questions are nothing but a stall and should be recognized as such. It will be a favor to the child to call his bluff. Parents who are intellectually inclined are perhaps more ten than not, can be stated "Am I safe?" or "Who will take care of me?" When the two-year-old asks, "Has Halloween got a mommy?" her misunderstanding of Halloween (which will soon be straightened out) is less important than her preoccupation with mommies. "Mommies take care of people. Everything should have a mommy. Will my mommy take care of me?"

Around two, children's repeated questions about where the water goes when the toilet is flushed may originate in a fear that they will fall in and be swept away with the water. The three-year-old who exclaims with real anxiety "What is the moon doing up there *at breakfast?*" is expressing typical three-year-old concern with having things in their proper places. At three, you are just beginning to learn that there is order and system in the world. The moon belongs to the night. Suddenly it appears in the daytime. This is cause for alarm.

Listening with sympathetic ears, we may learn a lot about children's worries. A three-year-old, after ten minutes' conversation with a friendly stranger, asks soberly, "Do you have a bowel movement every day?" To be sure, if you are three, this is one way of establishing a social relationship. But such a question may also sound a warning. "Mother! Better let up a bit on the toilet training. It is becoming too important." Without humiliating the child, you can explain that there are more acceptable questions for establishing a common bond.

Why Is a Question Repeated?

Parents sometimes make the mistake of thinking that when a question is answered once, they are done with it. But the same question may occur again and again, in different words, or even in the same words. Such questions are likely to be especially important, for they show either that the child has hit a snag and needs help in getting straightened out, or that his ideas are shifting and developing. He is examining the subject from a different point of view. In any case you can avoid: "How many times do I have to tell you? . . . ;" "You know very well . . ."; "I've told you a hundred times . . ."

Respect Their Questions

It is well to avoid any of the replies that tend to make children ashamed, or that stifle further questions. Don't tease. Don't frighten. Don't laugh. Nothing is so precious as the dignity of a little child. Don't give a senseless answer, or a sentimental one. Not: "There's a fairy in the piano that makes the music come out." An evasive answer that looks like an easy way out at the moment may lead to trouble later on. You may occasionally need to say, "You'll understand better when you're older," but don't say, "You're too little to understand," or, "I'll tell you when you're older." These are question-stoppers. Perhaps the best principle is never to tell a child anything you will have to "un-tell" him later.

We want to preserve for children the joy, the excitement, the adventure of finding out, the thrill of wondering and of learning to think for themselves. We want them to feel that this is a comfortable, orderly world. We want them to learn that adults are friendly, helpful people to whom one goes with one's questions, and that it is all right to ask any question one wishes. These are the kinds of life-lessons we want children to be learning as they ask their questions.

HE STILL LEARNS
THROUGH HIS PLAY

L. JOSEPH STONE, Ph.D.

Chairman, Department of Child Study,
Vassar College, Poughkeepsie, N. Y.

THE five-year-old's play is earnest and active. Often it has aims of the greatest importance to him. Play is his essential way of learning. The most vital things children learn are not necessarily the ones grown-ups set out to teach, but rather what children themselves experience and find out. Certainly, parents and teachers must do some active teaching. But often they accomplish most when they clear the tracks for the child's own eager exploration. His seeking of information, his comparison of objects and ideas, his testing and tasting, his experiments with people contribute to his learning. This means we need to provide the materials, the setting, and the encouragement for his play.

When a six-year-old begins school, he is a fairly competent and knowing member of society. His skills and understand-

ing have gone far beyond what they were in the nursery years. The kindergarten period helped him consolidate and stabilize the achievements that had been slowly ripening. Thus the five-year-old has a great deal to put in order emotionally and socially before he undertakes the new problems of the Loose Tooth era of growth. Much of this he accomplishes through his play.

How Five-Year-Olds Play

Five-year-olds do many of the same kinds of things they did at four, but they are less helter-skelter, more poised and competent. Kindergartners enjoy activity for activity's sake, and for the sake of mastering the use of their bodies. The fives are more skillful than they were a year ago in the kind of active play that uses the large muscles. They are still not so skillful that such activities become boring. Running, rolling, hopping, skipping, swinging, jumping, climbing jungle gyms or trees, are all part of the five-year-old's program. Tricycles are used at high speed. If older children are jumping rope, the fives may try it, too, but without the older children's elaborate rituals.

Pretending Serves a Purpose

Most kindergartners take endless delight in interweaving dramatic play in their climbing, running, and jumping activities. Sometimes the dramatizations are the center of play that goes on for some time. Domestic play still holds first place. Doll carriages, trucks, and tricycles may be called on as props, while "Mother," "Father," and "Baby," with the occasional addition of other relatives, go through the drama of family life. If no grown-up or older child insists it is shameful, boys as well as girls will try out both the masculine and feminine roles. Any character from the adult scene, from doctor to garbage man, may be taken over, if he does something understandable and direct. Often this dramatic play throws a vivid light on the life of the grown-ups as the five-year-old sees it. Consider the rather melancholy role of Father as he is seen by these suburban children.

"Mother" is waking and dressing several "children." Enter a boy who demands a role, a boy not too welcome to this particular knot of children. They do not drive him off, but "Mother" says, "O.K. You be the daddy. Finish your breakfast and I must drive you to the station. Here is your briefcase. Good-bye," and the interloper is disposed of!

"Let's Dress Up"

Of special importance in dramatic play is being like the grown-up. "Dressing up" may be especially enjoyed. At home and at school it is useful to have a special collection of discarded grown-up garments that take into consideration

Clothes make the man—and the woman, too! Dressing-up is a never-ending delight. It makes play much more vivid, more real, and more fun.

Press Syndicate

Boats may not look seaworthy, houses may look flimsy in the five-year-old's pictures. But you can overlook techniques of drawing, if the children tell the story with gusto in their own way.

Let your youngster's painting hang in a place of honor, and he will feel the glow of being appreciated.

the boys as well as the girls. The boys at this age occasionally may want to try out the high-heeled shoes and the long dresses, and the girls may sometimes enjoy parading around in Father's discarded vest and hat. The dressing-up is often part of the make-believe dramatic play. Now the children use words like "pretend," instead of just *being* what they are pretending, as they did when they were younger. The emphasis on dressing up and pretending suggests again the pleasure of five-year-olds in understanding the world of grownups. The base of operations for children of this age is still the family. At school age, the base is provided by what the group of children their own age is doing.

How Do They Use Their Senses?

The play of the kindergartner continues to include pleasure in all his senses. When you are five years old, it is interesting to experience swinging, or whirling round and round until you drop. It feels good to test and taste and smell and feel the snow, the grass, the sand, the water, and the mud. The color itself and the mysteries of color mixing may still be raptly absorbing, quite apart from any plan of doing something with paints.

Kaleidoscopes and color tops satisfy the five-year-old, who is exploring with his senses. Soap bubbles offer delights we can comprehend only if we see through the five-year-old's eyes all the splendor and fragile perfection of a form he himself has created. Less understandable, perhaps, to grown-ups are the charms of the gurgles and tastes and slippery wetness that go with blowing bubbles. Fives still find honest pleasure in the smells, tastes, and feels that adults avoid or pretend not to notice. All these

158

enjoyments suggest the value and the fascination of "raw materials." The chapter on Toys and Play Materials, in this volume, has further valuable suggestions.

How Shall We Encourage Their Creativeness?

Five-year-olds are reaching the stage of pride in the product of their artistic activities. They are likely to draw stick or circle people and animals. Pictures of houses are usually complete with windows, doors, and smoke coming out of chimneys. Fives proudly display the products of their craftsmanship, and adult tact is necessary here. Acceptance and approval of these creations are more helpful now than criticism, or instruction in perspective, sizes, or choice of colors.

Many children lose interest in artistic activity at this period because adults set unattainable standards or prescribe in great detail what they shall do. Instructions like "Everybody draw this tulip" or "I'll show you how to make a better cow" destroy the pleasures of discovery. In a year or two, your youngster will begin to be highly critical of his work, but now you can give him the satisfaction of your approval. You can hang his work in a special gallery in the kitchen at home, or his teacher may display it around the walls of her classroom.

Are They Ready for Games?

Your five-year-old is just beginning to be aware of games with rules. He may try to keep up with the older children on the street who initiate him into the world of counting-out, hopscotch, or giant strides. The jumping, skipping, hopping-on-one foot aspect of these games is dearer to the heart of the five-year-old than the rules and rituals. The traditional group games of kindergarten are appealing, but they should not be allowed to take the place of free play entirely. London bridge, circle games, lotto, and other activities involving an awareness of simple rules, are just about the right speed for most five-year-olds.

How Do They Play with Language?

Five-year-olds are acquiring new words every day. It is not surprising that activity with language is a significant part of their play world. Sometimes we find them taking sheer enjoyment in the sound of a new word. Sometimes words are used with a special sense of what is "grown-up" talk. Listen to Jack and Danny perched on top of the jungle gym and giggling:

Jack: Its *lovely* to see you!
Danny: I'm so happy to see you.
Jack: How *are* you? How have you *been?*
Danny: Sorry I have to go so quick.
Jack: I hope you have a good time falling down and bumping your head.

They are both so overcome with laughter they nearly fall off the jungle gym. At other times, grown-up talk used seriously is the badge of the part a child is playing. Words have a special magic at this period of growth, and five-year-olds can convulse themselves and each other with the crudest of puns, and even with unusual sounds. The chapter His Language Is Rich and Fluent, in the section on four-year-olds in this volume, has much to say that applies to the five-year-olds also.

The way five-year-olds play with other children is an important part of the whole play question. You can read about it in a later chapter, He Gets Along Better with His Playmates.

Rae Russell

"The farmer in the dell, the farmer in the dell," chant the fives who are beginning to find pleasure in games like this that call for some co-operation.

Play Is a World of Practice

The five-year-old is improving in the ability to use his muscles and to control his body. Self-initiated drills are going on constantly as a part of play, to an extent that the most rigorous physical education program could not enforce! The very skill that a child has just acquired, and still performs somewhat shakily, appears to be what he most wants to use. There seems to be a built-in guarantee in the human organism that as it acquires, it will exercise and perfect new activities. Your five-year-old will "practice" these skills to the point of smooth co-ordination without criticism or teaching from you. Give him his beloved tricycle and wagon, and a safe place to climb, to swing, to slide, and he will do the rest.

Watch, too, the intensity with which he paints, draws with crayon and pencil, stitches, or builds with his blocks.

Through his play, he is making progress in using tools that he will need all through life. These tools will have a particularly important part in his school work.

How Are His Ideas Growing?

Through his play he is trying out ideas about number, time, distance, size, texture, strength of materials, and other properties of things in the world around him. The backlog of experience he is gaining in his play is contributing to his "readiness" for reading and other school work. The symbols he will use then will be meaningful if his experiences are rich now. You will find more about reading readiness in WILL MY CHILD BE READY FOR FIRST GRADE? in this volume.

You help your child immensely if you protect him from the early conviction of failure. Criticism or belittling at the wrong moment can put a blight on his eagerness to try new things, and can even create an unreadiness for, or a fear of, learning.

Understanding Differences

As children play together, they learn in time to take turns, to share, to co-operate. They find out where and how and to whom it is possible to say "yes" and to say "no," and when and how it is a good idea to stand up for their own rights. If parents and teachers use opportunities wisely, children can also learn through their play to accept differences in others.

Helping a child accept as a matter of course the idea that different people do different things in different ways is of fundamental importance. Countless chances crop up to point out the variety of customs and programs in different homes and neighborhoods, without implying that "our way is the right way." Even as respect for differences stems from basic self-respect, it is the beginning of respect for others—the essence of true democracy. Children Learn About Other People, in Volume 15, and When Children Are Anxious, in this volume, discuss this question in detail.

Play Contributes to Self-Understanding

One of the important goals of play—at five as well as earlier or later—is the opportunity afforded for self-understanding. The kindergartner is clarifying his notion of who he is. He is beginning to arrive at an understanding of the distinction between himself and other persons. He is getting hold of the notion that other person's thoughts, feelings, and points of view may differ from his own. This idea develops partly as he plays alone. It is important for each child to have an opportunity to go off by himself *when he wishes* with dolls or blocks, or other props of his choosing.

As he plays alone, he digests his experiences and comes to terms with them. In such play he makes things happen under his own control, for five-year-olds often feel powerless in the real world. As he plays alone, he can venture to try out his anger or his sorrow. He can try being powerful or fearful, or even try forecasting himself as a grownup.

In the development of self-understanding, the five-year-old begins to be conscious of names, especially of last names. He thinks of himself as belonging to a particular family or group. He may think of the "self" as residing in his head or in his chest. He is fascinated with himself as a growing, working individual. One five-year-old said, "I had the

F. P. G.

The fence will be painted only with water, but these young workers are co-operating in the undertaking, and that is the big step for kindergartners.

same skin when I was a baby. It fits very nice. It's me!" The five-year-old is beginning to be aware of the powerful feelings within him. You can help him realize that he shares this intensity of feelings with others and that there is no cause for feeling guilty because he feels terribly angry or frightened at times. At the same time, by stepping into play that seems to be getting too violent, you can help him learn that control of the expression, or the acting-out, of his feelings is possible.

Adults Learn, Too

Not the least important part of the kindergartners' play is the opportunity it gives us to learn about them. By watching their play, we may anticipate some of their difficulties, grasp their problems, and share their fun. If we can listen with the idea of gaining understanding, we can open to ourselves the rich, fascinating world of five-year-olds.

HE HAS
A CONSCIENCE

MARIA W. PIERS, Ph.D.

Child Guidance Consultant, Chicago, Ill.

WE MAY think it unfortunate, but babies are not born with a conscience. It is up to the adults, especially the parents, to implant that "still, small voice" in children and then nurse it along with praise, disapproval, and plenty of love. Raising a full-size conscience is time-consuming. The slowly ripened conscience is the strong and healthy one, but it takes from ten to twenty years to develop it. We should not expect to find much of it in a small child. By the time a child is five, however, his conscience is usually active, if not effective.

How Does a Conscience Grow?

Most mothers have always known that a baby needs milk, warmth, and cuddling, and that punishment has no place in his life as yet. So we place as few restrictions as possible on the baby. But, as soon as a youngster begins to get around under his own power, we begin to show him that some things are per-

missible and some are not safe or possible. Even the one-year-old is ready for his first spoonful of conscience. Usually his mother is quite ready to give it, too!

One-year-olds get around. Some crawl on all fours, some slide on their seats, and a few of them are even walking. As they get around, they usually get into trouble. They begin to grab flowerpots from the windowsills and eat what is in them. They throw slippers into the bathtub and rubber balls into the soup bowl. You simply have to do something about it. You pick up the baby and put the flowerpots on a high shelf. But that is not enough. You also tell the baby, "No, no. You mustn't do this."

A one-year-old hears quite a few such "noes" and "don'ts" and, fortunately, he is ready to take a reasonable number of them. After episodes such as this have been repeated frequently through the months, the toddler approaches the forbidden flowerpots with an anxious look on his face. He may turn around to see if his mother is watching him. It is at this point that the cornerstone of a conscience has been laid.

Mother's Face Is the Guide

During his second year, the small child learns a number of things which are "good" and a number of things which are "bad." He can only tell the difference between good and bad by looking at his mother's face. Other adults, including Father, are also guideposts, but Mother, in the two-year-old's eyes, knows best. If she smiles, that means "good"; if she looks angry, it means "bad."

Naturally, the toddler does not like it when his mother frowns, but it may be even harder to leave the flowerpots untouched. So the two-year-old hopes and fears that Mother will come just in time to rescue him from the temptation. Of course he does not put this notion into words. Yet his hope and fear may become so strong that, for just one moment, he takes over Mother's role. He frowns and says seriously, "No, no." But his hand reaches for the flowerpots and pulls them down after all.

By the time he is three, the small child knows better. He is not on both sides of such a question any longer. Instead, he makes decisions, even though the decision is often in favor of "bad," rather than in favor of "good."

Parents Are the Conscience

The years from three to five are not easy, in spite of the fact that the children seem so full of fun, and play with so much zest. It seems they must be having a good time and, in a way, they are. Yet they are beginning to feel that it is probably a lot nicer to be a grownup than to be a small child.

Three- and four-year-olds feel strongly about everything. They laugh and cry easily. They are extremely fond of people, or extremely angry at them. Whenever they are fond of someone, they wish they could have this person all to themselves. The four-year-old girl may become devoted to her daddy, and wish she could somehow do away with Mother and take her place. It is only a wish at first, and an angry, envious one at that. But, even so, it helps the little girl to learn from her much-admired and envied mother, and to take on or imitate her ways.

Much the same thing happens to the little boy. Of course, he always felt that his own mommy was a lot better, prettier, and more helpful than anybody else's mommy. But now that he is a big boy of three or four, he may decide that she really doesn't spend enough time with him. He wishes he were in Daddy's place. The only way to get there is to become like Daddy. At least that is how matters look to him, so that is what he tries to do. He tries to imitate Daddy's ways of thinking, acting, and talking. Most important of all, he begins to imitate Daddy's ideas about right and wrong. Boys often take after their fathers and girls often take after their mothers, as far as consciences are concerned.

All children, even those who are deprived of mother and father, must acquire a conscience from those grownups who love them and take care of them. The people who feed and clothe a small person, sometimes hold him on their laps and play with him, are the ones who have the power to make him conscientious. In these early years, parents also stand for conscience. They are the ones whose feelings the child copies.

Temptation to grab soft, wet earth in the flower pot may prove irresistible. But conscience has come into being, if an inner voice echoes Mother's "No."

Conscience is catching. Children get a sense of right and wrong from the adults who care for them and whom they love, admire, and want to imitate.

A child who has been loved from the beginning wants to be like those he loves. Gradually, he acquires from them the basis of a sense of right and wrong. By the time he reaches kindergarten age, this sense of right and wrong has become quite noticeable to the others in the family.

"Knowing" and "Acting" Are Not the Same

Does all this mean that the five-year-old can be held responsible for everything he does? No, he cannot be responsible in the same manner a grownup can. After all, knowing what is right does not mean that one can always live up to it, even if one is a responsible adult. It is often hard to understand why five-year-old Johnny teases a baby brother. Why does he bring so much

Strong pulls in opposite directions make it hard to live up to what is right when a child is only five years old.

dirt into the house instead of wiping his shoes on the door mat? Why does he dash across the street instead of holding on to Mother's hand, when he really "knows better?" All of us, though, can remember the many occasions when a grown-up has "blown his top," or has eaten the very thing the doctor has advised against, even though he "knew better." Human beings, especially young ones, just are not capable of living up to what they feel is right, all the time.

The five-year-old is not always good. Often he does not obey. Even the voice of his own conscience is frequently disregarded. But his conscience is active just the same. He worries about bad and good and he attaches "goodness" and "badness" to many matters an adult would never classify in that way. The fact that a table is hard does not make it "bad" to us, but to a five-year-old it does. "That table was mean, it hurt me," he will state, after bumping his head on the edge.

A New Conscience Is Strict

We often become annoyed with the self-righteous way five-year-olds pass judgment on the wrongdoings of others. Sisters, brothers, playmates are forever being labeled "nice" or "bad." Such stern morality seems out of place in one who so often gets into mischief himself. Why should Shirley slap her three-year-old sister when that young person stages a raid on the candy jar? Shirley herself is a frequent candy-snatcher. Exactly here, though, is where her conscience comes in! When she sees someone else do something wrong, something that she knows she could only with difficulty resist doing, her conscience makes her highly indignant. Her indignation is her way of proving that she really knows such behavior is unacceptable.

A great deal of the tattling of four-, five-, and six-year-olds is strongly tinged with this "There, but for the Grace of God, go I" feeling. Even as they report the wrongdoings, or fancied wrongdoings, of another, these youngsters are rejoicing in the fact that this time they were not involved. The reminder of all the times they may have been in similar scrapes may be a trifle alarming to them. All these feelings are appropriate for five-year-olds and show they are making progress in developing serviceable consciences.

Why Does He Worry About "Bad" Thoughts?

Finding fault with others is one of the beginnings of knowing right be-

165

havior from wrong. In due time, your youngster will learn to stop himself, as well as others, from doing the wrong thing. He will become capable of self-discipline. For the time being, he expects other people to stop him. He also expects and fears he will be punished for every "bad" deed.

A brand-new conscience sometimes works a bit too strictly, and may make a child feel that he deserves severe punishment, even for "bad" thoughts. A five-year-old *wants* to do many forbidden things, from sticking out his tongue at the lady next door to pouring ink over the new rug. He always has quite a few bad wishes and thoughts, and so he often suffers too much from a bad conscience. To make him feel better, we can let him know it is "all right" for him to *think*, or even *say*, without fear of punishment, many things he may not *do*.

Conscience Becomes His Own

One might think that such a conscience, ever-present and usually bad, would make the five-year-old the best-behaved child of all. But that is not what happens. He cannot by any means be left to make important decisions. His parents must make these for him, for some time to come. It is their responsibility to see that he gets enough sleep and the right kind of food, that he takes his medicine when he is sick, and that he wears an extra sweater when the temperature drops.

How Reliable Is Conscience, Size 5?

Even though he may be conscientious enough to keep out of danger, your pre-school child is not always able to judge what is dangerous. Climbing up on a third-floor windowsill, for instance, may look far less dangerous to Janie than it does to her more experienced mother.

But Janie can be counted on in other ways much more than she could have been last year or the year before. She is able to use the toilet by herself. She also knows where to put her toys, her clothes, and Mother's scarves and hankies. While she is not always willing to put her things where they belong, at least we can be sure, or almost sure, that she is not going to empty Mother's dresser drawers on the floor, or tear books. Janie has a lot more respect for neatness and order than she had when she was three or four. She does better, too, at sharing, and at respecting other persons' belongings.

Two years ago, Janie would have found it harder not to grab her older sister's beautiful doll. Now she is quite willing to ask first, "May I hold the doll for a while?" She is able to wait for her turn, and sometimes, but only sometimes, she can even accept her sister's firm "No, you may not," without tears. Janie now can play games such as "Old Maid" with the family, and she will not cheat—well, at least not always—when in danger of losing the game. She knows it would not be fair. And Janie is beginning to want to play fair. All these traits show that her conscience is maturing, but it still has a long way to go.

Shall We Take the Side of Conscience?

You certainly would ask too much of your five-year-old if you should put him in charge of his younger brother, or expect him to do the dinner dishes or perform jobs which are sometimes expected of, say, a third-grader. But you cannot afford longer to overlook all his misbehavior with the excuse, "Oh well, he is only a baby." A remark such as this suits neither you nor your five-year-old. He

This little girl got herself out on a limb because she still has only a foggy idea of what is dangerous. Protection, not punishment, is what she needs most here.

knows when he has done wrong. His conscience, still a little wobbly, needs the firm support and reinforcement of a grownup. Your five-year-old expects you to side with his conscience.

Most parents, naturally, do that by letting a child know when he has done something wrong, as well as by warning him to keep out of trouble. Often, though, there is no need for either reminder. Every day you, as parents, strengthen your child's conscience simply by being conscientious and responsible yourselves.

Five-year-old Tim watches his father working in the yard, carefully pulling out all the weeds, but none of the flowers, and he will feel, "I thought so. It's right, then, to pull out the dandelions, but it isn't right to pull out all the peonies." Tim learns from watching his mother that one has to give the baby his supper before looking at the television program. So his conscience was right again when it told him that taking care of people comes before having fun.

By the same token, Tim learns in time that it is right to help others, to wash when you are dirty, to pitch in with household jobs, to go to work every day, to put toys away in the evening, to brush the snow off the car. He also learns from others that it is wrong to lie, to steal things, and to hurt others.

What Is too Much Conscience?

The person who has been permitted to learn responsibility gradually and in his own time will probably not have too severe a conscience as an adult. But there are people who were rushed into being grownup and who worry so much about right and wrong, just or unfair, good or evil, that they have no time or strength left for other things. There are,

for that matter, some such five-year-olds. Worrying all the time over being good may keep these children from having fun, from being curious, from finding out what makes the world tick. Such worries may even prevent their learning anything, from jumping rope to spelling their names.

With such a child, it is a good idea to let him know that it is perfectly all right to make mistakes once in a while. After all, even grownups make them. A kindergartner with his conscience working overtime needs to be reassured repeatedly that his mistakes will not be held against him forever, or be the cause of ridicule. It is tempting for adults to make fun of a small child, but it does not make him grow up faster. Instead it makes him feel self-conscious and inferior, as if he were never quite good enough.

Do They Know Right from Wrong?

Most parents wonder if they have been strict enough with their young ones. Should Jerry, who is almost ready for first grade, be punished because he still cannot learn to let his dad's tool chest alone? Laura May has been told time and again not to push her baby sister over on the floor, and still she does it. Isn't she much too irresponsible, too disobedient, for her five years? Sam has been told not to take his third piece of candy, but he goes and helps himself when no one is looking. Will he grow up to be a thief?

Sam, Laura May, Jerry, and all the rest of them are "all right" if they do what is right once in a while. No five-year-old can or should be constantly well-behaved. His conscience is just the right size for him if he sometimes acts as he should. But only sometimes!

HE GETS ALONG BETTER
WITH HIS PLAYMATES

CHRISTINE M. HEINIG, M.A.

Childhood Education Associate,
American Association of University Women, Washington, D. C.

BY THE time your child is five, he will have made real strides in sociability. The demand of five-year-olds for the companionship of other children is a familiar story to parents.

When the fives play together and get into arguments, we need to remember that they often understand one another better than we understand them, even though they may not be able to put their understanding into words. They will learn from one another and take discipline from one another with much less resentment than they will take it from adults.

Of course, there are times when the situation appears to be beyond the children and you need to step in. But there are ways of entering into the five-year-olds' disputes without insisting that they take on our standards of politeness.

A Best Friend Is Important

It is not just other children that matter to the four-and-a-half- and five-year-olds. Friends whom they choose for

Pinney, Monkmeyer

Sheer exuberance, not wrath, is often the cause of roughhouse among the five-year-olds. Adults can help them find safer outlets for their high spirits.

themselves from among a group of playmates are especially important, for real friendships are formed in these early years. Discrimination in selecting a friend has grown to such an extent that the child of mother's best friend is no longer necessarily looked upon with favor. A best friend of his own contributes to the sense of security of the five-year-old.

When Jane and Jill are playing together, Jane will boast to Jill in the presence of Jill's mother, "Patsy is my friend and not yours." The two mothers should be careful now in what they say. It won't hurt Jill deeply to know that she is not Jane's best friend, even if she did wince when Jane made her declaration. She will take Jane's statement better from Jane than she would take an adult's apologetic explanation. Jane should not be scolded or made to say she "loves everyone the same."

It will ease Jill's feelings and give her a sense of security and comfort if one of the mothers says to both girls in a "take it for granted" tone, "Why, of course, everyone has someone for a 'best friend.' Jill has a best friend, too, but we are all friends, and we all play together sometimes."

Shall We Insist on Politeness?

The guidance of young children is simplified if we understand how much to expect of them. We can see them as growing individuals passing through a particular stage in their development. We will be more successful if we are not too eager to train children to behave "nicely" in ways which have no meaning for them. Jill and Jane can get along better with the matter-of-fact explanation of Jane's feelings than they would if the mothers made a moral issue of the incident. Forcing Jane to say the "nice" words will not change her feelings. If her feelings are bottled up, they may find release when Mamma and Papa are not looking. Maybe, then, she really will hit, pinch, or be just a generally inhospitable hostess and playmate.

Language Promotes Sociability

Children nearing the age of five have learned to express themselves in words. This is a satisfying social accomplishment because now they can communicate in words, instead of using fists, teeth, and fingernails, as they did when they were two and three years old. The physical attack of fives is more often "roughhouse" and "puppy play" than combat. When a five-year-old goes out of his way to fight with another child, look for some fundamental unhappiness in that child's life. Is he over-disciplined, or dominated? Does he come from a home where conflict and unhappiness are the rule? Is he undernourished, fatigued, or coming down with an illness?

The ability of five-year-olds to reason should be relied upon. Again, they understand each others' logic better than they understand the logic of grown-ups.

"Where is Nowhere?" came up in an argument around the "juice table" in kindergarten.

"I know where Nowhere is," said a cocksure five-year-old, "it's up in the sky —way up in the sky!"

"It's not," said another. "Couldn't be there because the sky is Somewhere."

"It's in the earth, way down in the middle of the earth," said another.

No argument, but a silence. It was a thinking silence.

Soon one bright-eyed boy said, "I know. What is a giant? A giant's nothing, there are no giants."

"So a giant is nowhere, and nowhere is in the middle of a giant's stomach."

The Fives Reason It Out

When five-year-olds can follow through to a logical conclusion in talk-ing about ideas, they certainly can be relied upon to settle most of their own social problems with each other!

Next time you find yourself in the middle of a battle with four- and five-year-olds, be content to observe for a while and watch the solution take shape. If you do have to interfere to halt the battle, wait until the screaming and yelling are over. When tempers are not quite so high, try playing the role of "chairman."

After each child has voiced his complaint, ask, "How do you think you could settle this?" Nine chances out of ten the children can reason it out satisfactorily and go on playing together again. They will be even better friends, and certainly stronger in themselves, than if they were obeying the truce terms of an "outsider."

How Do They Choose Friends?

Five-year-olds play together in groups. Their groups are organized around a common interest. Sometimes lines are drawn on the basis of sex, for at this age the interests of boys and girls are beginning to be more clearly divided. Similar physical strength and ability may

Imaginary boats turn into airplanes so rapidly that you may not be able to follow the turn of events. Occupants of the vehicle are in the know, and ready for such amazing changes.

Rae Russell

Friendships at this age ripen better with careful cultivation. Daily routines at kindergarten create the atmosphere that nourishes friendliness.

draw several children together and make them friends.

The slow child is often mercilessly left behind. The crybaby may be tormented, and the tattletale shut out. Children have techniques of their own for effectively excluding unwelcome playmates. In such cases, some adult guidance may be called for to help the excluded child. Children's ways of playing are loosely organized, and are subject to change with any whim. New rules are made spontaneously to suit a need, a sense of humor, or a brighter idea.

Children understand one another so well that often, without explanation, the pattern of play will shift continuously, yet nobody seems to lose the thread of its meaning. It bothers the fives not one bit that unfinished beginnings of thrilling adventures, as well as a litter of toys and play materials, are left in the wake of these activities.

If you listen to them you may hear something like this in any back yard.

"This is a train and I'm the engineer. Sit down everybody. All aboard. Here we go for New York," says Bill.

"Hey, this old train is no good. It's breaking down. We're coming to a big

river. Hey, you guys, we're in a boat. Look out everybody, the waves'll get you soaked," chimes in Harry.

For the space of three minutes the passengers appear to defend themselves bravely against wind and water, and then, miraculously, they are in a space ship. Never mind how they got there! A space ship suits their needs at the moment and by common consent they are already half way to the moon! Of such stuff are the friendships of the fives made. Let no adult try to impose the rules of the real world on these pretendings that further friendliness.

How Can We Help the Fives Make Friends?

The desire of kindergartners to play with others who have similar interests gives us a good cue here. If we want to help five-year-olds to make friends, we can provide the kind of experiences that furnish good ideas for play. If young children are to be interesting to their age-mates, they need to see something of the animals and plants, the things and people, that make up their world.

You are contributing to your child's popularity and his capacity to get along with other children when you take him

172

on the kind of excursions described in EXCURSIONS FOR YOUNG CHILDREN, in this volume. The teacher who often makes the effort to take a group of children to see the big scoop shovel digging out the foundation for a new building will find that play ideas will eventually follow this common experience. Children can see and understand through first-hand observation what the truck, the driver, the shovel, the engineer, the carpenter, the mason, and the foreman, are doing. Then they will be able to co-operate, to share, to take turns in dramatizing this experience with their own wagons, tricycles, blocks, and hammers.

Friendships must have something to feed on. Interesting experiences shared by parents and children, as well as between children themselves, are the stuff of which good companionship is made. Such experiences lay a foundation that can withstand differences in personality, short tempers, or schedules that make it hard for the children to get together.

Why Do They Get Along Better in School?

Children get along better with one another when they are welcome and provided for. A kindergarten, because of the philosophy upon which it is based, is designed to be a "garden" for children under six. It is a good place for children to grow. There they are usually busy, happy, and co-operative. They can reach out in a friendly way toward others. The teacher, because she has prepared this garden and set aside her time to cultivate it, often becomes the four- or five-year-old's new love.

How Home Can Provide a Welcome

Daddy can make other children feel welcome in the yard, even when he is working in his garden, his workshop, or his garage. Mother, too, can arrange her house and schedule to allow for making playmates feel comfortable and wanted. Children under six who have playmates of their own age, a place planned for their play, and things to play with keyed to their size and interests, can be expected to get along well with each other much of the time. They will need only occasional, and, as a rule, undirected supervision. You can train your ear to

Lucien Aigner

Two's company, but three's likely to be a crowd, when kindergartners play in the backyard. Two, four, or five children do much better than three.

listen for the sounds that warn of approaching trouble, and step in to prevent major crises.

The Child Who Does Not Fit into the Group

There are always children with special needs. The child whose development may be a bit slow, or markedly accelerated, may not fit in with his age-mates. The child who has personality problems because he is not as strong, as happy, or as fortunate as the average child, needs special understanding and guidance. In this connection you may want to read THE HANDICAPPED CHILD AND YOUR CHILD, in Volume 12.

The crybaby and the troublemaker, the belligerent fighter and the child who is always in the background, need special nurture and understanding. Usually, strict discipline is just the wrong prescription for these "specials." They need love more than anything else to solve their problems. But they are likely to behave in ways that harvest the least love. It is worth making an effort to give these children some sympathetic attention.

You may be surprised to find that the neighborhood bully who has been making your child's life miserable will be far less of a nuisance if you include him in the back-yard group, instead of shutting him out sternly. Maybe he is a bully because nobody ever gives him a kind word. Listen to these children and follow the leads they give you in their childlike behavior. Books, teachers, guidance workers are ready to help you understand all children better, but especially the troubled ones, if you use the counsel they offer. We all have a degree of responsibility for the children in the neighborhood as well as for our own.

This We Can Do

The job of helping young children to get along better together is fascinating, but it takes a big measure of common sense and a sense of humor. You may have found some things that will help children get along together. If you were to list these points, they might add up to something like the following.

Take time to find some companionable friends for your child to play with often.

Give children experiences together that have meaning and interest for them, and they will play together more happily.

Do things with your children and with their playmates. These experiences can lead to happy play and prevent those doldrums that herald a squabble.

Set up simple rules for play, but keep them flexible, attainable, and practical.

Keep the groups small, especially in a home, and particularly indoors.

Try to have either two children together, or four or five. Three make a triangle with friction points, even among youngsters who are four or five years of age.

Let children have the chance to settle problems for themselves, but be ready to give a helping hand as counselor.

As a parent, or as a teacher, be willing to study the child who is different. His behavior often shows you what help he needs.

And speed the parting guest! An overdose of a playmate, like any other overdose, is likely to end in a minor catastrophe. The old adage can be applied to sociability as well as to food—"The time to stop is when it tastes the best."

Parents Grow on the Job

Both parents and teachers, to be successful, should be able to learn from their experiences. Remember where you have had failures in trying to help a child and then think out a better approach. You can grow on the job, if you are willing to learn from your mistakes.

NORMAL DIFFICULTIES
IN EARLY CHILDHOOD

Rae Russell

As a child grows from babyhood to the age for starting school, he learns a great deal about fitting into many different situations and accepting many kinds of people. Each child finds some circumstances harder to cope with than others.

Each child reacts in his own way when problems are too much for him to handle. Some of the solutions our children try out are useful and win our approval. Others are not useful to them or comfortable to those around them. Fumbling efforts to balance their needs with our demands often lead to behavior that cannot be permitted because it interferes with the children's own welfare or that of others.

The worries, the resentment, or the fears that are troubling a small child may get in the way of his sleeping, of his eating, of his eliminating, or of getting along with other people or with himself.

In whatever form or in whatever degree trouble may show up, we can only give our children real help, if we get at and alter the cause of the trouble. Most of all, we need to accept the fact that troubles are an inevitable and invaluable part of growing up.

"MY CHILD DOESN'T LIKE TO EAT"

Lucien Aigner

MARY M. ALDRICH

Co-author with C. Anderson Aldrich, M.D., of "Babies Are Human Beings" and "Feeding Our Old-Fashioned Children," Winnetka, Ill.

THERE are some children who, over a long period of time, have no interest in food, fight over eating, disrupt mealtimes, worry their families, and even become medical problems. This is a hard situation and it is good to know that something can be done about it. Mealtime does not need to be a battle.

Eating need not be made a moral issue. Refusal to eat does not mean that a youngster is stubborn or "bad." It is merely a sign that something has temporarily gone wrong. Eating is one of life's greatest pleasures. It is meant to be fun. Children should be rarin' to go at the sound of the dinner bell. So if you have a child who is a mealtime problem, go over the suggestions in this chapter with an open mind. They have been chosen because other parents have found them useful. They may start you on the way to a solution.

First Aid for Appetites

Perhaps your child needs a medical check-up. In any case of persistent poor appetite, you will first want to rule out illness. Any illness that hangs on, even though it be slight, could cause a loss of interest in eating. It is good sense to start by getting a thorough medical examination for your child. Only a doctor

177

Armstrong Roberts

Satisfy that "eleven-o'clockish" feeling with fruit or juice. Then there will be no struggles over anti-snack rules, and no loss of appetite at mealtime.

develop. A cocker spaniel will never be a Saint Bernard, no matter how much you feed him. The same holds true for children. Some children will always be relatively small and some relatively large, so don't try to make a child bigger than Nature intended him to be.

Timmy Eaton's father was brought up in a home where every meal looked like Thanksgiving dinner. "And a good thing, too," says Mr. Eaton. "Don't I stand six foot two in my stocking feet, weigh a hundred and ninety pounds, and never been sick a day in my life? No skimping at my table." Food, and a lot of it, will make a man out of Tim, his father maintains.

Unfortunately, Mother Nature does not agree with Mr. Eaton. Timmy is a wiry little fellow, and small for a three-year-old. He clearly takes after his mother's side of the family, who are the "sparrow type," as Mr. Eaton is fond of saying. He will probably never be a husky football player and he may never need a lot of food to stoke the engine.

But Mr. Eaton is firm. Since Father is a ham-and-eggs man, Timmy must clean up a plate of ham and eggs, too, and no fooling, even though ham and eggs at breakfast are more than Tim can stomach.

The seeds of a rip-roaring appetite problem are in this situation. Forcing a child to eat more than he can manage is a one-way road to trouble. The doctrine of the "clean plate" is not a sound one, if the plate is always heaped. Some persons will be small eaters all through their lives.

is competent to find a possible low-grade infection, or an ailment that has been overlooked.

Is Your Child Being Overfed?

Overfeeding can be the cause of poor appetite. It is foolish to urge a child to eat beyond his inclination to do so, in an effort to fit him into a physical pattern that isn't his.

Each child requires a different amount of fuel for his growth. Each can be well nourished within his own capacity to

Does He Need a Change in His Diet?

Often simple changes in the kinds of food eaten will improve appetite. Foods that are too rich, with too much fat, may

178

make a child less eager to eat. A small child can live comfortably and happily without the sauces, gravies, pastries, and whipped-cream desserts that the grown-ups consider delicious. Meat, eggs, vegetables, milk, fruits, and whole-grain cereals are the best bet for a child. Milk is a basic food and most children love it. But some of these children with poor appetites will drink more if the top cream is removed. The chapter KEEPING YOUR YOUNG CHILD HEALTHY, in this volume, will give you more complete information about a nutritious diet.

Too many sweets or sweet drinks can interfere with appetite. Not that it's always easy to be firm, when other children in the neighborhood are allowed to have them! Of course, one can't always be thumbs down on a lollipop if it's offered. Children need to feel that they are like everybody else. The point is to try for a happy medium, and not let the sweets department get out of hand.

Is He Getting the Wrong Kind of Snacks?

Children are going to eat between meals. The question is, what shall they eat? Nonfilling foods make better snacks. An apple, a glass of fruit juice, or a piece of raw carrot or celery may interfere with mealtime eating less than milk, especially for children with poor appetites. Food just before meals is seldom a good idea. It is better to plan for a mid-morning or mid-afternoon snack as a part of the regular program.

One shouldn't be too hidebound about this question of snacks. Again, it's a matter of striking a happy medium. Asking for something to eat, and getting it, gives a small child a sense of well-being that is food for the spirit as well as for the body. It does no harm to break down and give a child the cooky he begs

for when you are touring the supermarket with him. In the midst of all that plenty, why shouldn't he have a bit?

What Is Appetite?

A child may get into a jam over eating simply because his parents do not know that appetite is a special device of our body machinery, set up to guide the proper intake of food. Like breathing, swallowing, and all the other marvelous arrangements of the human body, it works without urging. Even in young children it should be treated with respect.

Can Appetite Be Trusted?

Many persons think that a small child could not possibly select the right kinds and amounts of food, or decide when he has had enough. But if a wholesome assortment of simple, natural foods is offered him, his appetite will do the job. He will usually choose the foods that are needed for his growth.

A careful experiment with a group of babies and young children was tried over a period of years under controlled conditions. Each child was offered at mealtimes a tray containing a variety of natural foods. By "natural foods" we mean foods not combined into puddings or casserole dishes. For experimental purposes, each food was served separately. Meat, vegetables, cereals, eggs, sweet and sour milk, fruits, and sea salt were put before the children at every meal. Each child's selection of food, as well as his weight, health, and physical development, was carefully recorded. When the experiment was over, it was found that appetite *could* be trusted. The children had eaten the right proportions of each kind of food necessary for proper nutrition. Furthermore, they had all

Cheerful, noisy confusion is not apt to diminish a small child's zest for his meal, but tension in the air, or enforced silence, will give his food the taste of dust and ashes.

Some children enjoy meals with the family while they are still in the high chair. You may enjoy this, too, if yours is an easy-going household, not readily upset by untidiness in eating.

Rae Russell

made good records in their growth.

It would not, of course, be convenient to offer a child as varied a diet at home as was offered in the laboratory. But this experiment has something practical to say to mothers. A healthy child usually can be allowed to take responsibility for his own eating, *if he is given a wholesome and varied diet.*

Appetite Varies

The amount of food a child eats will change from day to day and from meal to meal, just as is true of the grown-ups.

180

His stage of growth, his energy needs, and his total feelings all influence how much and what a youngster will eat.

As every mother knows, some children need a little food often. Like Pooh in the children's beloved Christopher Robin poems, they are always looking for "a little something." Other children prefer fewer and larger meals. This variation is perfectly normal.

Many little children have "runs" on certain foods. Don't be upset if your child wants peanut-butter sandwiches every day in the year, or sticks to bananas for dessert until you cannot bear to look at one. This, too, is normal. There is really no reason why a young child should not have the food he likes, provided it is food that should be in his diet anyway. Some children are conservative and like only a few foods. Most children have special likes and dislikes—and why not? Tastes will broaden later.

Some children of two and three may not be hearty breakfasters. Granted that a child who is to spend long mornings at school needs a good breakfast to tide him over, still, the smaller children need not be forced to down big bowls of hot cereal, if it seems to go against their wishes.

It's well to remember that with children, as with grownups, a cold or a minor illness usually decreases the desire for food. In fact, if a child suddenly loses his appetite, a mother might easily guess that he is coming down with a cold. In this case, offer him food, but do not insist that he eat it. He will get hungry again when he feels better.

In the second and third years, children normally eat less food than do year-old babies. At this period, growth slows down a bit. Less energy is needed and the urge to eat is not so demanding. If food is not forced, the youngsters will be coming back for second helpings when they are a little older.

"Soup's On! Let's Eat!"

The atmosphere at mealtimes may also be a definite cause of trouble. This does not mean that the cheerful uproar of the ordinary home at suppertime is likely to interfere unduly with a small child's appetite. The average happy toddler calmly goes on eating bread and butter, even if the hunt is on for Grandma's lost glasses, if Sister has three phone calls, and if Brother is in a hurry to get to his Cub Scout meeting.

But there are some distractions that will disturb him and in time cause an appetite problem. Too much talk about his food and too much concentration on whether he is eating, what he is eating, and how he is eating will stymie any child.

Little children need to be happy at meals. Eating at the family dinner table is fine if the adults are cheerful, enjoy their food, and can endure slow and sloppy eating. It isn't what goes on around him that usually bothers the two- or three-year-old. It is the way the important people in his life make him feel about eating that determines his reaction to food.

Table Manners, Size Three

When children eat at the family table, manners come in for a going-over. Now good manners are indeed important. But it is useless to think about them until a child has learned to eat easily all by himself. At two, three, or even four, a child has not the muscular co-ordination to be neat and efficient in eating. One has to expect messy faces, spotted bibs, and an occasional overturned milk cup. Literally, there is no use crying over spilt milk.

This is the time for a child to learn to *like* to eat. Manners can, and should, come later. Making an early issue of manners can lead to refusal of food. The chapter WHAT KIND OF MANNERS FOR OUR CHILDREN? in Volume 15, has more to say about table manners.

Hints for Smoother Mealtimes

Children, like adults, enjoy food that tastes good and looks attractive. This is not hard to give them today. Processed and easily prepared foods make it simple for any mother to serve meals that would have taken hours of work in the so-called "good old days."

Even at two years of age, children have their own ways about food. Some like to keep everything strictly separate on the plate. Others are eager mixers, and it really does not matter. Carrots and prunes stirred together may not be your dish. But it may be most attractive to your small daughter.

Serve small portions and let the children come back for more. Introduce new flavors and textures gradually. A spoonful is enough for the first try. So many tastes have to be acquired. If your child doesn't like raw carrots at first, remember how long it took you to be enthusiastic over oysters or squash.

Toddlers may need a little help toward the end of the meal. When interest lags, it is time to stop. There is not much nutritional value in those last three mouthfuls anyhow. Your youngster is not putting something over on you by not eating them.

Certainly when a child gets into the habit of loitering endlessly over his meals, it's good sense to bring them to an end after a reasonable time. To say

cheerfully but definitely, "That's all for this time," will make him understand that eating is business as well as pleasure.

Change Routines to Improve Appetite

Sometimes when a mother is thoroughly discouraged about a youngster who won't eat, a change of scene may help. If he has been eating at the family table, try feeding him by himself. His room, if he has a small table and chair there, might be a welcome change. The kitchen table before the family eats, or the back porch, will help to break the pattern that has grown up and needs to be altered. If he has been eating alone, promotion to the family table may be the answer.

If a mother has tied herself into knots over the question of eating, her child may be more relaxed and better able to enjoy his meals if somebody else takes over temporarily. Grandma, Father, even a willing neighbor who comes to the rescue can be most helpful.

Worry Can Hamper Appetite

A mother who worries about her child's eating does not improve her child's appetite. A youngster senses his mother's anxiety even though she does not put her worry into words.

All mothers want their children to eat well. When a child seems hungry, people are likely to think he is healthy, and healthy children are always a credit to their parents. Actually, many healthy children are not big eaters.

Every mother loves to give food and appreciates it when that food is well received. When children will not eat the food that she has painstakingly prepared, it is hard for her not to take it personally.

"I don't want to grow up big and strong! I want to be pale and interesting!"

A youngster who has been feeding herself independently can be allowed occasional backsliding, if she is especially tired or needs the reassurance that comes with spoon feeding.

But we need to get over that way of thinking. Mealtime is a time when it pays to be casual.

A Child Can't Eat When He's Afraid

If your small child is steadily refusing to eat, he may be anxious. Although we sometimes forget it, little children are people. They respond to fears and worries just as adults do. If there seems no other reason for persistent lack of appetite, it is wise to take a look at what is happening to the child in his family and with his playmates. You may get a lead about the cause of the difficulty this way, without going overboard looking for trouble.

Even a small child has his own problems to work out in daily living. Like the grownups, he must learn to deal with them. With his limited experience, he often misinterprets ordinary events. He worries for fear Father or Mother might be going to leave him, or that they do not love him any more. He worries about cross words between the grownups that he does not understand. He even worries about the big six-year-old down the street, who throws his weight around in the back yard. He worries about new experiences, such as starting kindergarten.

Of course, not all children have these worries. Most of the time they work them off in their play or get them out in words. But some children hold them in. Worries attack the weakest point, and, with some children, appetite is the weakest point. These are the children who refuse to eat.

If you understand what is happening, you can often get a clue. Until you do, don't insist that your child eat. Relax the pressures. Let him feel that you love and trust him. Don't make your love, or any of the things he enjoys, depend on his "eating like a good boy." Encourage him. This kind of treatment will help him to open up and tell you what is bothering him.

Is He Telling You Something Is Wrong?

Refusal to eat may indicate that a child is not getting what he needs. Perhaps he isn't getting his share of attention, because his parents are busy with other interests, or with other children.

"George won't eat. He's just trying to get attention," is the statement you sometimes hear. And, in a sense, that is true, although children are seldom conscious of such a motive. But George may be entirely right in his struggle to be noticed. He may really be the forgotten man in the family set-up. A child needs loving attention just as much as he needs food. An appetite problem can often be helped when Father and Mother arrange to give more personal attention to the child.

Perhaps, however, a child is getting too much attention of the wrong kind. Maybe he's being "managed" within an inch of his life, or hovered over until he can't call his soul his own. It takes considerable humility for parents to look at these family situations squarely and co-operatively, and make the necessary changes. But experience has shown that sometimes a right-about-face attitude is the only thing that will bring peace.

Happy Children Are Hungry

A child's distaste for food may indicate that something is wrong in the relationship between his parents which affects the whole climate of the household. Children, like house plants, are sensitive creatures. Without the right sun and soil and atmosphere for growing, they wither. No child can thrive in a home where Father and Mother are constantly bickering and arguing and trying to get the better of one another. But they can take almost anything in their stride, if Father and Mother are generous with each other and are united in values that are bigger than themselves.

These children who won't eat almost always need more fun in the family. There is a natural tendency for grownups to handle the problems of children by getting grimmer and grimmer. But, as all good teachers know, a light touch gets results, a sour face gets you nowhere. Many an appetite problem would be nipped in the bud, if parents and children could only learn to laugh together.

SOME CHILDREN HAVE TROUBLE SLEEPING

MILTON J. E. SENN, M.D.

Director, Child Study Center, Yale University,
New Haven, Conn.

Walter Chandoha

ALL children, at some time or other, have trouble sleeping. The same statement may be made about parents. Like eating, sleeping is one of the important things people do, or are supposed to do, quite regularly every day of their lives. In fact, eating and sleeping are related to each other. When one is proceeding in good order, the other is likely to be doing the same. If there is trouble with a child's appetite, in the taking of food or in digestion, normal sleeping behavior may also be thrown out of balance.

Sometimes the sleep of a baby or a child is going along as it should, but parents become unnecessarily worried. They do not know what to expect. They think something is wrong because a baby or small child changes his sleeping habits. Probably this is the most frequent reason for parents becoming alarmed at their child's sleeping. It is important then that we try to understand something about *normal* sleep, be-fore we consider the usual reasons for children who have trouble sleeping.

What Is Sleep?

Sleep is more than the opposite of wakefulness. Scientists who have studied sleep know that in falling asleep every person passes through certain stages. There is a more or less gradual giving-up of wakefulness. Then there is a period of light sleep, followed by the real, deeper sleep. There are similar stages in reverse when one awakens. As a human being falls asleep, the sensations he has may be pleasurable, or unpleasant and even frightening.

It is easier to give up wakefulness and activity at some times than at others. No individual, whether infant, child, or adult, likes to bring to an end interesting and satisfying play or work. When a person is sick he may fear sleep because it will take him out of contact with what is going on around him. He feels uneasy, and is even frightened by the

185

thought of what might happen to him while he is asleep.

What Changes in Sleep?

In going to sleep, many parts of the body change their activity. The temperature changes inside the body and in the skin. There are also changes in the rate at which the body produces heat and energy, as shown by differences in sweating. It has been found in studying children as they fall asleep that the temperature of the skin rises for a short while. Along with this there is production and evaporation of sweat. This may be why many babies and children show a flushing of the face, and sweating, soon after going to sleep. Perhaps they kick off the covers in an effort to cool off. Here is a hint to parents not to cover a child too warmly when he is put to bed.

Babies Have Their Own Way of Sleeping

The way infants and children sleep differs from the way adults sleep. The positions your baby assumes may seem most uncomfortable to you. He frequently turns his head far to one side and places his arms and legs in odd postures. These positions are normal for him. He also shifts his position often. The young baby makes trembling and sucking movements of his lips, fluttering motions of his eyelids. His body and feet may twitch. When he is old enough to move about, he "cruises" around his crib until he finds a side or an end against which he can fit snugly. Even when asleep, the baby may make whimpering noises in his throat, and as he grows older may cry out or talk. While this is all normal, crying-out and talking are done especially often when the baby is sick or when he is uneasy, worried, or frightened. Restlessness in sleep may be caused by hunger or discomfort, or may be due to being too warm or too cold. It may be caused by real pain.

How Much Sleep?

The number of hours of sleep required is different for each person. This does not mean that we know how much every person needs to sleep in twenty-four hours. Tables telling how much sleep is required at a certain age may be not only useless but upsetting.

In general, young babies sleep more than older ones. Then, too, they sleep during the day as well as during the night. But nobody knows enough about sleep requirements to say precisely how much sleep every infant or child needs. This is an individual matter. It changes with growth, and even differs from day to day, depending on many things. Probably the most common reason for the inability of some babies and children to sleep is that they are forced or expected to sleep when they are not ready to do so, or more than they need to.

But babies and children do not always know, or are not willing to admit, that they need rest and sleep. When fatigued or sleepy, they may, by their activity, give the impression that they are able to continue full steam in play. An overtired child, especially, may fight sleep and become overactive. Every parent knows that such a youngster is difficult to calm down. This is the reason why parents should not overstimulate a youngster with intensive play or exciting stories just before bedtime. Quieting, comforting stories or play with Mother or Father are always in order.

Causes of Wakefulness

When children have trouble sleeping, it may be that the sleeping arrangements are not good. A safe and comfortable sleeping place, with enough room for the baby to move around, is, of course, the first requirement for good sleep. Sleeping garments that are too warm or that interfere with the natural movements of his body may make a small child restless. Although some sleeping bags are comfortable, others are too snug and confining. They may even be dangerous if they fit too tightly around the neck, or if they interfere with the baby's breathing when he gets into one of his favorite, distorted positions.

Households do not need to stop talking or working when a small child is put to bed. Babies should not become accustomed to absolute quiet while they sleep. Rhythmical or steady noises are not usually disturbing. In fact, they even seem to soothe some babies. But youngsters, like adults, may be disturbed by sudden or loud noises while they are falling asleep, particularly if these are sounds to which they are unaccustomed.

Changes in the seasons influence the sleeping habits of everyone. In communities where daylight saving goes into effect in spring, babies who have been accustomed to being put to bed when it is dark outdoors seem to resist falling asleep while it is still daylight. Even when the window shades are pulled down to exclude as much of this light as possible, they fall asleep later than usual. There is also earlier awakening in the earlier dawn of the spring and summer months.

Does Daylight Interfere with Naps?

There is a difference between sleep at night and daytime naps. The infant may resist sleep in the evening when it is daylight, but he may easily go to sleep in the daylight of midafternoon.

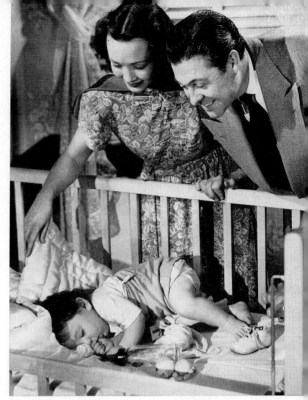

A favorite toy or cuddly stuffed animal to take to bed makes a darkened room seem far less lonely and scary.

The young infant readily takes daytime naps. Such sleep will be interrupted at first mainly by hunger and feeding time. Gradually, the growing infant spends time lying awake to look at the world around him, and to play. His naps become fewer, but last longer. In later infancy, he may take one nap in the morning and one in the afternoon. By the age of two or three years, he usually naps only in the afternoon. At four or five years of age, he has usually given up his regular afternoon sleep. It is interesting that sleep in a nap may be less restless than night sleep.

Wakefulness a Sign of Illness

Sleep problems are too often considered deliberate and willful attempts on

187

When jealousy or resentment of a new baby must be bottled up, small children are often troubled by bad dreams or wakefulness. Letting them express feelings in words may help to diminish worry.

the part of the child to "get back at" his parents in a teasing or annoying fashion. Looking at sleep difficulties in that way is not helpful to anyone concerned. When your baby or child has trouble in going to sleep or remaining asleep for a suitable period, look for a reason, but do not decide it is stubbornness. Many children and infants show restlessness in their sleep as the first sign of physical illness. This may be due to fever, pain, or general discomfort.

What Effect Has Change?

Sleeping in a new crib or bed, in a new room, or in a new house may be dis-

quieting and even frightening. Changes of routine daytime activity, such as new ways of feeding, visits from strangers, or a new baby sitter, may be upsetting, even though unavoidable. In fact, any change in the routine or the personnel of the household may cause a change in sleep behavior.

Of course, the coming of a new baby to a family will have an influence on everybody. The brothers and sisters may be accepting and happy about the new arrival, but at the same time they may be troubled, jealous, and insecure. New babies in the home are a frequent cause of sleep disturbance in a two-, three-,

Worries and fears often come out in nightmares. Then a young child needs comforting and his parents need to look for the cause of his anxiety.

or even five- or six-year-old who cannot put his feelings into words. The chapter Sometimes Rivals, Sometimes Friends, in Volume 12, discusses the handling of this problem.

Some Wakefulness a Part of Growing up

Like all behavior problems, sleep disturbances *may* have emotional causes, but every sleep problem does not mean that something is wrong with your child or with you. Most of the time, sleep difficulties are a temporary part of the growing-up process.

Children who are going through periods of extreme physical growth are always under something of a strain, and this strain may show up at times in an inability to sleep readily or soundly. A small child who is having difficult new experiences in eating, talking, toilet training, or other kinds of learning, may be a poor sleeper for a time. Sometimes you can ease up on the pressures and improve the whole situation, sleep included. When your child is not sleeping well, see if your standards in some part of the daily program are too high. The newness of an experience, even though it is pleasant, carries with it some elements of fear for many children.

When They Call for Mommy

Between the first and second birthdays there comes a period when youngsters seem to be particularly concerned about separation from parents. One of the common causes of sleep disturbances in young children seems to be this fear. On being put to bed, a child may call for his mother and insist that she stay with him until he falls asleep. Such a youngster may awaken during the night, cry out, and again demand that one of his parents, usually his mother, stay with

him until he again falls fast asleep.

You are not spoiling your child if you go to him when he calls. He needs to know that you are available. It may not be necessary to pick him up. A few words of reassurance from you may be enough to convince him you are not about to vanish. The confidence in your tone when you say "Now you can go to sleep" helps him, too. If you know that his wakefulness is not his fault or yours, you may be able to be more patient in dealing with it. It is just possible that he needs more of your company during the day. Then he may find it easier to leave you at bedtime.

If a separation of several days or weeks from his parents is necessary during the second or third year, a child should be told about the separation a day or two in advance. He should know and like the adult who is left in charge. A sudden, unannounced absence of a parent is likely to seem like the realization of his worst forebodings. Poor sleeping, changes in eating habits, and other disturbances may show up as a result of his worry.

During the second year, when worries about being left without Mother or Father are present, nightmares may appear. It is at this age, too, that daytime naps may be given up temporarily for a few weeks, or even months. Usually, children resume daytime naps if you keep on with the routine of putting them in their beds at the usual naptime.

What About Bedtime Rituals?

Getting a child to bed in a cheerful frame of mind is discussed in the chapter Guiding Him Tactfully, in this volume. All small children need time to settle down at bedtime, but some time after the first birthday, many children seem to take on presleep rituals. They cruise around the crib, rock their bodies, and nod their heads. A slightly older child may demand that Mother stay with him. He may ask for a drink of water, for something to eat, or to be taken to the toilet. He may find it impossible to go to sleep without sucking his thumb. He may insist on holding a favorite teddy bear, toy, or blanket. Let him have the toy that comforts him.

Do not try to discourage his thumb-sucking forcibly. He needs this kind of support at the moment when he must be separated from the company of the adults who are so important to him. Taking away his favorite toy, prohibiting thumbsucking, or ignoring his need for the little ceremony of being tucked in, having the shade pulled down, being kissed good night, may lead to more severe sleep disturbances. Any change in the going-to-bed routines may be unsettling or disturbing, for these young children are extremely conservative!

Many parents ask, "Will these bedtime ceremonials become a permanent thing?" As a rule, children try to give up these rituals when they are able to do without them. When you see your youngster trying to leave some of his babyish ways behind, you can help out. "Should we let Teddy sleep on the bureau tonight?" or "How about putting your blanket in the wash?" may give him the chance to make the transition he is trying to make. A four-, five-, or six-year-old can often relinquish his babyish ways if he takes over the responsibility for putting himself to bed.

If you understand that the separation at bedtime is really hard for a child, you may be more willing to give him time to settle down. His little ceremonies bridge the gap between the delightful hour when he has his mother and father, and the lonely moments before he sleeps.

Early Wakening

Your child may sleep well for several hours, but awaken before you think he should. Some children are fully awake and "raring to go" at anywhere from 3:00 A.M. to 6:00 A.M. (particularly on Sunday mornings and holidays), those hours when the parents often feel that they, themselves, are getting their best sleep. The distinction between "early in the morning" and "the middle of the night" is a fine one here! With the young baby, the cause of awakening may be hunger or thirst, which may be relieved by giving him food or water. The older infant or preschool child may awaken because he "can't sleep."

Should You Let Him Play?

These children are often safe if they are given light in their rooms and are allowed to play alone with their toys or books in bed. Perhaps you are uneasy about letting your child go unsupervised this way. After some time of sleeping "with one eye open" you will probably find that the child may play for a while and then go back to sleep.

The toddler who can crawl out of his crib may be a hazard if left to his own ideas of play. You may need to limit his excursions to a single room. A gate across the doorway is often the easiest way to do this. A room may be considered safe if you have removed any objects and materials with which the child could hurt himself. You may need to spend some time with him. Try standing or sitting at the crib-side for a few minutes before holding him. This is hard on you when you are sleepy!

It is difficult or impossible not to be

The early riser may play quietly in his room, but roaming the house is usually dangerous. He needs the protection of a gate across the doorway.

annoyed or angry. But such feelings are recognized by the child and may keep him from settling down to play or sleep. If parents can take turns being with a child who, morning after morning, wakes up early, it may be less hard on them. Sometimes these periods of early awakening last a day or two, and sometimes several weeks. You may wonder if such attention keeps the early-awakening habit going, since the child gets so much enjoyment from it. It usually works the opposite way, particularly when you try to help the child go back to sleep. Encouraging him to stay alone and play by himself really does help him drop off again. Shaming a child, or letting him "cry it out," is not recommended. It usually does not work. When it does seem to work, you may

"He's Up!"

see new, but equally unpleasant and difficult, behavior develop.

Sometimes you may find a partly satisfactory compromise in looking at books, reading to the child, or listening to music. You can sit next to him, or you can even both lie down. Sometimes such an arrangement has put both parent and child to sleep. When this is the case, one wonders if the physical closeness of child to parent was the sleep-provoking agent.

Should He Get in His Parents' Bed?

Certainly, all children at early ages want to crawl into bed with their parents, for the parents' bed seems warmer, or more cuddly. On occasion children want to join the parents because they are curious and wonder what the parents are doing. Sometimes this is permitted for reassurance and for security when the child has some unexplainable fear. While taking an infant or child into their bed may seem the easiest way for parents, such an arrangement has serious drawbacks. In the case of an infant,

191

he may be physically injured by falling from a bed or by being rolled on by the sleeping parent, or he may be suffocated in the bedclothes. Once infants and children experience the pleasure of sharing a bed with adults, they want more of it. A habit may become so fixed that it is hard to break. In the long run, parents find it easier to solve sleep problems in other ways, even though the share-the-bed approach appears at the beginning to be easiest.

Of course, the occasional morning romp in bed with Mother or Father may be a lot of fun for everybody. That is an entirely different matter.

What About Bad Dreams?

Most children come to a period of development when they dream often, and even have nightmares. The sleep of the child in the years from two to five is frequently broken by bad dreams. In fact, these children seem to dream of frightening things more often than of pleasurable ones. Dreams represent a carry-over of daytime life and experiences. They act as safety devices for getting rid of feelings we cannot tolerate easily.

Children of this age have worries that are completely groundless. They misunderstand some of the things that are happening to them and their bodies as they go through ordinary training and learning. At the time of toilet training, children may express their fears and discontent by words, in play, or in dreams. It is not unusual for such a child to awaken in panic, and, when talked with later, to say he saw animals that were about to hurt him.

How Can You Handle Nightmares?

When such nightmares or panics occur, the best thing to do is to awaken the child and encourage him to tell you about his dreams. You can reassure him by telling him everything is all right, and, if he seems to need you, sit by his bedside until he settles down again. Sometimes a hall light to break the gloom of the bedroom gives a youngster comfort. A child may demand a favorite toy to hold, or may suck his thumb in an effort to comfort himself, just as does a child who wakes without bad dreams. Such finger-sucking should be permitted to him.

On the day following a nightmarish night, you can talk to your child about his dream. Perhaps he will be able to talk out his fears. He may, in play, re-create the situations he finds of great concern. These may be frightening, exciting, or even pleasurable events. This does not mean that he should be pushed into talking or playing out these experiences, or urged to dig into thoughts he would rather try to forget. You can examine his daytime activities and see if they are too strenuous, worrisome, or tension-producing. Rearranging his daily schedules and activities often results in sounder sleep and fewer bad dreams.

Good Life Makes for Good Sleep

The basis of good sleep is, then, not so much in what happens at the time a child is put to bed or during his sleeping periods, as in what goes on during the waking hours of each day. Anything that helps a child develop and grow in as healthy a manner as he has the possibility of doing, anything that assists him and his parents to get along with each other in mutually enriching and satisfactory experiences, will provide a foundation for a happy and creative existence. Good sleep is but one segment of such a life.

SOME CHILDREN RESIST THE TOILET

GUSTAVE F. WEINFELD, M.D.

Psychiatrist, Institute for Juvenile Research; Attending Pediatrician, Children's Memorial Hospital, Chicago, Ill.; Consultant, Staff, Highland Park Hospital, Highland Park, Ill.

Suzanne Szasz

PARENTS are so eager to have their small children take responsibility for going to the toilet, that any setback or breakdown in learning the accepted bathroom procedures is likely to be discouraging. If you understand some of the reasons why toddlers and even three- and four-year-olds sometimes resist toileting, you will be better able to handle these normal difficulties.

Rebellion—Sign of Growth

It is reassuring to discover that growth and development are responsible both for a child's compliance and his rebellion to our standards of toilet behavior. HELPING YOUR CHILD LEARN TO USE THE TOILET, a chapter in this volume, discusses this problem.

The child of two or three may refuse to conform to demands that he eliminate at a time and place of your choosing, because he has reached a stage of development where he wants to exercise his independence. Look at it from his point of view. He regards his stools and his urine as his, and when he eliminates is a matter for him to decide. Rebellion of this nature may be looked upon as a healthy stage in the child's development. He is beginning to catch on that he is powerful, too. You need not worry about this rebellion. Under favorable conditions, he soon has his fill of satisfaction with this power. He learns that it is better, after all, to do as Mother wishes, for her appreciation is more valuable than his "I'll show them" attitude. But this is not the only reason for toilet difficulties.

Are Physical Defects Ever a Cause?

A physical defect can be the cause of toilet difficulties, but only in a small group of children who soil is this the case. When there is a physical basis for resisting toileting, you will have plenty of other evidence that something is

Suzanne Szasz

When a child refuses to use the toilet, try to find out what is troubling him. Elimination may have become frightening because it is painful for him.

wrong. Physical defects of the urinary tract or the bowels may have been acquired, or the child may have been born with them. Your doctor or your clinic will want to make a thorough medical examination to find out the exact nature of the trouble. Then steps can be taken to correct the condition. For instance, children who dribble urine day and night are highly suspect of this type of defect.

Children who are mentally retarded also have difficulty in acquiring toilet skills. This does not mean that you should suspect mental dullness just because a child soils or wets. The number of soiling children who are retarded is

extremely small. When retardation is the cause, there will always be other striking evidences of it. There will be a delay in the first smile, sitting up, walking, and talking. Even these children ultimately achieve control, but they do so at a later age than normal children. Training programs for these children should be adapted to their potentialities. The section on "Mentally Retarded Children" in the chapter SPECIAL NEEDS OF VARIOUS HANDICAPS, in Volume 12, will be useful to read in this connection.

Elizabeth Hibbs

If you are relaxed and casual in your attitude toward toileting, your baby will be likely to follow your lead.

Why Do We Stress Elimination?

The youngster who is resisting the use of the toilet usually has reasons for doing so. His feelings toward bowel and bladder control will determine how he uses the potty or toilet. These feelings of his reflect our own feelings about the whole question of elimination.

Most parents were taught in their childhood that regular elimination is essential to good health. Medical men will tell you that the dangers of constipation have been stressed too much.

A mother reared in a toilet-conscious society finds it difficult, if not impossible, to adopt a casual attitude toward these matters in her own child. Fortunately, modern science has demonstrated that many ills previously attributed to constipation are almost always due to other causes.

Does Constipation Injure Health?

Children can go without a bowel movement for astonishingly long periods of time without ill effects. The only unfavorable aspect of constipation is that the longer the stool remains in the intestines, the larger and harder it becomes. This may produce pain when it is passed. When this occurs, the child may develop fear of having a bowel movement and will withhold the stool in order to avoid the pain. Regulation of diet and harmless, pleasant-tasting lubricants given *at your doctor's direction*

will quickly correct the difficulty. Cathartics such as castor oil should *never* be used except when ordered by your doctor.

Resistance May Be Imitation

Some people have strong feelings that the waste products of the body are offensive. They find it difficult to change the baby's diaper and to clean the baby afterwards without having feelings of disgust. Such feelings do not escape the infant, and he reacts accordingly. Most mothers fortunately do not have such strong feelings. They will clean a soiled infant quite casually and cheerfully.

Mothers are well aware how their own attitudes are reflected by the baby. On days when Mother is irritable, the baby will be fretful and tense. If Mother is always that way, the baby will tend to be that way, too. When Mother is happy, relaxed, and casual, the baby cries little, eats well, and sleeps quietly. If Mother is tense about diapering and anxious in her toilet training, the baby will react by resisting with the muscles and nerves controlling his elimination.

Do Feelings About Elimination Affect Personality?

If Mother fears or is repulsed by things messy and odorous, she will quickly reveal her feelings to her baby. He will learn from her that his bowel movements are something to be resented and shunned. Some such infants grow up occasionally to be the kind of

This youngster is comfortable, for the toilet seat is not shaky. Children are sometimes afraid of falling off a high toilet, or are really worried by the idea of being flushed away.

adults who are meticulously clean and miserably unhappy over anything messy or disorderly. Other infants may react in the opposite way to this kind of motherly training. They become defiant and take on an attitude of rebellion. They soil long after the average child has learned to keep clean. This messiness of infancy may remain a part of their characters throughout their lives. They may become like certain extremely sloppy, messy adults we all know.

Harsh Training Makes Trouble

John, at the age of nine months, had been completely trained. He had not soiled his diapers for more than six weeks. Then his mother found him in his crib one afternoon with hands and face covered with his bowel movement. She scolded him severely and cleaned him up while he cooed happily. About a week later the experience was repeated. This time she really became angry and soundly spanked his bottom. Then John became severely constipated for long periods of time.

This mother was able to recognize the error she had made. She had imposed training before her son was old enough to understand what was expected of him, or before he had the ability to express his toilet needs in words. He was confused about what his mother wanted. To John, it looked as if his mother was angry over his having a bowel movement. As children so often do, he had misinterpreted the reason for his mother's displeasure.

After three or four days of constipation, this baby would finally soil his diapers. His mother, realizing that a new approach was needed, patiently changed them without any expression of displeasure. She placed a low potty chair in

his room. She watched for his rhythm of passing urine and bowel movements and, at the same time, encouraged him to sit on the potty chair without removing his diapers. Gradually he became accustomed to this new piece of furniture. Then, when he was due to have a bowel movement, his mother placed him on his potty chair, saying, "Make bowel movement." Shortly he did this regularly. After this skill was well established, she did the same with his urination. If this mother had not been patient and understanding, the situation might have become increasingly difficult for both her and her baby.

Can a Child Sense Our Deeper Feelings?

Most parents feel that they are supposed to love their children every day—twenty-four hours a day completely. Nobody can feel such love all the time. Most of us are afraid to admit to ourselves that there are moments when we do not like our children, but these moments really come to us all. Instead of facing our feelings, we try to hide them. We try to make up for our "wrong" feelings by being too attentive and worried about our children, in an effort to prove to ourselves that we really do love them. It would be so much easier and better for our children if we could only say to ourselves, "My annoyance and displeasure with this youngster are only natural. I don't have to prove to myself that I am a good parent."

Children are much more sensitive to feeling tones than adults are. But even adults become suspicious of those who are oversolicitous of their welfare, and they are made uncomfortable by such hovering. The child feels uneasy if he is smothered with anxious attention. His uneasiness and mistrust may express itself in a number of ways, but the most frequent is wetting and soiling.

If Training Is Mismanaged

Sometimes well-meant, misdirected efforts may defeat their own purpose.

Teddy, a three-year-old boy, wet at night and soiled during the day. He had been trained for bowel movements at six months. At the age of fourteen months, intensive training for bladder control was begun. He was taken to the toilet regularly every hour and a half during the day. He usually wet his diapers immediately after this. About this time, he began to soil again. At first his failures were casually accepted. Later his mother's anger and disappointment with him mounted and a pitched battle between them ensued.

His mother saw she was not making any progress, and wisely consulted a qualified counselor. Teddy's mother was told to remove all pressures and bend her energies toward relaxed care and affection. Such an attitude, she was told, would be much more helpful in getting the youngster to use the toilet. It worked out just that way.

Not all cases respond so quickly and completely, but when one way of handling the situation proves useless, it is only sensible to try another. Someone trained in dealing with children's problems can often give a discouraged mother a new point of view.

Sometimes the cause of the trouble is not so deep-seated. Many parents lose sight of the fact that the small child views the world from a different level from that of the adult. Toilet-seat heights may frighten the child and make him feel insecure. When one is frightened, all muscles tense. The frightened child will scream in rage, stiffen, and throw himself into a state where he cannot or will not move his bowels or urinate.

Can You Be too Casual?

Many children seem to "train themselves," but actually it rarely happens without some encouragement and teaching. The numerous incentives toward cleanliness in our world have their effect, even if parents are indifferent to a child's learning. The expectations of children's playmates, their playmates' parents, and other adults set a standard for their behavior. They find out as soon as they play with other children that using the toilet is one way of being like grown-ups. For these reasons and others, some parents feel that they should do nothing to teach their children control of elimination.

Debby's mother had been the victim of severe toilet training when she was a child. She was determined that things would be different for Debby. She didn't expect her to ask to go to the toilet until she was quite old, and, therefore, she was unaware of all the signals of readiness Debby had given. It was not until Debby was three years old and her mother was embarrassed to have the little girl in diapers that she began some training. It was not easily achieved, because by now the child believed she was supposed to soil and wet. The signs that point toward a child's being ready to use the toilet are discussed in the chapter HELPING YOUR CHILD LEARN TO USE THE TOILET, in this volume.

New Babies and Toilet Problems

One little four-year-old boy who was an extremely clean child had been toilet-trained since he was six months old. He had a bowel movement daily without

F. P. G.

A child's problems can often be avoided if we recognize that facts adults take for granted are frequently distorted in a child's mind. Whole truths simply explained can usually avoid such problems. The chapter He Learns About Differences Between Boys and Girls, in this volume, may help you in making explanations in such an instance. If a child has been confused and anxious for some time, he may not respond quickly to a simple explanation. Advice from your doctor or a child guidance clinic may be necessary to help him.

He Wants to Be a Baby, too

No matter how well a young child is prepared for the birth of the new baby, he is never free from some anxiety after the baby arrives. The chapter Sometimes Rivals, Sometimes Friends discusses this in detail in Volume 12. Watching mother feed and cuddle the baby kindles in him the desire to be a baby himself again. There are numerous ways of acting out this desire. Some children will deliberately wet and soil, as a bid for the same kind of attention the baby gets.

Other children have too much pride to act out their wishes by such conscious acts. These children will wet their beds while asleep, or soil their pants while they are preoccupied in play. In this way they feel that it is not really their fault that their good habits have lapsed.

fail after his first meal of the day. His mother became pregnant and, because of her threatened miscarriage, had to remain in bed during the first six weeks of her pregnancy. During this time he was cared for by his grandmother, who believed that bowel regularity was absolutely essential to "good health." The child's emotional life now became focused on his bowel movements. He was high-pressured by his grandmother. At the same time, he thought that he had been let down by his mother because she no longer took care of him.

He reacted to this combination of circumstances with fear and anxiety. In an effort to solve his problem in a confused childish way, he withheld his stool. Mother had something inside of her, he had been told, so he would keep what he had inside of him. His anxiety was increased because he associated pregnancy with his own problem of taking in food and expelling body waste.

These are the very children who seem to have the least jealousy of the baby. They are afraid to express this jealousy directly, but have to do so by other means.

Jealousy is not the only reaction a child has to the new baby. Some children feel angry at their parents for bringing a competitor into the home.

If your child begins to soil and wet after the arrival of a new baby, he is not being "bad." He is really trying to tell you, in the only way he can, that he is troubled. If you understand his feelings, that alone will do much to set his fears at rest, and his anger will be lessened. The way you act toward him, more than what you say, will convince him that the baby is not a substitute for him and that your love for him has in no way diminished.

A Departure May Cause Setbacks

A young child usually reacts to separation from someone he loves with fear and anger. Fear comes from the loss of the feeling of security the loved person provided. He is angry because he feels deserted by the loving and departed individual. These reactions not infrequently show up in soiling and wetting.

Ben had been using the toilet since he was two years old. When he was nearly three years old, his grandmother, who had taken care of him much of the time, moved to another home. He was unable to understand this sudden separation from someone he had loved. He felt his grandmother had left because

The walk down the long, cold, dark hall is more frightening than Mother's disappointment over a wet bed. A flashlight or a hall light may help.

she no longer loved him. Also, if she could so easily disappear, his parents might do likewise! His babyish behavior in soiling and wetting showed clearly that he was trying to tell his parents how desperately he still needed their care and protection.

Fears at the Root of Difficulty

Between the ages of two and five, a child learns that boys and girls are made differently. This is an important and necessary kind of learning and it is desirable that children see other children of both sexes nude, in a setting where an adult can answer questions that arise. The chapter HE LEARNS ABOUT DIFFERENCES BETWEEN BOYS AND GIRLS, in this volume, discusses this question in detail. Often, especially if their doubts and questions have not been given satisfactory answers, little girls fear they have lost an important organ. Little boys

worry that they might lose one. How this will come about, and why, differs in every child's thoughts. The anxiety over this problem frequently shows up in wetting during the day or night.

Adequate reassurance of these children, and simple sex instruction, may be all that is necessary to dispel their fears and make it possible for them to stay dry at night. Some children will not respond so easily and you may need more skilled help with them than you can provide yourself. If your child fails to respond to the advice your doctor gives you, then you may want to avail yourself of help from a specially-trained adviser in a child guidance clinic, if that is in any way possible.

What About Night Wetting?

Some children do not learn to stay dry at night until around the age of three or three and a half. In some boys, it may be even later. The chapter HELPING YOUR CHILD LEARN TO USE THE TOILET, in this volume, has some practical suggestions for encouraging a child to stay dry through the night.

When a child who has been able to go through the night without urinating starts wetting frequently again, some worry is usually at the root of his difficulty. That is also true if a child four years old or over has not been able to achieve night dryness. Punishment or anything that shames a child is worse than useless.

Such a boy or girl needs confidence in his own ability to achieve that desirable state of dryness. He needs to know you have confidence in his ability to achieve it, too, and that you will stand by him and accept him even if it takes a long time for him to achieve it.

The disturbances in a child's life, such as a new baby or the departures of persons close to him, that have been discussed as the cause of daytime wetting, may be the cause of nighttime wetting too. In fact, any change in the usual routine or any upset may show up in a loss of control of urination at night.

Look at the Practical Arrangements

In our effort to find an emotional cause, we should not overlook some of the obvious practical reasons for failure to stay dry at night. It may be that a small child is sleeping in a cold room. If he awakens needing to urinate, it is just too cold to get up and go to the toilet. The bathroom may be down a long hall or on another floor. For a small child to get up and go through the dark hall may be a fearsome business. Even Mother's disapproval for wetting or soiling seems less dangerous than that walk in the dark! Sometimes a simple arrangement, such as giving the child his own flashlight, leaving a light in the hall, or letting him have a potty in his room, may be the answer. Cutting down on liquids in the late afternoon or evening is not usually a good plan, for there is a chance of making a child uncomfortably thirsty, and anxious, too.

The child who continually wets or soils where or when he should not is usually doing so in an attempt to solve a problem. From his limited and childish view of things, that seems to be a possible way out of a difficulty. We can help most if we can discover what that problem is and remove the cause. Until we can help him out of his difficulty, he needs our patient support. In general, the more satisfactory all the other phases of his daily life are, the more readily will the toileting problem be worked out.

DIFFICULTIES IN LIVING WITH OTHERS

EVELINE B. OMWAKE, M.A.

Associate Professor, Child Study Center,
Yale University, New Haven, Conn.

W HAT a child sees, hears, and feels as he grows from babyhood into childhood makes the world appear encouraging and full of opportunity, or frightening, discouraging, and overwhelming. Many of the daily conflicts and misunderstandings fall into two groups. There are the problems a small child meets in "communicating" with others, and in understanding what they expect or want. There are, too, the difficulties he encounters in his early contacts with discipline.

Why Are Children Rude?

The fact that children learn to speak at all is strong evidence that they can adapt to unpredictable demands. Through the child's second year, any addition to his vocabulary is prized and repeated. But it is not long until he discovers that, having learned to talk, he must now learn when *not* to talk, and what *not* to say. While he is trying to master these confusing matters, he may run into difficulties because, by adult standards, he may be rude, shy, or untruthful.

Fortunately, to a great extent, children develop a sense of their audience, and learn easily to regulate the flow of language and the choice of words to the situation. Sometimes they slip. Then they unintentionally embarrass their elders and are bewildered themselves. They may not have even the faintest

201

idea as to what is wrong with what they said.

A three-year-old girl whose family had been openly criticizing their doctor met him in public one day. Her mother said, "Tell Dr. Black how glad you are to see him." The little girl answered, "But I'm not glad. You said we don't like him any more." Her response was honest, direct, and made in good faith. Far too much diplomacy was expected of her. It would hardly make sense to punish a child for being rude under such circumstances.

How Can You Teach Sincerity?

The problem of being honest, polite, and sincere may become a serious dilemma. The child who replies over the telephone, "Mommy says she isn't here," is reporting accurately. Though she may be double-crossing her mother, she is doing so innocently.

Through hearing adults talk, and learning what to say under certain conditions, children come to differentiate between "lies" and "white lies." To learn that one is a serious offense and the other an act of diplomacy is indeed difficult. If children make mistakes, if they are evasive or untruthful, or lay the blame on someone else, the responsibility is probably not entirely theirs.

You can help children make the distinction between honesty and politeness. You can explain, "We try not to hurt people's feelings." You can also make it seem safe to tell the truth.

Sometimes children are untruthful because they are desperately anxious to please their parents. A three-year-old who is timid about going down the slide in nursery school, but who is under pressure to be big and brave, may report at home, "I went down the slide a million times today." Here, as in so many instances of untruthfulness, you can help your child most by asking yourself, "Why does he need to be untruthful?" Then, perhaps, you can modify the conditions that make him feel it is necessary to alter the facts in order to win approval.

Are They Really Unco-operative?

The children's own expressions suggest the universality of some of the difficulties they meet in growing up. "Do it myself," or "Let me do it," brings to mind immediately the picture of the two- or three-year-old who wants to be given the necessary time and tolerance at least to try to show that he can do his part. He is not dawdling or loitering as he experiments with the mysteries of the heel and the toe in his sock. The "Watch what I can do" of the four-year-old, and the same child's "Go away from here," are just other ways of saying that he feels his own importance as a person. You need not set it down to disrespect or rudeness.

"What does she take me for?" and "What does she think I am?" are traditional expressions of irritation and frustration at parents and teachers who have set standards so high that they cannot be maintained, or who fail to see children as the children see themselves. These expressions may be signs that we need to relax the pressures on the two-, three-, or five-year-old.

Learning to Control Anger

In general, it is easier for children to depend on language for expression when the situation is calm than when it is tense. At such times words leave them, and they communicate by more primitive but no less effective methods. From the point of view of a small person, hitting, biting, spitting, scratching, kicking, and the like are easy ways of solving conflicts with other children. When the child is feeling angry or is threatened, he is literally speechless in his rage. The other child involved may also be in too much of a rage to hear what is said. Between these two, fists are likely to fly.

A two-year-old figures that a quick bite is sure to make another two-year-old release a toy. The bite does not mean the same thing to the child who bites as it does to the one bitten, or to an adult. Grabbing a bike, a doll, or a carriage from another three-year-old is much more effective than saying, "It's my turn." Kicking over a block building is a quicker and surer way of saying, "You're playing too close to me—move over." Eventually, the right words must become a part of the children's personal play equipment.

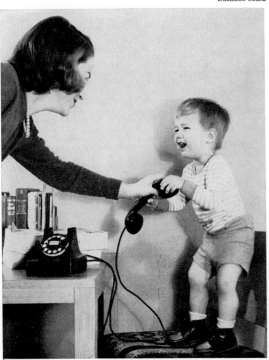

Suzanne Szasz

How Can You Show Them Better Ways?

You can give children real help if you say the phrases for them and lend what physical assistance is necessary to solve the problem. "He wants to use it when you are finished." "You use it a little longer and then it will be his turn." "He doesn't like it when you play too close. He is afraid you will spoil what he is doing." These help interpret to the one child what the other wants, and suggest what he can do about it.

To the attacking child, you can say, "He's using it now. You can have it soon;" "Hitting makes him angry;" "Tell him you want it when he is finished." These phrases do help, even though the situation in question may not clear up immediately. It may be necessary to continue being referee as long as the children are together.

Keep your statements clear, short, and simple. If too much explanation is offered, the children are likely to stop listening. They want to get on with what they were doing. That is one reason they used the "quick method" in the first place.

Physically separating the children is often necessary. Producing another similar toy, or suggesting a variation of the activity, is as much a part of the adult's job as helping find the right words and phrases.

It's Hard to Learn the Rules

Discipline, as it has meaning for children, might well be defined as a system

The difference between tactful evasion and the downright lie is too involved for a small child. He has no grasp of our embarrassment when he says, "Mother says she isn't home now."

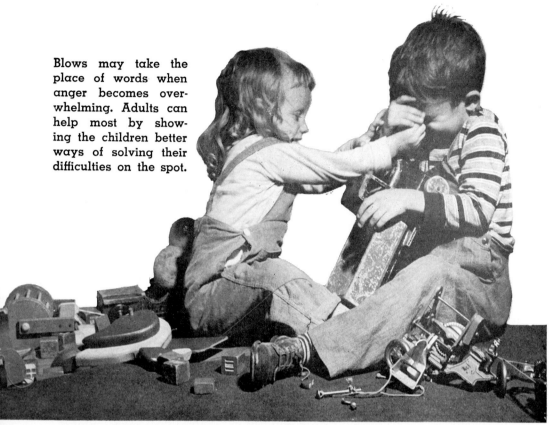

Blows may take the place of words when anger becomes overwhelming. Adults can help most by showing the children better ways of solving their difficulties on the spot.

of behavior one must learn in order to grow up successfully. Learning how to grow up to be the kind of person you are expected to be, and still remain yourself, is the basic conflict.

Fuller use of understanding, good sense, patience, and experience is important in good discipline. Learning the rules is hard for children because the rules vary, depending on who is in charge.

Can They Understand Different Standards?

Some people tell the children they must be little ladies or gentlemen. Others say that they have to be tough to get along. Some say that they have to learn to hit back. Others say that they must never hit, or at least never hit anyone smaller, or defenseless. Perhaps it is a

good thing that children do hear different viewpoints. But for young children it must be particularly confusing to find that one kind of behavior pleases one member of the family and a different kind pleases another.

Sometimes home and school standards and values differ. It takes a skillful parent or teacher to recognize that there is a difference in attitude toward a certain form of behavior, and then to accept the differing opinion. Finally, to explain one's own point of view without destroying the child's confidence in the other person's opinion takes consummate tact. But it can be done.

They Can Respect Differences of Opinion

One child said to her teacher, "Mommy said that here it's up to you, but at home we have our family way of doing things." Another little girl said to her mother, "My teacher said that families decide things like church and bedtime."

A respect for differing emphases and opinions can usually be presented in such a way that children, while they may be temporarily confused, at least can have the feeling that you can stick to your own opinions, but should respect those of other persons. Only gradually can children be expected to learn how to act in many different kinds of situations.

Will They Outgrow Selfishness?

To be able to get along with other people without losing their own individuality—to please themselves and others—is a difficult assignment all children must attack. Giving and taking, starting and stopping are so difficult because children's natural, normal impulses are often in direct conflict with the demands of other persons.

For instance, sharing is hardly a natural impulse for the two-year-old, but often he is expected to give his favorite toy to a visiting child. If ever there is a time when it is right to be selfish, it is when one is two years old. This is the stage in development when a child is most concerned about himself, and least concerned about other persons.

At three, the sharing comes somewhat more easily, but to share with grace and good manners is too much to expect as a regular thing. A great deal of trouble can be avoided if you keep a few "sharing toys." Bring them out when other children come to play. Then the favorite doll or car of the host or hostess can be put away for the afternoon and need not be shared.

At three, it is natural to be attentive to something that is of interest to you. To pay equal attention to the wishes of another is more than a three-year-old can manage.

How Much "Picking Up?"

Children of this age can spend endless time seriously and purposefully caring for their dolls and going through the motions of being careful housekeepers. This seriousness and intentness does not necessarily hold true for the picking up and putting away at the end of playtime. The interest and effort can sometimes be sustained if the adult enjoys the process with the child, as a game, and does not make it become the child's chore.

How Much Respect for Property?

At two, three, and four it is natural to investigate and explore, but not to be discriminating about your explorations. It is natural to cherish your own possessions, but not to respect other people's privacy or their property.

At this period, it is natural to go after what you want with the most direct approach possible. As a result, children may take what does not belong to them. When a three- or four-year-old takes another person's possessions, he is rarely "stealing," in the adult sense. Sometimes children take something that does not belong to them, but not because they particularly want that object. This situation is another matter, and is discussed in the following chapter, WHEN CHILDREN ARE ANXIOUS.

How Can You Handle a Tantrum?

Children seem to learn the controls involved in respect for property, and even for persons, in a surprisingly short space of time. Some learn more readily than others, it is true. This learning is not without cost. At some time, most children pay for these controls in temper tantrums, tears, irritability, and the various other signs of strain.

You can understand the tantrums and the tears as necessary features of growing up. Then you can handle them so as to avoid even more frustration and strain, and you can prevent the accumulation of angry feeling from being damaging. Matter-of-fact acceptance, a state of feeling easier to define than to achieve, helps the child to keep the cause of the trouble in its proper place. This means you need to be aware when an outbreak is brewing, and try to steer it toward the room or part of the room where angry behavior can do the least harm, away from the object or person provoking it. You can refrain from shaming, ridiculing, or threatening further consequences. You can restrain your impulse to "rub it in" or to point the moral. As soon as possible, try to re-establish friendly relations, with an eye to the child's need to "save his face." As soon as the worst is over, it may help to take the troubled child on your lap, and let him know you do not hold a grudge.

Admission of mistakes on your part can also be a wholesome experience for all, and does not necessarily undermine the confidence of the child. When tantrums are frequent, and you feel that some discussion may help to clear up the reasons, it is well to choose a time when the child is calm and rational, and can talk. Do not choose a time when an issue must be settled.

Preventing Tears and Tantrums

General irritability and such indications as frequent crying suggest that the demands of life are more than the child can comfortably cope with. Nagging, comparisons with other children of sunnier dispositions, questioning as to why he is that way only make matters worse. They tend to increase the child's discontent with himself. It is more helpful to adjust standards, but with necessary limits and restrictions made clear and enforced. You can allow plenty of time and scope for the activities that a youngster finds most satisfying.

Patience in waiting for the plan to show results is an important part of changing any situation to ease tension. Results are usually not immediate. When people say they have "tried everything" and "nothing works," a study of the situation frequently reveals that the change was expected to show up within a day or two. A week, a month, or even more, might have proved enough time to allow for the child's feelings to change. Only then could his behavior be expected to improve.

Can They Understand Reasons?

For the two-, three-, and four-year-olds, the consequences of an act are the major concern. The children learn to refrain from hitting because adults do not approve, and the other child is likely to hit back. "My Mommy doesn't let me," "My Mommy will spank me if I do," are the usual reasons offered by a three-year-old if he is asked why he did not do something he wanted to do.

Usually, by the time children are about five, they have had enough social experience and are sure enough of their own place to be concerned about other persons. There are fleeting moments when they can recognize social values for their own sakes, and will reason about the behavior of their friends as it affects others. They may say, "If he won't do that, we can't have our juice," or "we can't go out to play," suggesting that they see behavior as a group problem.

How Do You Secure Co-operation?

Much of the time, children like the feeling of pleasing us, the adults, by doing the things we want them to. But we have tended to take advantage of this tendency, in order to guarantee co-operation. It is poor teaching to ask a child to put away his toys so that he "will be a good boy." It is not particularly wise, either, to urge him to finish dinner, go to sleep, play quietly, or keep his clothes clean because, if he does, it will please people. One child tried to express her feeling about this when she complained at the suggestion that a nap would help her irritability, "It might make me weller from sick, but it won't make me gooder from bad."

It is true that children love the feeling of being considered "good," but asking them to perform duties for the sake of approval does not help them understand that there are practical reasons involved.

Nursery-school and even kindergarten teachers have for years been saying, in effect, "do it because we all do it here." To say to the child who throws his food, "We don't do that here," does help the situation and does give him an idea of what is expected in nursery school. But if you say, "That's not a good idea because someone will have to clean it up," he is just as likely to stop. He may also get the idea that the demand is more than pure whimsey on the part of foolish adults, and that it may apply in places other than nursery school. To say, "You take a nap because everyone takes a nap," may be all right some of the time, as long as the child also has a way of connecting naps with his need for rest.

Do We Overstress Being Big?

All children have difficulty in feeling satisfied with themselves as they are at

Korling

When the calm comes after the storm, it is good to know Mother loves you, no matter how bad the behavior was.

the moment. Children who never are content unless something new and different is in the offing come by this restlessness naturally. It is so easy to prod children through their growing years by highlighting the advantages of the years ahead! We tend to overdo this stress on "when you are older, you may . . ." As a result, hardly any young child is satisfied with his age as it is. Most three-year-olds would much rather be four than three. Privileges are in store for them after that next birthday, and to be bigger and older is important. This is particularly crucial for the three-year-old if there is a younger child in the family, because to be a baby also has certain advantages. His view of the world may get to be like the White Queen's in *Alice in Wonderland*, "Jam yesterday and jam tomorrow, but never jam today." There are obvious privileges that go along with being two or under, if one happens to be three and is expected to be giving up the babyish behavior that once brought so much attention and approval.

Parents and teachers both need to check themselves, for it is a temptation to gain co-operation by exploiting the age feature. Behavior excused because a child is too young to know better does not add to his respect for his own age, any more than does the promise that at a later age things will be better.

They Need Chances to Backslide

Sometimes, when a child cries, resists, or goes to pieces more than usual, he is reminded that he is "too big to behave in such a way." Often, by way of punishment, he is told "If you are going to act like a baby, you will be treated like one." The principle here is sound enough, since what he really needs is extra support and comfort, and someone to take over for him. It is true that he wants and needs to be treated like a younger

child. This should be offered in recognition of his need—*not* as punishment to make him feel ashamed of having slipped back a little.

There Is a Strong Drive to Grow up

The natural drive to move ahead—to grow bigger, to be able to do more things, to be more independent—is strong. Good stage settings help children to develop at their own natural rates. Prodding is rarely necessary if the learning conditions are favorable. Appropriate standards, encouragement, tolerance of mistakes, toys and equipment scaled to size all encourage growth. Help over the hard spots and opportunity to investigate, explore, and find answers to questions are good and necessary aids to getting along with others.

Much has been written about accepting children for *what they are*, but accepting them for *the age they are* is rarely emphasized enough. We do not need to hold out the bait of the glories and privileges of the year ahead to hurry them toward it. They will get there, anyway, under their own steam.

"Each age has its own satisfactions" can be demonstrated daily. Then the middle child will not feel that his is a mean age, a tiresome, in-between age.

WHEN CHILDREN ARE ANXIOUS

MARY FISHER LANGMUIR,
Ph.D.

Formerly Chairman, Department of
Child Study, Vassar College,
Poughkeepsie, N. Y.

Ewing Galloway

To be a young child means to be loved, to be taken care of, and to be cherished. It also means, part of the time, to be unloved, to be kept waiting, and to be punished. This light-and-dark of the early years colors and patterns feelings and behavior all through life.

The light—the being cared for and loved—helps make it possible for children to like and accept themselves and others. The dark—the being unloved and punished—helps create the fears, angers, and hates all human beings carry out of childhood into maturity.

As long as life lasts, there is darkness as well as light in each human spirit. Fear and anger and hate take many forms and find many outlets. Yet the need to be loved and to love is never lost, never completely satisfied.

Some Anxiety a Part of Growth

In spite of everything we can do, our children will have to experience much that, in our love, we would wish to spare

them. Even if it were desirable, it would be impossible for children to know only security, love, and happiness. Children are human, born to human joys and sorrows. As we all realize from long personal experience, anger and fear and jealousy are as much a part of being human as courage and love and kindness —and ever so much easier to rouse and keep alive.

Learning to understand and control destructive feelings is the task of a lifetime. Actually, this learning begins in infancy. It continues all during childhood, as adults try to make children behave in ways which society requires and approves. It is still going on when the children become the adults.

Learning to do right and to become "good" is always complicated, painful, and often heartbreaking. So much is expected and demanded. There are so many penalties and such rich rewards. Always the basic fear of losing love, which to the child means losing protection, is deep and penetrating. It colors much of his behavior. This fear, which begins in the early weeks, is one part of learning to wait, to be alone, to stop crying, to please adults, to do what is required.

Fear of losing love is particularly strong during the first two or three years, when training in cleanliness is under way. Continuous worry about pleasing parents who are too strict can lead to much sorrow. Many of the difficulties children and adults have in living with themselves are born of such worry.

Where Do Worries Come from?

Being anxious not only begins early but stays with us throughout life. Reasonable fears easily become unreasonable. Anxiety takes many forms. It seems to lie in wait even for those of us who appear to be most fortunate and most successful.

Why these persistent, way-down-inside fears? Why do they trouble young and old? Why do they keep us or our children stirred up, even when we know we are "just worrying"—that there is "really nothing the matter"? Why do we feel vaguely or sharply dissatisfied even when we get what we thought we wanted most? Why are our children fearful or worried some of the time, whether they take naps or not, whether they do well in school or not, whether they are "good" or not?

There can be no single or simple answer to these whys. How old a child or a person is, for example, often plays a part. There are such things as "developmental fears," which are part of certain

Bravado, acting wild, or being destructive may be a way of covering up fears. Punishing the behavior is useless. Find the cause and you can help a child.

Elizabeth Hibbs

stages of growth. These fears are not necessarily outgrown with childhood.

The Source of Some Worries Lies in the Past

Other reasons for our own or our children's fears and anxieties lie in the past as well as in the present. The particular thing we worry about may be as up to the minute as this year's taxes or Johnny's last report card. *Why* we worry is ancient history.

To understand our own and our children's worries, we must always look to the past as well as the present. Strange though it may seem, even a new-born baby has a past. In fact, the past is always with us. It is easy to get caught in this past. The chapter YOU HAD A FAMILY, TOO, in Volume 12, suggests how we can avoid having our children caught in the web of our pasts as well as their own.

Anxiety Is Part of Helplessness

The fact that human babies are born helpless makes some early anxiety inevitable. To be dependent is always to be anxious. It is true that an infant can breathe and suck and cry by himself at birth. But he must be kept warm and safe, and given something nourishing to suck, if he is to survive for long and have something to cry for.

The very weakness and littleness of infancy spell helplessness. Helplessness means dependence on people who are not only bigger and stronger, but *willing*. And there is the rub. There is where the fear arises. Help may not come in time. One may be left. In fact one *is* left, over and over again. Sometimes people are willing. Sometimes they are not. Life, at best, is precarious and uncertain. The fear of being deserted is as ancient as the human race. It is not confined to infancy.

Learning to Handle Anxiety

If anxiety begins at birth, so, too, does learning to handle it. One of the first and most important things a baby learns is the language of human action or behavior. Weeks and months before he can recognize words, he has learned the difference between being helped soon or kept waiting. He feels the difference between being handled gently or impatiently, between being talked to and enjoyed or being left alone.

Whenever parents get tense and anxious, babies are apt to become demanding and fussy. Their world has darkened. Their parents have changed. This happens whenever family life gets difficult, as all family life does and must from time to time. As one young mother put it, "My baby always knows when I am worried and upset, almost before I know it myself!" All babies know these things, for they all learn the same universal language of behavior. They imitate our feelings, whether or not we really want them to.

Resiliency Is Catching

It would be impossible and unnecessary to pretend we are never upset. It is far better to admit it, to ourselves and to the family. Perhaps what we can strive for, in ourselves and in the atmosphere of our homes, is the ability to bounce back when we are down. Through what we say and do and feel, we can tell our children, when things go wrong, "Sure, this is hard. But it will get better. We'll come through all right." Then they will be finding out an important truth about living with their own worries.

Time and patience go into building a timid child's confidence. Help him become more sure of himself and courage to try the water will come at last.

Early Ways of Meeting Trouble Persist

Even though we cannot remember when we ourselves were most secure and least secure, as infants and young children, our behavior as adults still bears traces of our early learning and our early fears. Our bodies still remember how we felt when we were lonely and frightened and angry as little children. All our lives we may feel threatened and tense whenever a woman gets sick, or silent, or driven, in her anger, or a man gets punitive or explosive. If these happen to be the ways our own parents behaved in family crises, long-forgotten feelings will be awakened inside us when we encounter such behavior in our later years.

Even our adult ways of getting along with stronger people and weaker people still tell the story of how we learned to handle our early anxiety. How to get help, how to be taken care of, how to avoid trouble were all learned when we were quite young. Some of us learned to get what we needed by fighting for it; others by withdrawing from any conflict and being good. Or perhaps we went off by ourselves and tried not to care or not to want anything. Perhaps we changed and varied our ways as we grew, perhaps not.

Those of us who were most secure as

little children are almost certain to carry less anxiety into our adult lives than do our brothers or sisters, or friends, whose early years happened to be harder and less satisfying. The same is true of our own children.

In spite of everything we can do, living *is* harder for some babies and some children than for others. Knowing and accepting this fact as one of the important basic differences among people will help us live with ourselves and our children more realistically and more sympathetically. Directly and indirectly, such understanding will help diminish our own anxiety, if only because it will help us recognize it. We cannot change feelings whose existence we refuse to accept or must deny.

Anxiety Grows with "Badness"

So far, we have stressed the anxiety that is part of every child's early dependence. Needing to please stronger and more powerful people is an inevitable and costly part of dependence. If we should ever forget how important needing to please adults is, we have only to remember how angry or hurt or desolate we felt as children when a brother or sister or cousin got more praise and approval at a family reunion. "Why couldn't you shake hands nicely the way your cousin John did?" "Didn't Katie look just lovely? *She* wasn't chewing the collar of her dress."

It helps us to help children if we can remember that rivalry between brothers and sisters is really an asking for reassurance that each one *will* be taken care of, that there *is* enough love to go around. The jealousy children show is always fear and hate. When one child is praised or specially favored in a family, the other children often feel disapproved of, unloved, and even unwanted.

This can happen in a classroom as well as at home. The more liked and loved a teacher is, the harder it is on other children to have one child become teacher's pet, or even receive special praise. Not to be praised is often to feel blamed.

"Badness" Means Losing Love

We can easily see, if we will only try to remember, that jealousy and rivalry are all tied up in children's minds with "badness." Not that they think jealousy and rivalry are bad, even though we adults try to teach them just that. Children think *they* are "bad." They believe that their "badness" is why they are not as loved as the other "good" children, the preferred brother or sister or the baby.

Quite early, children learn that being "good" and being loved go together. They also learn that *not* being loved is the penalty of being bad. In the logic of childhood, not to be approved of and loved is to be "bad."

In spite of a great deal of talk and reading about constructive ways of discipline, most of us still control children in the same ways our parents controlled us. This is both conscious and unconscious. We give love and show pleasure when children are good. Baby eats well, and we smile and give love with his cereal. He throws his food on the floor, and his hand is slapped.

A two-year-old who brings Daddy's slippers when he is asked is hugged and praised. "That's a good boy—a big boy!" But if he brings instead the watch from the bedside table, he is scolded. If he happens to drop the watch on the way, he may be spanked. "No! No! That's Daddy's. Bad Boy!"

Fear Feeds on Itself

Such incidents happen many times every day. They are the stuff of life, a part of living and learning. But whenever children do bad things, their fear of not being loved, of being punished, is inevitably increased. Fear always makes a person fight, defend himself, punish himself, get even, or run away. That is what fear is for, to stir up some kind of action to relieve a painful or intolerable state of tension.

When children are bad, they become afraid. When they become afraid, they usually behave worse—or they turn their fear into some kind of anger against themselves. Sometimes we mistakenly call punishing themselves being "good," but it is being "good" at too great cost. The cost is greater anxiety and the need for more defenses.

How Can We Ease Fears?

Fear of the dark is often one form of self-punishment. A child is worried about something he has done or thinks he has done. He is afraid of his own anger. He fears that punishment is coming from somewhere. What more likely place to imagine dangers than in the lonely dark, which is mysterious anyway?

We can relieve children's worries about their own misdeeds to some extent. It is often comforting to a child to know that others, too, have occasion-

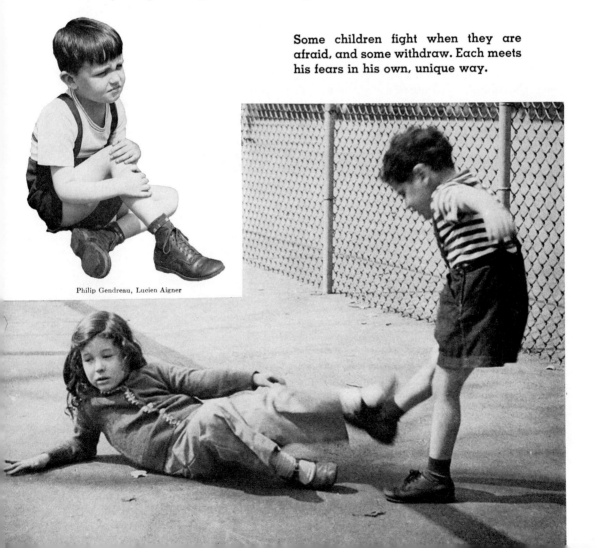

Some children fight when they are afraid, and some withdraw. Each meets his fears in his own, unique way.

Philip Gendreau, Lucien Aigner

ally been in trouble, but have not lost the love of their parents. Sometimes a few stories about Mother's or Father's own early mischievous behavior may go far toward reassuring a small child whose recently developed conscience is overactive. This may do more to ease fear of the dark than lights in the hall, or an open door; but night lights and other devices may be useful as supplementary help.

Signs of Children's Anxiety

The many ways children show us that they are anxious and afraid are all part of the language of human behavior. Some of their defenses and ways of releasing tension are learned by imitating us. Our children may lose their appetites, vomit, or get sick headaches or nervous stomachaches whenever they are upset, just as we do, or did.

Other ways may be quite new to our particular families and may seem to be their own inventions. They may blink, or stutter, or cry overeasily. If everyone else in the family can show a controlled front to the world, even under fire, this is particularly disturbing. But whatever their individual ways, all children use the same basic materials in designing their defenses against their own shortcomings and the world's demands.

Children all have restless, growing bodies, wonderful imaginations, and minds that are trying to understand and to solve problems. As they grow, they also have deep and almost desperate needs to be valued, and to do things well. Children are not born to fail or to feel inferior. The less adequate they feel, the more tension and anxiety they experience. The more successful experiences they have, the more they tend to become confident and courageous.

Since all learning involves going from not-knowing to knowing, from being inadequate to being adequate, some anxiety is a necessary part of all new tasks.

Anxiety Has Many Disguises

Fortunately for our peace of mind, children's differences in sensitivity and ways of behaving are not entirely a result of experiences, and what we did or failed to do. As many earlier chapters in CHILDCRAFT have pointed out, children vary greatly, even at birth, in their requirements and needs.

The discomfort and the near-panic which some babies can experience when they are hungry, or cold, or too long alone are part of their physical make-up, their inheritance. Such children may always be more sensitive, more quickly angry, more easily anxious. They may need to cling to infantile patterns of comfort longer than other children do.

It was a good day for parents and children when experts "discovered" that it was harmful, not helpful, to restrain babies and children from sucking their thumbs. But it was a bleak day when thumb-sucking and such other so-called "nervous habits" as sucking, biting, chewing, picking, and clutching themselves began to be regarded as signs of insecurity. Then parents felt they had failed as mothers and fathers, in not making their children secure. True enough, these ways of behaving are signs that a child is anxious. But that is only part of that larger truth: to be a child is to be anxious some of the time. Occasional signs of insecurity are no reflection on a parent.

Fears Due to Real Events

Sometimes, through nobody's fault, children are exposed to experiences that are truly frightening. Often, a small child must face a situation that is unfamiliar and therefore seems dangerous to him. Adults can usually make such situations easier for a child to meet.

Suppose a three- or four-year-old accidentally fell into deep water, was trapped in a burning house, or was chased by a large or angry animal. It is possible that a youngster in the care of a calm, trusted adult might not be much disturbed. For everyone, fear sets in at a different point.

When a youngster has an upsetting experience, it is best to admit, "Yes, this has been scary." Knowing that other people, even big, strong people like Mother and Father, have been scared is reassuring. You can emphasize the idea that people do get over such frights. It is never a good idea to say that "only babies are afraid," or make fun of a child who is timid.

Dwelling on a frightening experience is not desirable, but you can allow a child to talk freely about what has happened and ask as many questions as he wants. Getting feelings out in the open in words is better than bottling them up. Telling a child "don't think about that," "forget it," is not helpful, no matter what his fears are.

Some children may bring their fears out in play rather than in conversation. The child who has undergone painful treatment in the doctor's office finds relief in playing doctor himself. Some children find it easier to express their fears by painting pictures of an upsetting event. Others will enjoy making up a story about a child who is afraid. Perhaps a boy or girl will create out of his own imagination another child or an animal who is easily frightened and whom he must protect. Remember

Christopher Robin's imaginary friend, Piglet in *Winnie-the-Pooh*, who was "a very small animal and easily frightened"? Sometimes the imaginary creature may be a strong one who protects the small person. These are all useful devices in living with an ever-present unpleasant memory.

Preparation May Avoid Fears

If a new experience is in the offing, whether it be a trip, going to nursery school for the first time, a visit to the barber, or staying over night at grandma's, you can talk it over in advance. Acting out what will happen often proves highly successful. To a child, a new experience presents many more "unknowns" than it does to us.

Whenever it is possible, let the new experience be tackled gradually. In no sense of the phrase is it wise to "plunge a child into the water to sink or swim." Even the neighbor's friendly collie can be approached cautiously, if a two- or three-year-old is doubtful that this is a "nice doggie."

Let a youngster go to the barber shop with Daddy to watch him have a haircut before his own is cut. Take a five-year-old to visit the school building and meet the teacher before he spends a morning in kindergarten.

Sometimes children are unreasonably fearful about thunderstorms, riding in elevators, or other events that must be faced frequently. Your own matter-of-factness about both the event and their fears can be helpful. Giving a child something pleasant to do may take his mind off his troubles to some extent. Being allowed to push the elevator button has been known to make the ride almost bearable to a fearful youngster. An activity that reduces the feeling of

An anxious child may try to comfort himself

. . . by sucking a thumb

. . . by twisting a lock of hair

. . . by crying or pouting.

being overwhelmed and contributes to the feeling of being able to do something about the situation is helpful.

Sometimes parents wonder whether to force a timid and unwilling child to go to a party, to go in the water at the beach, to ride on a merry-go-round, or to do any number of other things that grownups are sure he would enjoy if he only gave himself the chance. There can be no hard and fast rule about how much pressure to exert, but there is seldom anything gained by forcing a reluctant child against his will.

Helping Anxious Children

The behavior that shows us that our children are having difficulties in learning the rules and in living with themselves is not new. It is as old as the human race. What *is* new is our understanding of such behavior. What is also new is our faith and hope that the burden *can* be made lighter. Those who have studied children tell us that children can be helped to grow up with less guilt and less fear—and with more capacity to love, to enjoy, and to create.

. . . Then he needs comfort from understanding parents.

217

When we ask, "How can we help anxious children?" we are really asking, "How shall we live with children? How can we help all children?" Every chapter in CHILDCRAFT that helps us understand the needs of children and the normal problems of growth can help us keep our children's anxiety from becoming unbearable. Everything that has been said about not expecting more of children than they can do, giving them opportunities to succeed, and being generous with praise for small successes will be useful in preventing anxieties.

Excess Is the Danger Signal

The difference between more-anxious and less-anxious children lies in the extent to which they behave in any certain way, rather than in the behavior itself. For example, many children have a favorite toy or a blanket they take to bed. Some children, when they are tired or troubled, will look for that toy or blanket and carry it around with them. They may even chew the blanket a bit. If such behavior helps them over bad moments, it harms no one. But occasionally we may see a child who cannot play happily or carry on any real activity because, week after week, indoors and out, he must have that toy or that blanket in his hand. Without it he goes into a state of near panic. It is not *wanting* that blanket, but the *extent* and the *intensity* of that wanting, that guide us in deciding what this behavior means.

When a child cannot play, eat, sleep, or get along with others happily, because one kind of behavior always gets in his way, special and expert help is usually required. Our concern is not just with stopping that behavior. Generally, that only drives a child to find some other way of relieving tension.

The continuous behavior may be relatively harmless, like sucking a thumb or twisting a lock of hair. It may be more upsetting, like persistent destructiveness, aggressiveness, stuttering, running away from home, certain kinds of untruthfulness, bed-wetting, or extreme shyness. More than one of these signs of anxiety usually shows up when anxiety is really severe.

If Expert Help Is Needed

Many of us may need extra support or expert help at one time or another, when anxiety becomes too great a burden for our children. Fortunately for today's children, getting help for emotional problems is coming to be almost as normal a part of raising a family as seeking medical help when our children come down with measles, or fall and break their arms.

At long last, emotional health is becoming as important as physical health. For we now know that childhood anxiety can become so burdensome that growth is slowed down, the ability to learn is interfered with, and the capacity to enjoy is seriously impaired. The chapter FAMILY GUIDANCE SERVICES, in Volume 15, has suggestions for finding help.

Love Is Still the Cornerstone

Most of all, we protect and safeguard our children against too great anxiety by giving love—not by taking it away. As a wise and kind psychiatrist used to say, "Children are never so in need of love as when they are unlovable." It was true of us when we were children. It is true of our own children. It will be true of our children's children. Men—and the children of men—will be saved at last by Love. For Love alone can cast out Fear.

FIRST EXPERIENCES AWAY FROM HOME

A. Devaney

33. WHAT LEAVING HOME MEANS TO A SMALL CHILD

34. TRAVELING WITH YOUNG CHILDREN

35. WHAT NURSERY GROUPS OFFER

36. IF YOU WANT A PLAY GROUP

Small children are usually somewhat home-bound and home-centered. First ventures away from home seem almost like a journey to the moon, for the outside world is a bewildering place.

You want your child to have confidence in the world and to feel at home in many kinds of places and situations.

As nursery groups, especially those managed co-operatively by parents, become more available in all communities you will want to consider what makes a "good" group for your boy or girl.

You can plan the short visits, the longer trips, the first experiences in play group or nursery school, so that they will tend to strengthen confidence and further growth, if you understand what leaving home means to a youngster. Through this planning you can often reduce the bad times that are unavoidable and make the inevitable moments of insecurity bearable.

WHAT LEAVING HOME MEANS TO A SMALL CHILD

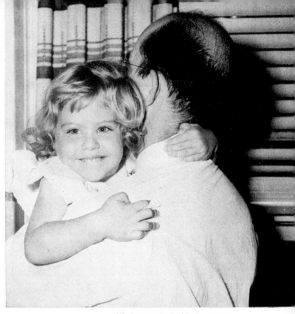

VIRGINIA MESSENGER STAPLEY,
Ph.D.

Head, Department of Family Relations and Child
Development, Oklahoma State University
of Agriculture and Applied Science,
Stillwater, Okla.

All photographs in this chapter are
from the Oklahoma A and M College

Leaving home will mean something different to each child. Some children say, through their actions, "All's right with the world;" "Give us a chance to go any time, any place, with anyone." Others seem to be saying, "Everything strange is suspect. The world is full of giants. We don't know the passwords. We want to be cautious. Therefore, we want to cling to the familiar."

The behavior of the majority of children lies between these two extremes. The satisfaction children get from leaving home depends on the unique make-up and the past experiences of each child. Behavior will be as different as the number of small children you know. If you can accept a child as he is, give him time, help, and encouragement, he will probably learn to enjoy himself away from home for a few hours in a way that will be satisfying to him and to you.

What It Takes to Leave Home

If many of your child's experiences have been satisfying, your child is likely to approach this new one—leaving home —comfortably. A feeling of confidence and friendliness is important if a child is to feel safe about leaving home. The child who has confidence in himself, who has trust in people and in the world, can usually take short separations from home in his stride. The development of a sense of basic trust is discussed in the section on THE INFANT in this volume. The chapters WHAT CHILDREN NEED FROM LIFE and DISCIPLINE FOR SELF-RELIANCE, in Volume 12, are also good reading in this connection.

What Are Signs of Readiness?

Sociability need not be forced. You can watch for signs of readiness and help your child take the new steps gradually. He is beginning to show he is ready to play with other children when he is interested in new people. When he is delighted to see a child, when he moves near him readily and with confidence, and follows him around, he will find the pleasure of companionship tends to outweigh the strangeness of new surroundings. When he enjoys going with his parents where all feel at ease—to grandparents' and close friends' homes—he is probably ready for further adventures.

When you see these signs, you can help your youngster reach out bit by bit. But you can still allow him to return to "home base" in every sense of that term when he wants support. Then he can go comfortably. The "mamma baby" who cries and has a difficult time going into other homes, or to Sunday School or nursery school, may be the child who was plunged too fast into new situations.

Mother Goes Along at First

Some young children may not appear to need their mothers as they start to Sunday School, to nursery school, or to a playmate's house. Usually it is wise for you to be on hand at a first visit, at least until the youngster gets acquainted. It is possible that the child who shows no reaction is in as great need of his mother as the one who cries.

Perhaps your child is sufficiently independent to be comfortable if you are in the next room or in another part of the building. You can take the lead from the youngster, in leaving. You can assume in a cheerful way that he will enter into the other children's play and be happy.

Are Mothers in the Way?

You may be eager to stay with your child but be afraid you may be in the way, or may not be wanted, especially at school. More and more, teachers have come to believe that parents, particularly mothers, should remain to help children in this adjustment period. With some children, Mother will need to remain until the child knows the teacher well enough to get the support he needs from her. This is usually the case in the nursery school. It is coming to be an accepted practice in many kindergartens and first grades, as well.

If a mother stays around for a day, or for several days, neither mother nor teacher need fear that the youngster will want her to stay always. When a boy or girl is sure that Mother will stay for a while, he feels more secure. When he feels ready, he will be able to let her go. As one mother put it, "Bobby fairly pushed me out of the door when he was ready to be on his own."

Shall They Take Toys with Them?

The first time three-year-old Peggy went to Sunday School she clung to her own hat and coat for dear life. Naturally, Peggy could not join in any activities, hat in hand! When Peggy said good-by, her teacher suggested that next week she bring a toy to show the other children. Here was a happy way out of the difficulty! With her familiar toy dog to cling to, Peggy was more willing to hang up her hat and coat. Showing the dog to the other children proved to be a good icebreaker for Peggy, too. Since the toy dog was a link with home, the teacher did not insist Peggy let the other children play with him.

Something from home to talk about, to show, to cling to, is proving useful as a source of comfort in nursery groups, and even in kindergartens and first grades. It can be equally good as a prop for the small child who goes on a brief visit.

Good-bys Are Important

When you do leave your child in new surroundings, never slip away. Children develop trust in people, and in the world, as they find they can depend on people. If you always tell your child

"Where Mother is, there I am at home" is the feeling of most small children. Take a cue from nursery schools, where mothers are encouraged to stay around until their children feel at ease.

good-by before you leave, you are helping build trust. The child who knows what to expect is better able to take what comes, even though he cries.

You can assure your youngster you will return. If you state the time in relation to an activity, like "after your outdoor play" or "after lunch," you help him to understand and accept the idea. You might leave something familiar behind, like a coat or a scarf, as evidence that you will return, for that, too, adds to security.

When Leaving Home Seems Hard

Unexpected, sudden changes that involve separation from home and mother are likely to be distressing to a small person. But emergencies do arise, when such separation is necessary. In our concern over the emergency, we may sometimes fail to see how things look to the children.

A sudden death in the Carson family made it necessary for Mr. and Mrs. Carson to be away from home during the day for a few days. Two of Mrs. Carson's friends immediately volun-

teered to share the care of the three small Carson children. The first day, going to one house for lunch and a nap, then to another for play in the afternoon and supper, seemed like a lark to the children. The second day they were frightened. When Mother and Father finally came for them, they sobbed out their fears, "Will you and Daddy have to go to Grandma's every day for always now?"

In making explanations, the Carsons had omitted the one detail that would have helped to reassure the children. "This is for today and tomorrow. Then we'll all be together again like always."

Whenever it is possible to talk over any departures a day or two in advance, it is wise to do so. Then children can get doubts, questions, and worries out in the open.

They Might Miss Something!

Almost any unusual situation or crisis in the family can be expected to dampen the willingness to leave home. Some such situations are caused by visitors, family projects, and new babies. The child feels himself a part of his intimate group—his family. He "belongs," and therefore wants to participate when visitors come. A family project may not appear unusual to the adults, but from the child's viewpoint it may be more appealing than the unknown experience away from home. Any kind of workmen in the house, anything interesting being delivered, is more fascinating to a small person than a three-ring circus.

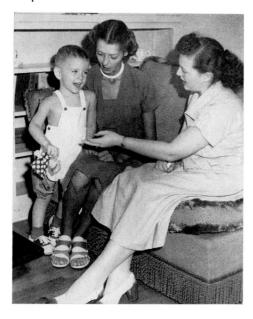

If a child has a chance to become acquainted with his teacher before going to school, it will be easier for him to feel at home in his new surroundings.

Adjusting to a new baby is hard enough, without adjusting to leaving home and Mother. This fact needs to be weighed when you consider sending a two- or three-year-old to a neighbor or a relative. The chapter SOMETIMES RIVALS, SOMETIMES FRIENDS, in Volume 12, discusses the new-baby question fully.

When a Child Won't Leave Home

Many preschool children go through a stage when they are unwilling to go to other children's homes to play, no mat-

Even with careful preparation, parting may not be easy, but his teacher reassures him as he waves good-by, "Mother will be here after story time."

ter how enticing the prospects. Even birthday parties are no inducement to leave home. You can afford to ignore the issue for a while.

Sometimes children have a vague sense of uneasiness that makes them want to stay at home. Perhaps they are worrying over something they have done. If they would, or could, talk about their worries, adults might have a better chance of helping them. Perhaps they have found some experiences away from home too uncomfortable. Perhaps they have that fear, so common to two-, three-, or four-year-olds, that they may be deserted by their parents. Repeated assurance, in words, that Mother and Father will be on hand, come what may, is often a comfort. While you wait for confidence to return, you can interpret clues to your youngster's behavior and watch for signs of readiness for new experiences.

How Can You Give Him Courage?

Give him opportunities to release his feelings through many kinds of creative materials at home. Finger paint, dough,

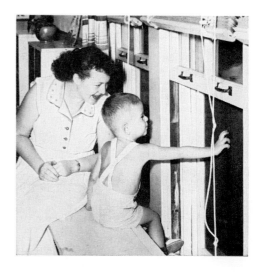

clay, sand, wood, all help him work out the nameless fears that will not come out in words. Encourage him in vigorous outdoor play. Take advantage of his desire to be independent at home. Let him share in family activities of many kinds, day by day. Let him have other children to play with at home.

Arrange to spend as much time with him as you can. Without making him dependent on you, try to see that the experience is satisfying for him—that he has fun. Then start as you would with a much younger child. Arrange for some short experiences away from home that you know will be gentle and pleasant. Accompany him on visits as long as he wants you to do so. Take the attitude of "pretty soon I know you will want to go alone," and have confidence in his ability to overcome his homeboundness. But accept the fact that it may take months of patient support to make him sure enough of himself to be able to enjoy experiences away from home.

Confidence Comes Slowly

When children refuse to leave home

When something especially interesting is afoot at home, small children are reluctant to leave. Who says there is anything more important for four-year-olds than watching painters at work?

they are usually feeling uncomfortable, troubled, worried, or afraid. If they go, feeling like this, they gain little from the experience. Forcing will only increase the fears. When they enjoy leaving, they go readily.

You cannot reason a tense and anxious child out of his unwillingness. He cannot actually hear your reasons. Discussing his unwillingness in front of him, or shaming him, has disadvantages. You do not want to give him or others the idea that he is shy and unsociable. You want to provide experiences away from home that will lead to satisfaction and wholesome development, but you are not pampering your child if you let him go at his own pace. The path of development of outgoing self-confidence and friendliness is not a straight road. It has many twists, detours, and even cutbacks. On these detours and cutbacks your children especially need your patient, affectionate encouragement. At such times, home and the right to stay there are immensely comforting.

Leaving home and Mother seems worth the effort when he becomes absorbed in the delights of pounding clay, or in other pleasures nursery groups offer the three- and four-year-olds.

225

TRAVELING WITH YOUNG CHILDREN

CARMEN STONE ALLEN, B.Ed.

Mother and Author, Atlanta, Ga.

TRAVELING with young children can be accomplished with a minimum of discomfort, but it does require advance planning and preparation. Long before the date of departure, make a list of everything your child will require. If you are traveling with a small baby, sterilized bottles head the list. For any age child, be sure to include a warm sweater and blanket, a waterproof bag, toys, comfortable clothing, food for meals and snacks, a big package of cotton, and a thermos of boiled water. If your youngster is trained to use the toilet, take along his own toilet seat. Whether you go by automobile, train, plane, or bus, you will find these things essential.

Comfort by Car

If you go by automobile, many of your problems are simplified. If yours is a short trip, there are advantages to driving at night. Babies or toddlers can be put to bed at the usual time, and moved to the car when you are ready to start. All but the most hardened night owls fall asleep right away, stay asleep through the move, and scarcely wake until morning. If your baby is breast fed, you can start right out on any kind of trip with no misgivings. If you have a complicated formula, your doctor will probably be willing to change it to evaporated milk and water if you explain the situation to him. Try out the new mixture for at least a week before you leave, to be certain that it agrees with the child.

What Food Along the Way?

If your trip by car will last only a day,

You may not travel light, but you will travel comfortably if these are included in your "needed on the journey" list.

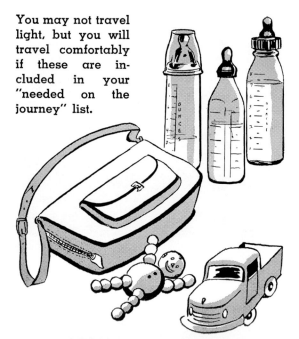

make up the usual supply of bottles for the baby. Pack them in a portable refrigerator, or make one with a cardboard box lined with newspapers and packed with ice. You can carry along a small portable stove, or you can ask a restaurant to warm the bottles when you stop for meals.

If your motor trip is a long one, carry a thermos filled with boiled water, and make up one feeding at a time. Never put a formula in a thermos, or in bottles that cannot be kept at refrigerator temperatures. Cans of baby food are a boon because they are sterile, but throw away all leftovers unless refrigeration is practical. Give the child only boiled water from the thermos. On a long trip, get permission to go to the hotel or restaurant kitchen to boil another supply.

If your baby takes noise, lights, and people in his stride, feed him in the restaurant where your food is being prepared. Use dry cereal mixed with evaporated milk and boiled water, and open fresh cans of baby food. If he prefers peace and quiet, feed him the same menu in the car. He may not eat as much, he may demand food oftener, and he may develop a finicky appetite, but do not be alarmed. He will return to a regular eating pattern when the trip is over. New foods should never be introduced until you return home. Be firm about friends and relatives giving him anything he is not accustomed to having. It is better to hurt Aunt Clarissa's

feelings than to have your child sick.

If you are traveling with two-, three-, or four-year-olds, be extremely careful about foods that spoil easily in hot weather. Stick to bottled pasteurized milk. Use packaged crackers or cookies for snacks, and peel any fruits you buy along the way. Small children may want to eat more often, and may eat less at regular meals, while on a trip.

Back-Seat Playroom

If you can give up the back seat of the car, your small child can have a perfect place to sleep and play. Build up the space between the front and back seats with luggage, wooden boxes, or a framework of planks, until the entire area is level. Pad this part with blankets, quilts, or a mattress. Put a waterproof sheet over the top, and pad the door handles with pillows to prevent bumped heads.

Fasten the rear doors, if you have to do it with log chains. Fasten them for your baby's safety and for your own peace of mind. You now have a safe, comfortable space where any small child whose head does not bump the top of the car can sleep and play. Even for the infant who will sleep in his basket, this space is wonderful for changing pants and for dressing. Parents on the smallish side have been known to occupy part of this space for a short nap themselves. Hard-bottom car seats that fit on front seats of cars are helpful for a change of scenery and posture. Canvas hammocks

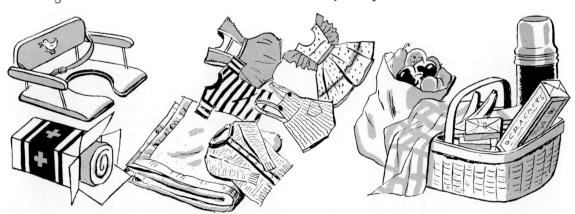

for babies are also satisfactory for beds.

Carry all the children's supplies and clothing separate from your own. Disposable diapers are a blessing to travelers. By the time all the children's things are stowed away, there is never much room for Papa's and Mama's things, so plan on traveling light. When you leave, you will be amazed at how closely your car resembles the covered wagons of earlier days!

How Shall You Dress the Travelers?

The traveling child should wear loose, comfortable clothing. The lovely handmade outfits with laces and ruffles have no place on a trip. If your son or daughter wears jeans and a two-gun holster at home, there is no reason he should not wear them in the car, or even on a plane or train. Save the tailored broadcloth job until you arrive and want to show him off. Self-service laundries, where a load of soiled clothes can be washed and dried in less than an hour, are lifesavers. When you pack, select materials that need no ironing, and you are all set.

Do let the child be comfortable, and don't worry the life out of him by trying to keep him spotlessly clean at all times. On any form of transportation, and for any age child, it always pays to have a box of cotton or cotton pads. Since a thermos of boiled water should always be within reach anyway, it is easy to swish away the top layer of grime.

Never, never bathe your baby in a public rest room. It may not be sanitary. It will do no harm if your baby skips an all-over bath, even for a few days.

How About Playthings?

On a long car trip it is not possible to dump a baby in his back-seat playpen and expect him to be happy watching the scenery whiz by at sixty miles per hour. He needs toys. Some of them should be his beloved old ones, but there should be lots of brand-new ones, too. These may be from the five-and-ten-cent store; in fact, some of them may not be toys at all. One little girl, aged eleven months, was kept happy for thirty minutes with a package of red bias tape. Another was entranced with a flat sink stopper with the ring removed. The newness will last longer if toys are doled out one at a time. Put the discarded one back in the box for another hour.

In Case of Illness

If your child develops an illness while motoring, call the local American Medical Association, and ask them to recommend a doctor. If the Association is not listed, and there is no hospital, ask the

"As snug as a bug in a rug"—that's your baby when the back seat of your car is made solid, soft, and safe for him to sleep and play while traveling.

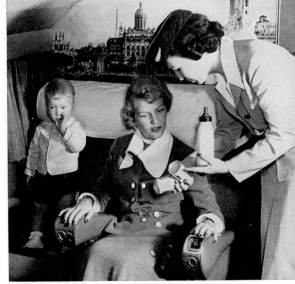

Heating baby's bottle or fixing lunch for two-year-olds is all in the day's work for the stewardess. Small children and mothers traveling on the airlines get top priority in service.

chief of police, the sheriff, or the minister of your preferred church to recommend a competent medical man. People everywhere are genuinely sympathetic toward small children, and are more than willing to help. It is always wiser to get competent medical advice before continuing an automobile trip with a sick child.

On Trains, Planes, and Buses

If you are traveling alone with a baby or small children, it may be easier for you to fly. The cost may be higher, but time and energy saved can be worth it. You can make up the amount of formula needed, pack the bottles in your sterilizer, and give them to the stewardess. She will refrigerate them and bring them warmed when you want them. She will hold your baby while you eat. In fact, most stewardesses like small children so much, they hold them every chance they get. If you write the air lines in advance, many of them will prepare a boxed meal for your toddler. Such lunches usually contain milk, a dry cereal, jars of meat, a vegetable, and a fruit. There is no charge for this service.

What Services Will Trains Give?

If you travel by train, and can possibly afford it, go by Pullman. There is less crowding, better service, and more comfort. By writing to the passenger agent, find out in advance what services are offered, and state any special problems you have. You will be surprised at how much service you can get by making inquiries before you start.

If there is a diner on the train, you can make up the necessary bottles of formula, pack them in the sterilizer, and hand them to the porter. He will keep them cold, and bring you a warmed bottle when requested. If the diner does not stay with the Pullman all the way, it will be necessary to carry boiled water and evaporated milk and make up individual feedings as needed. Give the porter a rubber sheet to put on the berth, and put the baby to bed at his usual time. There is plenty of room in a lower berth for the baby's basket. Follow all the familiar routines that you possibly can at bedtime. Pat-a-cake, a song, a story, or cops and robbers— whatever it is, try to make it seem like home. Young children are more set in their ways than any eighty-year-old, and they feel safer with familiar routines.

If you go by coach, try to travel during the week to avoid crowds. Mix individual feedings as needed. It may be easier for you to bring your own food, or buy sandwiches, than to attempt the long trek to the diner. A detachable car seat with a hard bottom is fine for the toddler, and a car hammock can be

229

swung across some types of seats to make a safe, comfortable bed for the baby.

Buses and Boats

Bus travel is economical and comfortable. The bus makes fifteen-minute rest stops about every two hours, and about forty-five-minute stops three times a day, for meals. Unless you carry a portable icebox, it will be necessary to make up individual feedings as you need them for the baby. Carry a supply of food for yourself, too. Then, if the restaurant is crowded, or the baby takes too much of your time, at least you will not starve!

Steamship companies have excellent facilities for caring for young children. There is a ship's doctor. There are trained nurses and nurseries with experienced attendants. If you write in advance and state your needs, the steamship line will do all that it can to help.

In Emergencies

In any emergency, you can call on Travelers Aid for help. They will assist you to locate relatives, help you care for your children, and, if you let them know in advance, even meet you at the train. If you mislay your ticket, lose your pocketbook, or suspect that your youngest is coming down with the measles, you can turn to Travelers Aid for efficient, friendly help.

How About Routines?

When your son, who is a cherub at home, begins acting as if demons possessed him, do not be too shocked. Forget Discipline, spelled with a capital D, and substitute increased affection.

If your golden-haired daughter suddenly stops eating, shrieks "No!" at every simple request, and starts sucking her thumb and wetting the bed while you are traveling, do not despair. She will be an angel—or almost an angel—again. In fact, she will be one much sooner if she knows her mother and father love her no matter how she behaves. Do not be concerned if other people stare at outlandish behavior. This is no time to keep up with the Joneses.

Do not ever leave your child with strangers when he is asleep. He might wake unexpectedly and be really frightened at being alone with unfamiliar faces. Let him talk to strangers if he wants to. If they do not like him, they can always send him back to you.

Emphasis on traditional "good behavior" is not necessary for traveling toddlers, but familiar routines should go on as usual. If one o'clock is nap time, try to arrange for naps at about that time on the trip. It may not always work, but again it may. If bedtime is at seven, keep bedtime around seven. Try to have all meals at about the same time you do at home. Half of the children's objectionable behavior is caused by hunger. If regular meals are impossible, carry with you the food you always use for snacks. Fruit, crackers, and milk will stave off hunger pangs and bad tempers.

If you are taking your first trip with small children, do not expect to have the same kind of carefree enjoyment that you did when traveling as a couple. Traveling with children can be a pleasure to mature adults, but it does take thought and planning. Once you start, relax and do not worry. Ask questions, and ask for help if you need it. Everyone loves small children, and you will be surprised at the kindness and thoughtfulness of perfect strangers. Here's wishing you a good trip!

WHAT NURSERY GROUPS OFFER

FRANCES R. HORWICH, Ph.D.

Formerly Chairman, Department of Education, Roosevelt College, Chicago, Ill.

Post Dispatch, Black Star

NURSERY groups offer a two-and-a-half-, a three-, or a four-year-old a safe place to play, a variety of interesting play materials and a chance to learn to get along with other children, and to try out new ideas under wise and friendly guidance.

Why Nursery Groups?

Some people may ask why small children should not play at home under Mother's watchful eye, as they have done for countless generations.

Present-day living conditions are different from those of two generations ago. New customs and arrangements are needed to meet these changed conditions.

In the majority of homes there is not enough room in the house or apartment for the young child who needs to play actively. Traffic hazards and congested living combine to make it impossible for most young children to play out of doors unsupervised.

We have learned that, for happiness and for health, young children need carefully guided experiences in small groups of children of their own age. A nursery group can provide such helpful activities for your children.

How Nursery School Can Aid Development

For the youngster who is hesitant about playing with other children his own age or size, nursery school offers an opportunity to experiment in getting along with others under supervision. The youngster who is extremely dependent on his mother may find nursery school, with its attractive equipment and understanding teachers, the easiest place to take a first step away from home. The small boy or girl who does not find real enjoyment in using play materials may be stimulated by the activities of the other children and the toys he finds in the playroom. He may begin to use equipment with more spontaneity. Those who have studied children tell us that a youngster's shyness, dependence, or "do-lessness" may in itself be a sign that he is ready for the wider experiences of being in a group.

Varieties of Nursery Groups

The term "nursery group" can cover a wide variety of arrangements. Different set-ups have been worked out to fit community needs in different parts of the country.

In a neighborhood where many of the mothers work, there is a need for all-day care. To meet this need, *child-care centers* were opened, sometimes by a community center, by a church, or by the industrial plant employing the mothers. In this type of group, the center is open and the teachers are ready to take care of children by the time the mothers go to work. Mothers call for the children when they return from work. The program, including meals, rest, and play, is the same as in other kinds of nursery schools, but of course this center is open from early in the morning until six at night.

When we speak of a *nursery school*, we usually refer to the kind of group that serves a noonday lunch to the children after the morning session. Some nursery schools keep the children for a nap after lunch.

A *co-operative nursery school* is owned and operated by the parents and teachers. Usually, co-operative groups have a

Being left out is sad and chilling! In nursery school, the timid child can be drawn into a group, discover how to make friends, and realize the delight of companionship with his equals.

morning session only. The following chapter, IF YOU WANT A PLAY GROUP, gives a detailed account of co-operatives.

Play schools are groups for young children, usually lasting from nine to eleven-thirty in the morning.

Marks of a Good Nursery School

No matter what type of nursery group you select, there are some features that

Food, furniture, and conversation are planned to make three- and four-year-olds comfortable, and mealtime enjoyable, when noonday lunch is served.

Indoors or out, nursery groups provide materials small children enjoy, and a place to enjoy them thoroughly and wholeheartedly in good company.

you will find in every good group. Let us imagine that we are watching a nursery school in action.

When you walk into a good nursery group, you will notice that the playroom is a safe place for active children. Furniture, clothes hooks, toy shelves, washing and toilet facilities are the right size for young children. Everything is clean and in good repair, even though furniture and equipment show the wear and tear of hard use. The room is large enough to allow children plenty of space to play without getting in each other's way. The room is well ventilated and has an abundance of sunlight.

When you go to the outdoor play yard, you will see that it is fenced in. The gates can be closed and opened only by adults. The playground is protected from strong winds in winter, and provides some shade on hot summer days. There is plenty of space for the children to run and play vigorously.

What Kind of Equipment?

Outdoors there is sturdy climbing equipment, either a jungle gym or a combination of ladders. There are swings, too. That small girl over there is a newcomer who is gradually easing her way into climbing and swinging.

There is a variety of blocks, both indoors and out. No home playroom could offer so many sizes and shapes, or such quantities, as even this rather modest nursery school affords.

Let us go back into the indoor playroom, where some of the children are using the easel paints, and some are using modeling clay. All these materials suggest ways of expressing ideas.

Here is a low table with attractive books on it. One of the teachers is telling a story to three or four children. Nursery schools do not insist that everyone sit down for a set "story hour." But, in the course of the school year, all the children hear a variety of interesting stories and become friends with the characters in them. They ask questions, gain new interests, and grow in understanding of the world at large.

Later in the morning one of the teachers will sing simple songs with the children and let them experiment with sound and rhythm.

Do the Children Play Together?

A good nursery group arranges the problem so that children a year or two apart in age can play separately. No one insists that children play together, and they seem to drift in and out of groups. They just naturally have companionship and make friends here. If you watch, you will see a three-year-old on the outskirts of a group playing house. She listens for a minute or two and then joins in the laughter, and seems to be absorbed into the group. If the group had pushed her aside, the teacher might have made a suggestion. Since the children handled the situation without help, the teacher stayed out. Nursery school gives a child time to watch others in their activities and join them when he feels ready. He is encouraged to develop his own personality. He is not compared to, or put into competition with, others.

When children of about the same age are going through the day's routines together, it is easier for all the children to conform than it is at home. Look at Ruth, one of the four-year-olds, drinking her tomato juice. Paper cups with juice were set out on the table for the four-year-olds when they came in. At home, Ruth might have protested about tomato juice, but when everybody is drinking it, even a four-year-old wants to be in the swim! Without anyone talking about it, each child is unconsciously helping the others work out their problems. Children are learning to take care of themselves—to dress, to wash, to go to the toilet, to rest—without having an issue made of each step.

What Does a Nursery-School Teacher Do?

The nursery-school teacher can be casual, cheerful, and consistent with the children. She is not as tied up with each child as a child's mother usually is. If Ruth had not drunk her tomato juice, Miss Granger would not have felt that Ruth was defying her. At home, Ruth's mother might have felt Ruth was "getting away with something." Nursery-school teachers are friendly adults who help the children, without formal teaching.

If you watch a good nursery group, you can see that life is not made completely effortless for the children. For example, they face the unalterable fact that two people cannot ride a tricycle at the same moment. They learn either to wait for their turns, or to find something else interesting to do.

Different children will profit by different phases of the program, for each brings his special needs and special personality with him to school. Nursery schools will not solve "problems" in a week or in a month. There are a great many problems that cannot be solved by even the best nursery school. But you may hope for long-time gains built on the happiness, security, and growth the nursery-school experience offers.

Parents Go to School

Nursery-school teachers help parents through conferences—there should be at least two a year—, through visits in the home, and through casual conversation when children are brought to school and picked up. Some nursery schools have informal group conferences or larger meetings where parents can gain a better understanding of their children. Sometimes a picnic for mothers and children can be the occasion when mothers ask questions of the teachers informally. The program for parents is an essential part of a good group experience for the children. As the parents

One tricycle and two would-be riders —here is a dilemma best solved by taking turns. The youngsters have a chance to work out things themselves, but an adult in a nursery group can suggest the solution before fists fly.

F. P. G.

understand what the school is trying to do, they can sometimes adjust their own aims for the children. As parents find out that other children have the same difficulties their child has, and that other parents occasionally grow discouraged or irritable, they gain confidence in themselves. Many parents feel they enjoy their children more because nursery school has added to understanding.

What Do Parents Gain?

From the remarks parents themselves have made from time to time in different nursery schools, it is clear that they feel they have been helped in various ways. A better understanding of how children develop and of some of the ways they can be given security is the gain parents speak of most often. From watching the way children respond in the nursery group, it often becomes clear to parents how much more easily children will conform when they feel they are an important part of the group. As they see how children behave together in nursery school, parents begin to understand the relationships of the children in their own family.

Nursery schools can help mothers pool their favorite ideas on simplified clothing. Parents as well as children get new ideas for play materials, and for arranging and storing toys. Out of the nursery-school activities or the teachers' suggestions often come leads for family excursions.

New Ideas and New Friends

"Never in the world would we have thought of taking Tim to the firehouse. But Miss Olsen suggested it because he likes the toy fire truck so much, and now he's just about an honorary member of Engine House #19," one mother said.

Another mother at a neighborhood gathering said she found nursery school a lifesaver in the matter of birthday parties. "Miss Bigg's suggestions about managing the three-year-olds kept everything on an even keel. The best of it was, after I listened to her I realized my plans had been much too fancy. She showed me how I could keep things simple and still let those three-year-olds have a wonderful time."

Still another mother was loud in her praises of suggestions for keeping holiday celebrations simple and appropriate. These had come out of one of the group conferences at nursery school.

Not the least of the advantages is that the children make friends whom they enjoy playing with outside of school.

If You Need Special Help

Some children need special rest or other individual care. Usually the nursery school can co-operate with the parents in carrying out recommendations made by a physician. If the help of a specialist is needed because of some physical or emotional problem, the nursery-school teacher can be of assistance in directing parents to the source in the community that would be most helpful.

When Your Child Joins a Group

The quality of the program of the nursery school is important, and you will want to choose carefully. Nursery-group experience has been helpful to the great majority of children and to their parents, but nobody would claim it is a "must" for every child. There are, indeed, some times in a child's life when it may not be the best thing for him. Usually it is recommended that you do not start your child in a nursery group if it is his first experience away from home, or during the months just before or just after a new baby arrives in the family, or when some other decided change has come into the youngster's life. The age for starting depends on the groups available to you, and on your child. Some two-and-a-half-year-olds have been happy in a nursery group. Some children start at three, and the largest number start at the age of four. Sometimes even a good group and a well-adjusted child fail to click. It is not necessarily a reflection on either if that happens occasionally.

How Shall He Be Started?

The decision to send a child to nursery school is not to be made hastily. A young child needs plenty of time to "get ready" for school. He needs to be sure he is not being sent because his mother wants to get rid of him, and that he will not miss something wonderful and important at home. Of course, no child needs to be forced to go. Without glorifying what the nursery group will be, you can usually arouse genuine interest on his part. Parents and teachers can meet, and the child can be given a chance to look around the school before he is actually enrolled.

Give Him Time to Adjust

Mother goes along the first day, and possibly stays around for part of the time for several days, or even a week or two, until the youngster can be comfortable and happy without her. Attendance two or three times a week is sometimes advisable at first.

Parents can give the school an honest opportunity to help their child enjoy his group experience. Even though he may have a few unhappy days, when he goes to school reluctantly or stays at home, they should encourage him, and co-operate with the teachers. For some children, the adjustment may take weeks.

As the child goes through his period of adjusting to his new group, so, too, does his mother go through a period of adjusting to having her child away from her and in school.

A good nursery school can help a child live more happily and effectively because it supplements his home. It is a world especially suited to his needs.

IF YOU WANT A PLAY GROUP

ELIZABETH L. WOODS, Ph.D.

President, Southern California Association for
Nursery Education, San Marino, Calif.

THERE isn't a play group for miles around. How I wish we had something like a nursery school, or a group for the three- and four-year-olds." Thousands of mothers express that wish daily. More and more of them are doing something about it by starting a co-operative group.

The distinguishing feature of a co-operative nursery group is that the parents are in control of the project. They make the plans and the decisions. They assume full responsibility for both the financing and the day-to-day conduct of the play group. Mothers are on duty in each group. The aims, the program, and the equipment are the same as those described in the preceding chapter, WHAT NURSERY GROUPS OFFER.

Co-operative Nursery Groups

The growth of co-operative nursery schools and groups in America is amazing. Literally thousands of parents desiring nursery-school experience for their young children find that they are neither financially able to pay private-school fees nor are they eligible for partially state-supported centers. They are unwilling to forego giving their children the group experiences nursery schools provide, so they find like-minded parents who will co-operate in setting up a nursery group of their own. In different parts of the country we now find these co-operative schools in a variety of forms and in a variety of housing. Some are small groups carried on in the yard and home (or garage) of one of the parents. Some are housed in churches, some in rented or loaned property, some in community centers, and some in city parks.

While some of these co-operatives start without a trained director, they almost invariably come to realize, soon, that a well-qualified leader is invaluable. Few survive long without either a paid leader who has training and experience in nursery education, or an expert consultant who can and will give time and energy to helping with the program, equipment, reading materials, parent meetings, and counseling. The mothers and fathers still carry definite responsibilities, even when there is a full-time staff.

When a play group or co-operative school does not have such professional

Suzanne Szasz

Co-operative nursery schools often have their beginnings in a group that meets in someone's home. Four or five mothers take turns supervising the children.

help, it is a nursery, not a nursery school. When it does have guidance and leadership of this kind, the co-operative nursery school or play group has certain advantages over other types of nursery schools.

What Advantages Have Co-operatives?

The co-operative nursery school teaches the parents as well as the children. The parents learn, not only in planned discussion meetings, but also in the daily observation of children's behavior and its handling. The handling may be skillful and constructive at times, at other times, awkward and failing.

In a co-operative, you feel a genuine responsibility for the success of the school. You learn to work harmoniously and effectively with other parents, as well as with the leader.

Parents find that they increase their consideration for all children, instead of limiting their sympathies, affections, and emotions to their own. Parents invariably report an increase in their friends in the neighborhood and community, and they often speak of how life has been enriched for them by their co-operative association with other parents. The low cost, sometimes with no fee required, makes a play group financially possible to any parent.

Back-Yard Play Groups

The back-yard play group is the simplest kind of co-operative venture. It is a good starting point, if you want to make a modest beginning toward a real nursery school. The story of one mother who felt a great need for supervised play for her child is typical of the way these groups start.

This mother found in her small village a woman who had had training and experience in nursery education, and who gladly gave her counsel. Three other mothers living near and needing companionship for their preschool children readily agreed to take turns, one morning each week, in caring for the four children involved. Each took on a morning in her own home and yard. They found that each home could provide some special interest or activity for the children. One yard had an excellent tree for climbing. One yard already had a good sandbox. Another had an easel, and a fourth home had suitable records. All had some cars, wagons, blocks, and other toys.

The professionally trained and experienced woman whom they had consulted, whose boys were older and in school all morning, offered to take the fifth morning. Her wide experience equipped her to provide a rich variety of activities in music, storytelling, cooking, dramatic play, art, and nature experiences. The others visited her group as their time allowed, and learned from her.

The mothers found that they liked each other and shared basic ideas regarding a good day for children. Nothing is more important for success in such an undertaking than that those involved have the same attitudes toward children.

The consultant suggested that four quite young children make up a good group. If there are five, one child may be left out at times. It might be difficult for an inexperienced "mother-teacher" to keep more than five happily busy.

The mornings were carefully planned. Various activities, mid-morning juice and crackers, toileting, rest, and stories, that make up the usual nursery-group program were included. No fees were involved.

What Do the Children Gain?

There proved to be a number of assets for the children in this arrangement. They had a satisfying playtime in a small group of children of the same age. They had care and supervision by a mother whose main business for the morning was to keep interest high and to safeguard against accidents and keep them at a minimum. They had a planned morning, providing a variety of indoor and outdoor activities. Knowing other children's mothers well enough to like them and to be liked by them was also valuable. Often small children know other mothers only as reporters of their misdeeds!

What Are the Assets for Mothers?

For the mothers, there were assets, too. They gained widened understandings of child nature and needs. They had the assurance that their small ones were well cared for while they did many essential things in the house and outside. They also enjoyed relief from serious tension due to a twenty-four-hour-a-day job and the constant interruptions to their home activities.

They had time for more attention to fathers' or other children's needs; some possibility of social contacts with friends; necessary household shopping; doctor or dental appointments; a half-hour at the piano or the desk. "When do *I* have time to answer letters or keep accounts?" is the universal cry of mothers of small children. There was little or no expenditure of money for a service which is priceless, if it is good.

Can You Avoid the Hazards?

There are some points to have in mind that may keep you out of difficulties as you work out arrangements for your group. Try to select parents who are open-minded and responsible, who like each other, and whose children are not too difficult or too divergent in basic needs. If possible, select homes offering a variety of play equipment and space.

You will do better if you recognize the short attention span of young children. You will need to plan each day for six or more different activities which may be started as interest flags. Impress on parents the need for promptness both in calling for and in bringing the child.

Other children in the neighborhood who may be attracted and who may wander in and try to join the group may be a source of embarrassment. The mother in charge can explain that "this is the morning I take care of these children and you may come some other time." Make sure each would-be visitor's mother understands the situation. Here is the place tactfully to encourage other mothers to do what you are doing.

Try to find someone who can give professional help in organization and procedure. Many communities now have courses in family education given at junior colleges or other institutions. Many mothers participate in these courses. High-school graduation is the only prerequisite. The teacher of such a course might advise you on play-group problems.

You will want to find a time when the mothers can get together regularly to exchange experiences and discuss problems and plans. Write out, simply and clearly, the plan you agree to pursue, and how you expect to carry it out. Have a copy made for each adult concerned.

Reading materials can be helpful. Parents will find the guidance volumes of

When co-operative play groups bring you and your neighbors together, you discover you want the same things for the children and that your ideas for carrying out your aims are often similar.

Oklahoma A and M College

CHILDCRAFT as well as the materials in READING FOR PARENTS, in Volume 15, useful. Volumes 1 and 2 of CHILDCRAFT are excellent for reading aloud to the youngsters. Your public library can help you find additional materials.

You need information concerning local zoning and licensing laws if you have a real co-operative nursery school or play group. Some cities do not require either. Some have laws defining areas in which nursery schools may be located, and also ordinances requiring a license from either the Board of Health or the Department of Social Welfare. These rules seldom apply to a small, informal group such as the play groups described here. But it is safer to find out about the rules.

Organizing a Nursery School

A co-operative nursery school requires more organization than the play group. The following account of a successful church-housed nursery school may give you some ideas for setting up one of your own. A mother who had become concerned over her three-year-old daughter's difficulties in getting along with other children was the moving spirit. She knew something of co-operatives. This energetic and resourceful woman began a search for other mothers desiring nursery-school experience for their children, and for a place where a co-operative school might be housed. She tried playgrounds, clubs, and several churches, with no success. Then she found a minister with unusual understanding of children's and parents' needs (and great courage!) who responded to her idea with enthusiastic approval.

How Do You Get Community Support?

The first hurdle was not the last. The church membership had to be persuaded to accept the idea of sharing space in their building and grounds for use as a nursery school to serve children and parents without discrimination as to race or creed. Without the minister's wholehearted help, this could hardly have been accomplished. Then, the entire community had to be won over to the idea. To this end, announcements were sent to all the public schools in the surrounding areas. Interested parents spread the word among their friends. Another hurdle turned out to be that some parents lost their enthusiasm when they found that a co-operative really demands co-operation. Giving a certain number of mornings each month as teachers' aids, attending monthly business meetings, and enrolling in a training class for mother-participants were stumbling blocks to some people.

Difficulties were gradually overcome by persistent effort. Church and community backing made it possible to employ a nursery-school director. She was a woman trained and experienced in nursery education, and endowed with poise and a winning personality.

Why a Businesslike Set-up?

Constitution and by-laws were necessary to define purposes, policies, membership, and tuition. Tuition was $20.00 monthly for one child; $35.00 for two children in the same family. Of course, each school would need to set its own prices. The by-laws defined participation requirements, election of officers and approved chairmen of committees, and rules governing regular and special meetings.

The church donated tables and chairs. A jungle gym and a slide were given by an interested community member. The fathers gave endless help in every direction and the school opened with twelve children.

How Do You Keep a School Going?

Within three months, the enrollment had climbed to twenty-five, and an assistant teacher was employed. A president, vice-president, secretary, treasurer, membership officer, purchasing agent, and participation chairman were found to be essential. The latter had responsibility for scheduling the days for mother-teacher participation, and keeping count of the attendance. If a mother who must be absent on her day could not trade days with another mother, she hired a substitute (at $3.00) from a list approved by the director. Five mothers helped each morning. Because they were well known to the children, and recognized as "Stephen's" or "Susie's" mommie, they were enjoyed. Fathers participated actively in equipment upkeep and other work.

A great hazard to avoid, says the director, is not keeping the entire membership fully and clearly informed of all that goes on, in business and in programs. Any major changes must have the approval of members at a regular business meeting.

A real reward, says this same direc-

The success of co-operative groups is up to the parents. Mothers assist in taking care of the children, making doll clothes or curtains. Fathers repair toys or build needed equipment, and everybody in the venture becomes a willing and happy member of the ways and means committee.

tor, is the recurrent testimony of parents concerning their increased understanding of children's behavior and their enriched happiness in living with their own children.

This co-operative nursery-school program has now been made an integral part of the church's total educational program.

Using Available Resources

Another co-operative had the rare good fortune to find its first housing in a city elementary school during a summer vacation. The parents were permitted to use the fine, modern kindergarten room, its blocks, easels, and other equipment, and its playground with sandboxes, slide, and swings. A qualified director was secured.

When summer was over and regular school reopened, the group was made welcome at a near-by city playground, using the recreation building (not otherwise used in the morning) and, of course, the playgrounds.

This school is in session from 9 A.M. until noontime, with twenty-eight families (thirty children) enrolled. It now employs one assistant teacher, and each mother helps on five mornings of each month. Five mothers are assigned for each morning. They are responsible for sending substitutes if they are unable to come. Fathers are pledged to give the equivalent in time of one workday each month, making, repairing, or painting furniture or equipment. Two fathers who are physicians, and one mother who is a trained nurse, comprise a medical committee, and give professional help as required.

The usual officers and committee chairmen are elected by the parents, and reports of their activities are regularly submitted to the membership.

What "Training" for Parents?

The training program for parents begins with three meetings where the parents become acquainted with the underlying purposes and plans of the school. This presentation is made by the director, the assistant teacher, and the membership chairman. Plans are discussed, and rules and regulations are agreed upon by the membership. After this, monthly meetings designed to increase understandings of children's and parents' needs are conducted by the director and the assistant teacher.

A typical half-day nursery-school program is carried on. Its success is attested by the parents' satisfaction and the fact that this co-operative group is being welcomed back to the elementary school for the summer.

Fees differ from group to group. In a group in a Western city, there is an enrollment fee of $5.00, and a monthly fee of $16.00 for one child and $28.00 for two in one family, payable weekly ($4.00 or $7.00). Fund-raising drives, rummage sales, and other devices augment the school's bank account.

How Do Parents Take Part?

Mothers are regularly scheduled as teachers' aids in co-operative nursery schools. No group of more than six children is without an adult supervisor. Mothers do many "extracurricular" jobs, also. They can help create and mimeograph a "Guidance Manual for Mother's Work-Day" (with the children). They wash and iron the "dress-up" clothes and scarfs used by the children in dramatic play. When parties, dances, and fund-raising events are held, mothers assume scheduled duties. In some nursery groups, mothers successfully carry on such varied tasks as taking on extensive telephoning jobs, and writing poems and songs for the children.

Fathers are also active and enthusiastic. Records of their participation show that they design and build tables and play equipment, repair whatever may need repairing, make decorations, and contribute their professional skills and talents in many ways.

On a Sunday, when fathers could come, one school put on a typical nursery-school day, so that each father could understand better "what my child tells me from day to day about experiences at school." Enthusiastic response repaid this effort.

Of course, none of these projects was carried out without moments of discouragement, without days when those who took part wondered why they had ever undertaken this particular assignment. But on the average, and considering the long-time results, parents who have worked with a co-operative nursery group will tell you that it is more than a rewarding experience for them and for their children. They will tell you it is a thrilling adventure.

THE HEALTH
OF THE YOUNG CHILD

Elizabeth Hibbs

A sensible daily program of rest, activity, and food reinforces the tendency toward good health that is present in every child. Feelings play a part in well-being, and so does a cheerful attitude toward the whole question of health.

You can do a better job of keeping your young child healthy, if you understand what care and what protection he needs. The signs of good health and the signs of illness are worth knowing and noting. Your doctor and your dentist can be most effective in helping you keep your family healthy. If you give them your confidence, you can encourage your child to feel friendly toward them and co-operate with them in preventing illnesses, too.

Some illness is unavoidable. To a small child pain is frightening. When it occurs, your child needs good medical care. He also needs to know you will be patient and understanding.

KEEPING YOUR YOUNG CHILD HEALTHY

SALLY ANN PROVENCE, M.D.

Assistant Professor of Pediatrics, Child Study
Center, Yale University, New Haven, Conn.

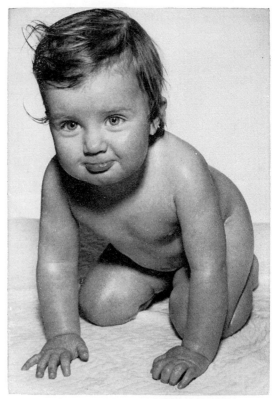

Korling

Good physical health is a precious asset. With good health, you can work and play with more zest and enjoyment. Without it, you may be both unhappy and inefficient. Millions of dollars are spent each year by persons in search of better health.

And yet, all in all, it is surprising how remarkably durable the average human being is. There is a strong drive toward good health in every child. This should be a source of comfort and assurance to parents who are eager to have children grow up well and strong.

Your child has an inborn tendency to stay well and to overcome successfully the illnesses which afflict him. His surprising vigor in surviving the difficulties of being a child is a never-ceasing source of wonder to all around him. And you can ally yourselves with this inborn tendency toward health by following the general principles of healthful living and by availing yourself of medical advice and care when they are necessary.

Signs of Good Health

We know now that health and normality cover a wide range of physical and psychological states. We can discard the idea that there is only one type of good health. We can look at some of the ways in which different children express their healthy state.

Johnny is thirty-three inches tall and weighs twenty-five pounds. Bobby is thirty-six inches tall and tips the scale at thirty-two pounds. Both are healthy young children, two years old. Each is growing normally according to his individual way of developing. But by the time they are six years of age Bobby may be five inches taller and fifteen pounds heavier than Johnny.

Any infant may triple his birth weight and grow eight to ten inches in length during his first year of life. If you have become accustomed to this rapid rate of growth in your baby, you may become worried when you notice that your two-year-old is growing much more slowly. From one to six years of age, the usual range of growth is two to four inches in height and three to six pounds in weight per year. There will not be another period of rapid growth until the years just before and during adolescence. You can relax and enjoy the slow, steady growth of your preschool youngster.

How Does He Grow?

The toddler has a long body and a big head in proportion to his arms and legs. He walks on a broad base. His abdomen is prominent, his feet look flat, and there is usually some bowing of the legs. At this age, as he also does later, the child adopts the posture and way of moving which keep his body in proper balance. Teaching posture has no value during these preschool years and may only confuse the child. In the latter part of this period, his arms and legs grow more rapidly than his body. He begins to lose some of the roundness and softness of the infant and toddler. He no longer looks like a baby. He looks more "leggy," more muscular, and more slender. His shoulders are slightly rounded.

Practice increases his skill in the use of his body. Co-ordination and mastery of his body for walking, running, and climbing come gradually. His skill in managing the larger muscles develops ahead of his skill with his smaller muscles. This is a way of saying that he can walk, climb, run, and throw a ball before he can button buttons, tie his shoelaces, or manage a pencil. He will do these things in the same order, but not necessarily at the same age or in the same way that other children do.

Children differ in movements as much as in rate of growth. Some children are vigorous, energetic, and robust in their movements. Some are more deliberate and placid.

These ways of being active are characteristic of healthy young children. Your own child's activity and tempo are characteristic for him, and you will become as familiar with his tempo as you are with the color of his hair. A healthy child will enjoy his play most of the time, though quieter or more active play will be characteristic of different children.

Is Skin Color a Sign of Health?

We need not demand that all cheeks be rosy. You may have a child who will never in a million years be apple-cheeked, or at least not until she gets her color in a small box at the cosmetics counter.

If your child's skin is clear and relatively smooth, and if his eyes are generally bright, you need not worry about color. But *changes* in color are important. If the child is usually pink-cheeked and becomes pale, or if he is usually quite fair and his skin begins to look yellow, you have good cause for feeling that something may be amiss. Then your doctor should be consulted.

Some parents worry because their children have dark circles, or a slight puffiness, under the eyes. It is true that some children have such dark markings only when they are ill or excessively tired. In these children, of course, they may represent one of the signs—sometimes one of the first signs—that they are "about to come down with something." Other children, in perfect health, have the appearance of darkness under the eyes. For these children circles under the eyes are not a sign of bad health. If your child is one who has this kind of coloring, never mind the critical remarks from Aunt Minnie!

By two and a half to three years, your child will have all twenty of his baby (or deciduous) teeth. The chapter YOUR CHILD'S TEETH, in this volume, discusses the way teeth develop and how they can be protected.

Food Contributes to Health

Certain basic foods provide a child with the elements needed for good growth and nutrition. They also furnish the fuel or energy on which the body operates.

These are the types of foods needed in your child's diet:

> Milk—one pint to one quart daily
> Meat, fish, or poultry—four to five times per week if possible
> Eggs—three to four times per week
> Vegetables (green or yellow)—two servings daily. Raw vegetables, such as lettuce, carrots, salad greens, and tomatoes, may be introduced at about eighteen months.
> Fruits (one fresh)—two servings daily. One should be citrus fruit (orange, grapefruit, any citrus fruit juice) or tomato juice.
> Butter or oleomargarine—two teaspoonfuls or more
> Bread, cereal foods (whole grain), and potato—once a day or more to furnish energy
> Salt (iodized) for seasoning

Select the foods from the wide variety available. Prepare them so that they do not lose their nutritive value in the cooking. A diet which contains these foods supplies your child's basic nutritional needs except for vitamins A and D. These should be provided for one- to six-year-olds. They can be given in the form of fish-liver oil or some similar preparation. For the young child, between-meal snacks of fruit juice or crackers are better than cookies, soda pop, or candy.

How Much Should a Child Eat?

Food lists are a mixed blessing. They help you to select wholesome foods for your child, but they may also make you feel that you *must* feed him all this every day. You might then be upset if he refused to eat. In feeding, it is the "long haul" that counts. You need not be upset by temporary loss of appetite, refusal of basic foods, or "jags" of eating just one or two things.

Vitamin preparations other than vitamins A and D usually are not necessary

Meat, fish, butter, eggs, and cheese—
Children will thrive on foods like these.

Fruit and vegetables, cereals and milk
Give them complexions as fine as silk.

All this is basic to their diet.
In tasty dishes, they're glad to try it.

for children who are eating a reasonably well-balanced diet. They are helpful and important when a child consistently eats an inadequate diet. There is one other good use for them. If you are extremely concerned about your child's eating, it is better to give the vitamin supplement and relax than it is to try to force him to eat.

Not all children need the same amount of food for growth and development. Nor is there any one certain amount that is "right" for all children of the same age.

You will be concerned, understandably, about your child's eating from time to time. Try to think of the results of his diet, and not of the number of spoonfuls he takes. If he seems healthy in ways that have been presented in the beginning of this chapter, you can have peace of mind about his eating.

More detailed discussion of eating and of some of the ways of making mealtime pleasant are given in "My CHILD DOESN'T LIKE TO EAT," in this volume.

Signs of Good Digestion

Digestive upsets will occasionally occur with all children. These may be in the form of vomiting, pain, or diarrhea. These occasional bouts do not as a rule indicate anything more than a temporary disturbance. If your child is able to eat most things without becoming upset, and if his bowel movements are normal in color and appearance, you can assume that his digestive system is in good order.

Bowel movements are usually yellow or brown in color and soft in consistency, but formed. Some children have one or two bowel movements each day. It is normal for other children to go three or four days without one.

Unless the passage of the stool is difficult or painful, this condition need not be a cause for concern. If you are disturbed about constipation, talk to your doctor or your public-health nurse. You might do more harm than good with some old family remedy.

During the preschool years a child gradually masters bowel and bladder control. Temporary lapses of control are common in times of illness, excitement, or emotional upset. Single "accidents" are common for several years after control has been established, and are not a sign of illness.

If a child is consistently wetting himself in the daytime after two and a half years of age, or is still wet at night at four or five years of age, you will want to discover the reason. The chapters SOME CHILDREN RESIST THE TOILET, and WHEN CHILDREN ARE ANXIOUS, in this volume, may give you some helpful suggestions.

How Much Sleep?

The way we care for and live with our children can contribute to keeping them up to their own best level of health. One of the first questions that occurs to parents in connection with keeping a child healthy is "How much sleep should my child be getting?" A child from one to three years usually requires a total of from twelve to fifteen hours of sleep. From three to six years he needs about ten to twelve hours' sleep. This is only a rough estimate. Always remember that the amount of sleep needed varies widely from one child to another. The same child will require different amounts of sleep at different periods during these years.

A youngster's behavior, and eventually his general state of physical health, will tell you whether he is getting enough sleep. If your child is *usually* active, energetic, and not easily tired or irritated, he probably is getting enough sleep, even though he is not sleeping as much as the neighbor's children, or as much as his own brothers and sisters did at his age. If he is cross, irritable, and generally hard to live with day after day, it may be that he is always tired. But, of course, lack of sufficient sleep is only one of many possible causes for this kind of irritability.

Can You Prevent Overfatigue?

You will not need to count the hours your child sleeps if you provide a suitable time and place for sleeping and help him feel all right about going to bed. You do your young child no favor if you are haphazard about his bedtime, or if you permit him to choose it for himself. At the end of the day he is normally tired from the excitement and activity of living. He needs the help of a friendly adult and a familiar pattern if he is to settle down easily to a good night's rest. A regular time for going to bed in a bed of his own is important. It is better if he does not sleep in the same room with his parents or other adults.

You will find difficulties connected with sleeping discussed in SOME CHIL-DREN HAVE TROUBLE SLEEPING, in this volume.

How About Naps?

Most children need a daytime nap until they are five or six years of age. Some will take two naps in the one- to two-year period. This rest in the middle of the day is good for both your child and you. You will probably find that your child gets to bed much better at night if he has a daytime nap, or at least a rest.

Should He Stay Up to See Daddy?

Bedtimes should be arranged so that Daddy has a chance to see his child. Fathers are important people in the lives of children. They become increasingly so as these early years proceed. There is no reason to feel that all children *must* be in bed by 6:00 P.M. or 6:30 P.M., or some other hour set by an "authority." Select a bedtime for your child that can be kept fairly regular for him. Work this out according to your own family pattern of living.

Remember that an occasional exception to the rule about regular hours and routines is not serious. A trip to Grandma's or a party may extend past the usual bedtime. Such breaks in the familiar routine have their own place and their own value for the child.

Fresh Air and Sunshine

Out-of-doors play in the fresh air and sunshine contributes to good health, but it can be overdone. On a cold, windy day in a large city, a mother and a three-year-old boy stood on the sidewalk outside their apartment building. With them was an infant in a carriage. The three-year-old, who was jumping up and down to keep warm, said, "Mommy, can't we go in now? I'm cold." His mother, equally blue, looked at her watch and said, "Just five more minutes, dear." Only the infant, who was well protected by many layers of clothes and blankets, was unconcerned! This was an example of good advice gone wrong. Here was a mother trying hard to observe a "health rule." Her own good judgment could have told her fresh air on such a day did nobody any good!

It is true that young children can stand both heat and cold if they are properly dressed and the period of exposure is not long. If the air is too wet, too cold, or too hot for you to be comfortable, there is no reason to feel that your child will benefit by being out in it.

Consult your doctor or your well-baby clinic to find out how much sun bathing is advisable for babies and small children in your climate.

What Clothes for the Outdoors?

Your child, after he passes infancy, usually does not need more clothing than you do on a cold day. If he is actively at play, he will be overdressed if you bundle him up in layers of clothing. If the weather is too cold for him to be comfortable with a snowsuit, sweater, cap, and boots on top of his indoor clothing, it is too cold for playing outside. A child does not need three sweaters in the house. Clothing for young children should be simple, and selected with an eye to durability, washing qualities, and ease and comfort in dressing and wearing. The frills have a place but are not for day-by-day wear.

Prevention of Infection

Certain specific infections and diseases may be serious to your child, and can be prevented. Protection against diphtheria, tetanus (lockjaw), whooping cough, and smallpox should be given by your doctor, health department, or clinic, during the first year of your child's life. Most doctors feel it is wise to give a "booster" injection about one to two years after the first, to keep the protection at a high level. If there is an epidemic of some disease, or if your child has been exposed to it, your doctor

When it's broiling hot, or if the day is cold, gray and windy, don't be a fresh air fiend! A small child benefits most from the out-of-doors when he is comfortable and happy there.

— DAVI BOTTS

Even though your child was immunized in babyhood to certain diseases, ask your physician about "booster shots" before school days begin.

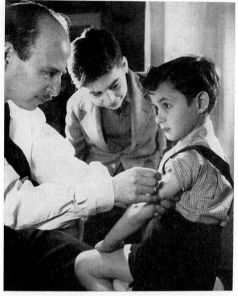

Lucien Aigner

or health department may advise a booster shot. A second booster dose is advisable just before a child starts to school, if he has had none for two or three years. Your doctor, clinic, or public-health nurse can advise you about the timing of such injections, and which preparations are proper for your child. Vaccination against typhoid fever is not necessary for all children but may be important in your community, or if you are planning a trip where you cannot be sure of the purity of the water and milk.

When Is Temporary Protection Wise?

There are, in addition, a few other instances where certain injections or medicines may be given to prevent infection. These are mentioned separately because the protection they give is brief and serves only for the one occasion. Red measles (big measles) may be a serious disease in young children. It may be prevented or made less severe by the injection of a material serum which your doctor can tell you about. The effect of this serum lasts only a few weeks and it is used when there is a known exposure to measles.

For advice about protection against other specific or contagious diseases that may be important in your community, you should consult your doctor or public-health agency. One other thing you can do to protect your child from contagious disease is to keep him away from sick persons. Deliberate exposure to childhood diseases, on the basis that "he might as well have it over," is not ad-

vised as best for your preschool child.

Regular visits to your doctor and to your dentist will help keep your child in good health. The question of how often medical checks should be made, and how you can build a good relationship with the family's medical advisers, is discussed in the next chapter, THE DOCTOR AND THE DENTIST—YOUR CHILD'S FRIENDS.

Accidents Will Happen

Some illnesses and accidents will happen to all children in spite of their parents' best efforts. Such mishaps are part of living and growing up and cannot be prevented. There is a difference between taking sensible steps to keep a child well, and hovering over him to such an extent that he worries about his health. You need not be filled with constant concern for your children's health and safety. Have fun along the way, for your children will be healthier if you really enjoy living with them.

Fred. G. Korth

THE DOCTOR AND THE DENTIST— YOUR CHILD'S FRIENDS

JULIUS B. RICHMOND, M.D.

Chairman and Professor, Department of Pediatrics,
College of Medicine, State University of New York.

THE health of children in the United States and Canada has been consistently improved in the last forty or fifty years. This has been due to advances in the training and information of our medical advisers. It has been due also to an increased understanding of what doctors and dentists can do to keep children in good health. Parents know now that their children's health can be improved through more frequent and more friendly contacts between children and their doctors.

Doctors and dentists contribute to the guidance of your child's growth and development so that he may fulfill his greatest potentialities as a healthy, useful citizen in later life. Doctors today are concerned with your child's feelings, how he gets along with other people, and how his mind develops.

We have added prevention of illness and the general supervision of children's health to the doctor's traditional responsibility—the care of the sick.

How to Choose Your Doctor

It is a good idea to have one doctor or one dentist take continuous care of your child, insofar as that is possible. Of course, from time to time a specialist of one kind or another may need to be consulted. But if you shift from one doctor to another, children have less chance to gain confidence in any of them. Nor will the doctor have as complete and thorough an understanding of your child.

Trust in the physician or dentist is basic to the development of friendly relationships. Proper choice of a well-qualified doctor is important for the establishment of such trust. The best assurance of a proper choice is to select a medical adviser recommended by a professional person or a professional society. In many communities, there are well-established, reputable clinics, properly staffed. Once you have selected your physician, give him your complete confidence. Abide by his judgment and recommendations, and carry these out carefully. Your feeling of trust is generally assumed by the child.

The child may transfer a feeling of trust in one doctor to another, if, for some reason, the child's doctor is not available. Again, your feeling about the change in doctors may be important in determining the child's reaction to the new doctor. It is well not to "oversell" any single doctor to yourself or to your child. It is safer to try to develop a friendly feeling toward doctors generally, based on friendliness to the physician you know.

In many clinics several physicians participate successfully in the care of a child, largely as a result of friendly attitudes on the part of parents and clinic staff alike.

Have Confidence in Your Doctor

If you have confidence in your doctor, you will understand that he does not make the same recommendations for every infant or for every child. No two children develop at the same rate. Doctors will advise parents at varying times to introduce new foods, to start toilet training, or to give immunizations.

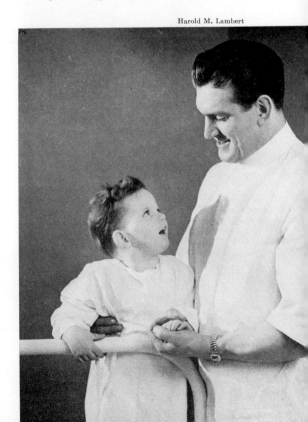

Harold M. Lambert

When the physician and his small patient are good friends, examinations are not frightening and even uncomfortable treatments are easier.

The children take their cue from you. Let them see you have complete confidence in your doctor and your dentist! Then they will feel more friendly.

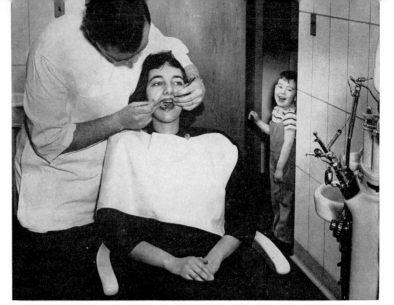

The dentist may become less of a bogey man if a child is allowed to play with such instruments as "the squirter" before any treatment is begun.

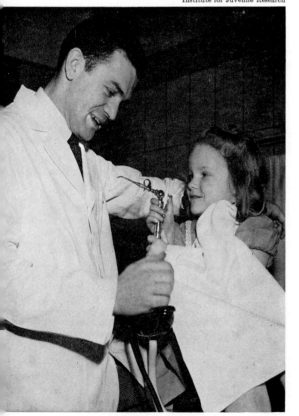

If you understand the importance of individual differences and the value of having a doctor take account of them, you will not feel that your doctor is "unfair" if he starts the baby next door on chopped foods while your baby is still getting strained foods.

Why Regular Visits?

There are some specific steps you can take in reinforcing the good feelings between your child and the doctor. One of the simplest and most effective steps you can take is to have your child visit the doctor and the dentist regularly when his health is good. This provides an opportunity for friendly contacts. Because the child is well, there will probably be no occasion for anything painful or frightening to be done. Indeed, the visit can be a pleasant experience. A mother who told her five-year-old she might choose a treat one afternoon received the astonishing reply, "Let's go to Dr. Bangs' so I can ride up and down in the chair and play with his toys"!

If your child and your doctor have become acquainted and developed friendly feelings, it will be far easier to secure your youngster's co-operation when he is ill. Children generally are irritable during an illness, especially if it is something acute. If the first meeting with the doctor takes place when a child is uncomfortable and distressed, you can hardly expect that the youngster will be co-operative.

How Frequent Should Visits Be?

The doctor who sees your child regularly keeps track of how he is growing in all directions. He can observe how his ability to express himself in words, his ability to meet a new situation or cope with his feelings, is advancing. Growth in these directions is as important as physical health, and is tied up with it, too.

Frequent short visits may be more helpful than longer, infrequent ones. The young child loses interest and becomes restless if the visit or the examination lasts too long. During these visits the youngster becomes acquainted with the instruments the doctor uses, and the way a physician makes an examination. He enjoys learning to name the doctor's light and the stethoscope—which he usually calls a "telephone"—as well as the instruments of the dentist.

How often a physician or dentist wants children to have check-ups varies with each practitioner. Visits once a month for general health supervision and immunizations, during the first year, are usually recommended. After that, check-ups twice a year are generally sufficient. Visits to the dentist should begin at the second birthday. Twice-a-year visits should be part of the regular program after that. The dentist will rarely need to do anything that will cause discomfort to your child at this time, but these visits do provide an opportunity for becoming acquainted. At

these times the dentist can explain to the youngster and his parents how to care for his teeth.

Preparation Smooths the Way

If you play "going to the doctor" or dentist, at home with your child, the way things are done will seem far less strange when he arrives at the office or the clinic. Children between the ages of one and three may show bashfulness or even fear with any stranger, including the doctor. Toddlers don't resist examinations because of any special prejudices against medical men, or a particular medical man! But if they know what the doctor will do, what he will look like; if you talk about the white coat he may wear and the reflector he may have on his head, his very appearance will be less alarming.

Many small children are afraid of riding in an elevator. Since dentists' or physicians' offices frequently can be reached only by an elevator ride, your toddler may need preparation for that as well. You can play "elevator" at home. You can let him push the button himself. It may make him feel safer if you hold him in your arms while you are in the elevator.

Your Honesty Promotes Trust

Honesty in talking about what the doctor or the dentist does is fundamental to the development of friendly relationships. Unfortunately, the traditional way to set a child's fears at rest has been to assure him nothing will happen, or that "the doctor won't hurt you." Formerly, many promises which could not be kept were made to children.

Since some discomfort if not actual pain may at times be connected with what the doctor does, a child may feel that his parents or the doctor are unreliable. The child who has been misled by adults' promises may place little trust in anything he is told afterward.

It is equally unwise to overemphasize the pain or discomfort that a youngster may experience. Should the treatment turn out to be not so bad after all, the child again feels that his parents have not given him the real picture. If you talk too much about how "this may hurt you a good deal" you may communicate your own anxiety to the youngster, for fears are highly contagious.

What Shall We Do About Tears?

A frank but sympathetic attitude on your part will tend to keep your child's confidence in you and make him more willing to repeat visits to doctors and dentists. Parents are likely to take pride in a child who can control his tears. Those who have studied children tell us that we have overdone the matter of trying to prevent children from showing their feelings readily and naturally. A few tears, even a slight shriek or two, are no reflection on a small person's upbringing, and relieve his feelings immensely.

One mother who handled her young children in a manner that inspired confidence said to them, "Look, nobody likes to get shots, but you know Dr. Mc-Mynn will hurt you as little as possible. Let's get it over with fast, so you can play with the little cars he has in his office. Maybe he'll let you listen through the funny kind of telephone he has around his neck. Remember you were going to ask him about the puppy he told you his little boy had."

To the older children, this mother would include some explanation of why the treatment was necessary—"It's much better to have it hurt for a minute than to take a chance on being sick.

What if Something Painful Is Necessary?

A doctor weighs carefully the decision as to whether or not a painful procedure should be undertaken. Your child's personality determines to some extent how he should be told about what is to come. As a general rule, it is not wise to tell a small child far in advance of the event, but he should know what will take place before he goes to the doctor's office. Simple, brief explanations are usually best. "That boil hasn't gone away by itself. The doctor will open it so it can clear up," or "He will take stitches in that cut so it will heal faster."

In most instances, sympathetic but firm restraint of the child, while the doctor carries out the treatment as swiftly as possible, makes for the least disturbance. Older children sometimes thank the doctor for getting things done so quickly. Certainly, if the relationship between your child and the doctor or the dentist has been friendly, carrying out a painful treatment will not interfere with it. It helps, too, if you let your child know you understand how he feels. "That wasn't so good, was it? Well, it's over now. Sure, you feel like crying, and it's all right if you want to." If the crying is dealt with sympathetically, and if your child knows that his fearfulness and anger are accepted, he will return faster to a more cheerful frame of mind.

Should "Bravery" Be Rewarded?

Some physicians or parents may offer rewards to children for submitting to examinations or treatment. Gifts are not generally necessary if the doctor has had an opportunity to establish a good relationship. Rewards in the form of

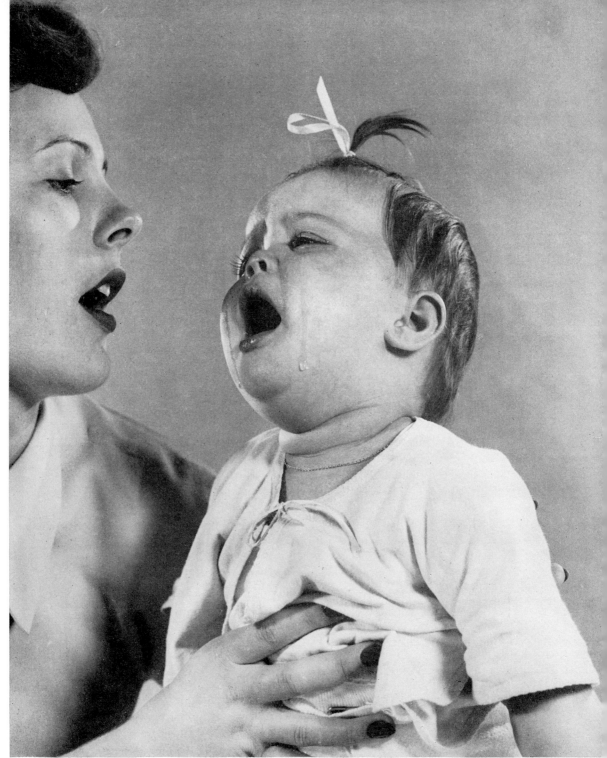

Maybe you have to bear it, but you don't have to *grin* and bear it when you are a year old. Tears and Mother's comfort are good for a baby who is in pain.

candy or toys have the disadvantage of giving the child the idea that he should be given a present for doing what must be done. "When we get through at the dentist's, let's call for Daddy at his office," or "Should we stop at Grandma's on the way home and see if she'd like to finish the story she was telling you?" gives the child something to look forward to. A pleasant experience ahead has none of the unfortunate features of the usual "reward," or of the bribe, which should always be avoided.

"Friend" or "Bogey Man"?

Of course, the doctor should never in any way be used as a threat. He cannot be assigned the role of "bogey man" one day, and be accepted as a friend the next.

It is often a temptation to use the doctor as the extra measure of authority to back up regulations you want to put across. "Doctor, tell Jimmy that he must wear his overshoes and keep his coat buttoned as I told him to," or "Shirley would not have caught cold if she had stayed out of those puddles when I told her to, would she, Doctor?" Such requests put the doctor in an embarrassing position. From a medical point of view, he may not agree that staying out of puddles and keeping coats buttoned would guarantee perfect health.

What is even more important, reinforcing parental warnings really makes just another parent out of the doctor. A physician plays a different part in the child's life. He can be more effective if your child sees him as a friend. He should be a special kind of friend and adviser. He can play his part in guiding your child's development best if he has your child's complete confidence. If he is regarded as an ally rather than as an other enforcer of everyday rules, his word will tend to carry more weight.

Let Your Child Speak for Himself

As soon as your child is old enough to answer questions himself, stay in the background during visits to the doctor's office. Your physician can learn much more about your child if he can talk to him directly. A youngster's answers to questions, and his description of how he feels, give the doctor a better picture of the situation than your interpretation of what your child wants to say. Let your boy or girl answer the doctor's questions himself unless the doctor asks you to add to what has been said.

As he talks to the child directly, a doctor may find out about feelings and reactions that surprise even the most conscientious parent. As your child grows older, your tact in asking if the doctor would like you to wait outside the consulting room will be appreciated.

The Dentist Is Just as Important

All these points apply to the relationships with your dentist as well as with your doctor. The chapter YOUR CHILD'S TEETH, in this volume, discusses the need for regular visits to the dentist.

Friendships of Lasting Value

The friendly relationships which develop between doctor and child are often deep and valuable to a boy or girl. More than one children's specialist prizes the presents his small patients have made for him out of sheer affection. This friendship may endure long after childhood is past. As persons who provide a unique kind of help in a variety of situations, the physician and the dentist can help guide a child toward his own best development.

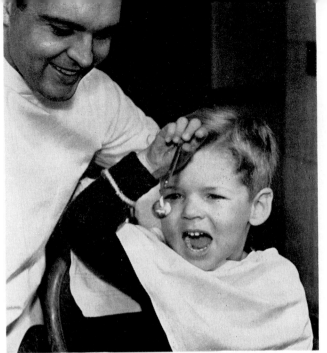

YOUR CHILD'S TEETH

J. H. SILLMAN, D.D.S.

Associate Visiting Dentist, New York
University; Bellevue Medical Center,
New York, N. Y.

YOUR child's dental health depends on diet, regular care of his teeth by your dentist, and good care of his teeth at home. Parents play a definite part in giving children sound teeth.

How Do Teeth Develop?

A tooth unit is composed of the crown, the root, the pulp (blood vessels and nerves), and supporting tissues. As early as two months after conception, the first, or primary, teeth begin to form in the unborn baby. By the time your baby is born, the crowns of his twenty primary teeth, and even part of the first permanent molars, are present. By three years, his first set of teeth is completely formed. Deep in the bone of his small jaws are also portions of more than twenty of his permanent teeth!

When Do Teeth Come in?

The first tooth you see in your baby's mouth may come in at six months. Generally, those in the lower jaw come in, or erupt, first. By the age of one year, your child will probably have the four upper and four lower front teeth, called the incisors. Around fifteen months, he will get his first molars, which are farther to the side of the mouth. The cuspids come through around the age of eighteen months. They are between the incisors and the first molars, and are more pointed. The second molars, the "back teeth," appear after two years.

Some children cut their teeth early, some later. If your child should be markedly late in cutting his teeth, and you are concerned about it, your dentist or physician will be able to advise you.

Your baby may have a receding chin at birth and for some months after that. As he grows, this should disappear. The scalloplike appearance of the incisors when they come in will even out with use.

Can We Make Teething Easier?

Before a tooth comes through, your baby will drool, bite, chew, and gnaw on anything that he can get into his mouth. He may also thrust his lower jaw forward or from side to side. This is his

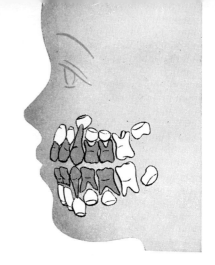

This is how a seven-year-old's teeth look. First teeth are shown in black. Permanent molars can be seen behind them. Notice permanent teeth developing at the roots of primary teeth.

way of trying to make contact between his gum-pads in order to help the teeth push through the overlying tissue. Rubber objects and teething rings of proper size and firmness are necessary to satisfy your baby's urge to bite. Your child may need your help in handling and using these objects successfully.

Because of their shape, the primary molars may cause more difficulty in erupting than other teeth. The exercise of chewing hard foods like carrot sticks, celery, and toasted bread is an aid to teething and jaw development. Your baby will be delighted to use his gums, even before he gets his molars.

A baby may be fussy while he is teething, but it would be a mistake to dismiss any signs of illness at this time as due to the fact that he is cutting a tooth.

Foods Build Healthy Teeth

The requirements for healthy teeth and gums are the same as for general health. Elements found in natural foods like milk and fresh, frozen, or canned fruits and vegetables need to be in every child's diet. Meat, poultry, fish, eggs, and butter are another important group of foods to include in planning your child's meals. Cod-liver oil and sunshine should not be overlooked in considering the building of strong teeth.

Milk is rich in calcium, minerals, and vitamins. So are green, leafy vegetables and citrus fruits. They also have the additional value of acting as cleansing agents and nourishing supporting tis-

sues. These foods are as important for your child's physical development as your love and encouragement are for his emotional well-being. Avoid serving overcooked foods. They are less nutritive, and because they are soft they have a tendency to stick to the teeth.

What Effect Has Candy?

Dental research has shown that constant or frequent use of candies is harmful to the teeth. There is no doubt that, as a nation, we consume an excessive amount of sugar per person. When other children are having candies, pastries, or soft drinks, it is extremely difficult to keep all such sweets away from your child. He likes the taste, and, besides, occasional sweets satisfy a child's emotional requirements. There are moments when the good effect of a lollipop on a child's spirits will outweigh any undesirable effect on his teeth.

If you make an issue of sweets, and try to deprive your child of them completely, he will only crave them more and obtain them elsewhere. He will feel deprived not only of sweets, but of your understanding as well. You can try to have candy infrequently at home, and avoid giving it to your child at bedtime.

Help your child to cultivate a "fruit tooth" rather than a sweet tooth. You

262

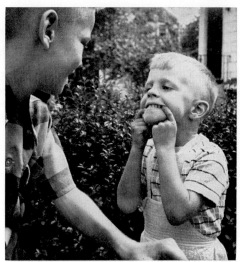

Rae Russell

"Lookit how many I got." Make sound teeth a source of pride, and children will co-operate in caring for them.

can partially satisfy his need for sweets with dried or fresh fruits, nuts, raisins, figs, and popcorn. Make more use of honey and unrefined sugars. Show your child what a wonderful treat it is to make and drink fresh, canned, or frozen fruit milk shakes.

What Effect Has Thumb-Sucking?

In most instances thumb-sucking has no permanent effect on the teeth, mouth, or jaws unless it is continued beyond the age of four. Even then it is probably only one of the factors contributing to the teeth not meeting in a proper bite. Yet, thumb-sucking has long been made a bugaboo for many parents. Most children suck their thumbs or fingers at times as part of their normal development.

Parents are pleased when their child confides in them or asks for help. A child who sucks his thumb is really doing just that. It is his way of telling you that he is in need of something.

Punishment, nagging, or any methods of mechanical restraint, will only make your child cling to his thumb longer and suck all the harder. In order to be helpful you should find interesting things for him to do so that he will be happier and more satisfied with his world.

How Can You Decrease Thumb-Sucking?

Feed your baby when he is hungry. Give him more of your love, good humor, and encouragement. Play, sing, and be joyous with him, if you want him to suck his thumb less. You will not spoil a baby or a child with love. If you could only be a child again for a day, you would be able to view his situation with more sympathetic understanding.

Think of the thumb-sucker rather than the sucking, and remember some babies need more sucking experience than others.

Most children want to stop sucking their thumbs. They just cannot do so until they outgrow the need for it. One child may take a little longer to be weaned from his thumb than another. As your youngster becomes more assured of your love and understanding, and has satisfactory activities inside and outside the home, he will gradually stop his thumb-sucking.

Caring for the First Teeth

Like other parts of the body, the teeth have a definite job to do. Your child must chew his food, and should take time to enjoy it. His teeth may affect his speech and also his appearance. Healthy teeth contribute much to a wholesome smile. Good dental health

Tooth brushing is an occupation after his own heart. It is a chance to mess around with water and pleasant-tasting paste or powder. Besides, if the grown-ups do it, it must be important!

can best be attained by planned dental care and regular home care, as well as by the right kinds of foods.

Decayed teeth can be painful and costly, and may lead to infection. Decay generally begins on the surfaces of the teeth where food collects for long periods of time.

The first set of teeth serves your child during his active period of growth. Neglect or decay of these teeth may affect his health during the time he is growing rapidly. If your child learns to take good care of his primary teeth, his permanent teeth will also benefit.

Home Care to Decrease Decay

See to it that your child brushes his teeth regularly as soon as possible after meals. When your child assumes the responsibility of caring for his teeth, it gives him a sense of his own importance. Brushing his teeth is one of the earliest things a child associates with the idea of being grown up and doing all the wonderful things that Mommy and Daddy do.

His own toothbrushes (to be used dry) in the colors he likes, an attractive glass for rinsing his mouth, his own toothpaste or powder, and a sturdy stool to stand on so that he can reach the wash basin give your child a feeling of achievement and pride in ownership and belonging. Although the actual brushing of his teeth may at first be awkward, your child will soon learn the proper technique from you or from his dentist. The kind of dentifrice used is not as important as how the brushing is done.

Do not oversupervise and do not expect a thorough job right at the beginning. Encourage his efforts and let him know you are proud of him. Not only his teeth, but also your child's whole personality will benefit.

He will enjoy and welcome these experiences if you give him the right start. One child who had just that day gone with his mother to buy a brand-new red toothbrush and tube of toothpaste, went up to his mother at a birthday party, tugged at her dress impatiently and said, "Mommy, now can we go home so that I can brush my teeth?"

What Is the Fluorine Treatment?

Fluorine, in the form of fluoride, offers a practical means of helping to prevent dental decay. Children who from birth have lived in communities where drinking water contains small quantities of fluoride usually have substantially fewer cavities. Other communities have added fluoride to their water supply with reports of good results in the reduction of tooth decay.

If your community does not have fluoridation of its water supply, it is recommended that your child have fluoride applied to his teeth by his dentist, or dental hygienist. The applications should be made at the ages of three, seven, ten, and thirteen so that all your child's teeth may receive this beneficial protection as soon as they come through.

Visits to the Dentist

Your child's first visit to the dentist should be made a normal step in his growing up. Most dental fears are a carry-over from his parents or friends. You cannot reasonably expect more of your child than you do of yourself.

It is often helpful if you take your child with you—as a special treat—on one of your routine visits to your dentist. Arrange this visit beforehand with your dentist, so that your child will be allowed to come into the treatment room, sit in the dental chair, perhaps make the chair go up and down. He can be permitted to examine some of the instruments and familiarize himself with

Going to the dentist when Mother goes can be a special treat. Then a youngster can make friends with the dentist and have his teeth examined. Treatment can come at another visit.

both the dentist and the surroundings. This, coupled with a pleasant experience on his own first visit, will make going to the dentist a familiar and welcome experience, rather than a strange and alarming one.

A good relationship between your child and his dentist can be established from the beginning. The chapter THE DOCTOR AND THE DENTIST—YOUR CHILD'S FRIENDS, in this volume, discusses how such a relationship develops.

How Frequent Should Visits Be?

Your child should go to his dentist about two or three times a year, so that small cavities can be found and given preventive care. Starting your child on regular dental visits early will help to decrease decay in his teeth, and avoid the possibility of painful experiences. X-ray

Rus Arnold

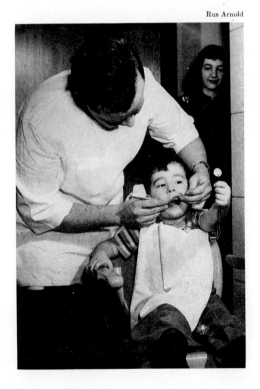

pictures are the best means of discovering tiny and hidden defects that cannot be found with hand instruments. Giving your child the right start toward good dental health will also keep the number of yearly dental visits to a minimum, saving time and expense.

In Case of Tooth Injury

Any damage to a tooth requires immediate dental attention, whether it be a first or a permanent tooth. A first tooth may break by accident. A healthy tooth rarely breaks on chewing, but a decayed tooth may crumble. A hard blow may injure the pulp and in time the tooth may become discolored, but, with proper dental care, a discolored tooth continues to be of service.

What Home Remedies for Toothaches?

Food debris wedged between the teeth may be the cause of toothache. Washing the mouth with warm water will be helpful. At times, cold water may help to relieve pain, if warm water is ineffective. Raising the pillow when your child lies down may also give some relief during the night. Take the child to the dentist as soon as possible, even if the ache disappears.

Caring for Permanent Teeth

The first teeth usually come out before the succeeding permanent teeth replace them. The root or roots of the primary tooth are gradually absorbed as the succeeding permanent tooth pushes its way to the surface. Then only the crown of the first tooth remains. Finally this crown will fall out.

Once in a while a permanent tooth may be displaced a little, leaving the roots of the primary tooth only partly absorbed. This tooth will not fall out.

In some children, certain permanent teeth are missing because they were never formed. In such cases, the primary tooth may retain its roots and, with care, may serve your child for many years. Permanent teeth come in during the years between six and twelve, except for the third molars (wisdom teeth).

With the aid of X-ray pictures, the dentist will be able to ascertain the state of your child's dental development. He will determine whether a first tooth which is late in falling out is interfering with the progress of the permanent tooth. Then he can advise you as to whether or not the first tooth should be pulled.

The same care that makes the first teeth sound helps to keep the permanent teeth in healthy condition.

If Permanent Teeth Are Out of Line

At times some teeth may come in out of line, and may correct themselves. If your child's teeth are out of line, the condition usually referred to as "crooked," his dentist will know whether treatment is indicated and, if so, at what age to begin. He may refer you to a dentist who specializes in the correction of the bite. Some children are self-conscious if they have a poor bite or crooked teeth. Personality can often be improved by having teeth brought into line. This process is familiar to parents as "straightening teeth."

The best service your dentist can render your child is to think in terms of his total needs, so that the youngster can fulfill a happy, healthy life. With your co-operation, he will be far better able to do this. Teeth are a priceless possession and should be cared for in a manner befitting their great value.

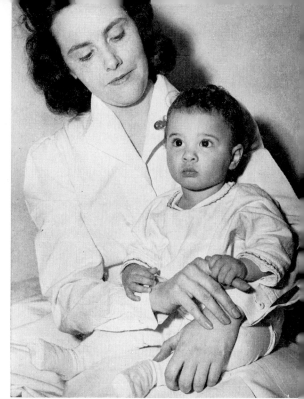

Rus Arnold

IF YOUR CHILD GOES TO THE HOSPITAL

MARY E. MERCER, M.D.

Psychiatrist, Department of Health,
New York, N. Y.

Every day, anywhere, parents bring their sick children to hospitals in order that they may get well. Then the hour comes when the parents must go home. It is hard for everyone. The parents are worried and worn out. Only their conviction that hospitalization is necessary to get their child back to health makes it possible for them to leave, with promises to return as soon as possible.

We all know that the most stable adult is not as mature or as sure of himself when he is lying sick in bed as when he is standing on his own two feet, feeling fine. The same thing is true of a child. His very illness makes him more dependent on his parents' help, presence, and encouragement than when he is well enough to go about his own affairs. At first the child is desperate in his separation from his parents.

Yet the hard fact that the parents must face and accept is that this seeming abandonment and temporary pain is the unavoidable price to be paid for health when hospitalization is needed.

Making Separation Bearable

Parents who have gone through this experience know these intense feelings only too well. They might ask, "What in the world can we do to make it easier for us all?"

Although there is no real substitute for you, his parents, it helps a child to have a member of the hospital staff present just before your first leave-taking. A child needs a person who has time to hold him when you leave and to comfort him in his immediate grief.

This helps in two ways. You are reassured in your own distress and helplessness if you can leave your child with a specific person. And there is no doubt but that it reassures the preschool child

267

to have his mother turn him over to the care of this person, even though he may object. You can say, "Now, Daddy and I are going home. Miss Brown will stay with you while you need her. We shall come back tomorrow" (or whenever the time *actually* is when you will return). Your child may seem to ignore Miss Brown, but her presence, any human presence, is more comforting than facing this separation alone. It is impressive how reassuring bodily contact and a quiet voice can be to the young.

How Should Parents Say Good-By?

The next step is up to you. It takes decision, but you must leave. The fact has been stated; now action is in order. The proper timing of your departure can be most helpful to your child. Somewhere between the extremes of "slipping away" without a warning or staying on and on and on, after the child has been told that you are going, lies the solution to a difficult situation.

How Can Hospital Staff Members Deal with Tears?

Another clear means of helping the child newly admitted to the hospital is to let him call for his mother without trying to change the subject. The child is consumed by the thought of her. Frequently, it helps him to have the hospital staff member say, quietly, "Your mother brought you here because you are sick. When you are well she will come to take you home. Your mother loves you. She wants you to get well fast so you can go home."

No matter how much the child may have abandoned himself to his unhappiness, he understands this kind of talk. It often brings about a silence brimming

Toddlers need their mothers, too, but in the hospital they will in time select a nurse or doctor as a temporary comforter.

Mother is the mainspring of a young child's wellbeing. If a baby must be in the hospital, mother should be with him as much as the rules allow.

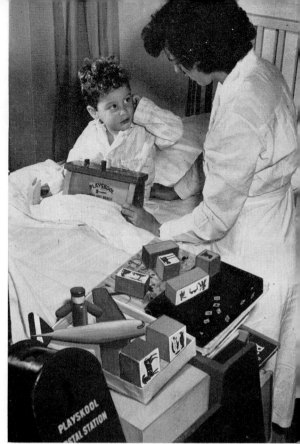

Toys are good medicine. The old, familiar ones are a link with home, while the novelty of new ones takes youngsters' minds off their troubles.

Rus Arnold

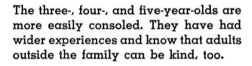

The three-, four-, and five-year-olds are more easily consoled. They have had wider experiences and know that adults outside the family can be kind, too.

with hope. The child will stare at the speaker to measure the truth of such words. Can this stranger be trusted? He may return to his tears, but with less pressure and need behind them. Parents who depart with their ears ringing with their child's desperate protest should be comforted to know that he is not completely inconsolable. Also, as these statements of fact are repeated from day to day and the child's health starts to improve, he usually settles down to the hospital routine with an increasing trust.

Tears have long been the earmark of the end of visiting hour on any children's floor. No one grows used to it. Many hospitals have found that it helps immeasurably to have a mealtime follow immediately after visiting hour. Food is a great solace, and for a moment it can take the child's mind off his loneliness.

Many a child finds comfort in having a favorite toy with him in the hospital. Certainly he should be permitted to have it if he wishes.

What About Toddlers in a Hospital?

Now this is all very well for the preschool child who speaks and can understand, but what about the toddler, who cannot put his feelings into words? What does hospitalization mean to him? It means only one thing: "My

269

mother has left me." Normally, at this age the child lives in an extremely close emotional partnership with his mother. He is not old enough to have enlarged his experience much beyond her. If the hospital situation makes it at all possible, the mother should visit the toddler every day. It would help him if she were to feed him, hold him, talk to him, and love him.

The hospital staff members play quite a different role with the toddler. He permits them to handle him, often after a protest. Should a mother be unable to visit her toddler for weeks, or months even, it is only after he gives up all hope of her return that finally he resigns himself to a half-hearted relationship with somebody else.

If the mother continues to see her child frequently, it becomes possible for this toddler to observe with a sober eye the efforts others make to be friendly. Then he will begin, at his own pleasure, to choose his favorites among the hospital staff. No matter how well he responds to a doctor or to a nurse, no one is in doubt for a second that his heart really belongs to his mother.

In that period of infancy where a mother and child are in the process of learning to love each other, a hospitalization should not interrupt the process, and this "couple" should be kept close together. A mother's visit to her baby is as much for her own sake as for his. These visits should be respected and continued on as free a basis as the hospital will permit.

The infant and the toddler are alike in their interpretation of hospitalization as the sudden and absolute loss of love of the mother. The sun has vanished. Other people and even painful medical procedures are nothing by comparison.

The preschool child needs his father and mother, but because his world is wider he can be comforted by other people, by words, and by touch. He has a better idea that there is a tomorrow, which may be brighter, but medical procedures hurt, and he is afraid. Physical pain can blot out every other emotion but terror. He needs much more support, preparation, explanation, thoughtfulness, and gentle, steady handling from the medical staff than he normally should need at any age.

Preparing for the Hospital

It is not easy for anyone to enter a hospital but, undoubtedly, the preschool child has the hardest lot. He is a keen observer, with a lively imagination but without benefit of much experience or many facts. He is all too likely to misconstrue what he sees happening to others as punishment. His attitude toward life seems to be, "If it can happen to him, it can happen to me." Under such circumstances, how can he possibly escape his own fears?

You need to prepare your child for hospitalization as matter-of-factly as the medical staff needs to prepare him for treatments. He needs to know, step by step, detail by detail, what is going to happen to him. You, his parents whom he trusts, are in the best position to do this for him. He should be told that you are going to take him to the hospital because he is sick, and when he is well you will bring him home.

It helps to describe the hospital and the step-by-step procedure of admission. If you do not know these details, find out for yourself so you can explain them clearly. It reassures your child to have you know a great deal about the place where you leave him. Always and always

Illness is confusing enough for a small child. Separation from his family when he is sick can be overwhelming. Unless hospital treatment is essential, children under six usually do best at home.

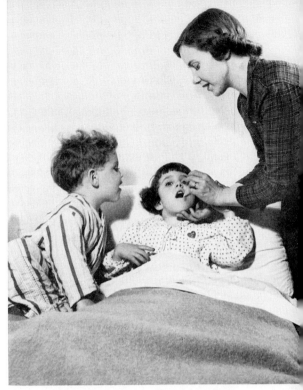

Elizabeth Hibbs

there lurks in his mind the paralyzing thought that you might not be able to find him again and he would be lost.

As your child is admitted, it is most reassuring to him to have you repeat the steps to be taken, such as, "You remember I told you that after you get in the wheel chair, the next thing we do is to go up in the elevator." Many hospitals ask parents to take the child's clothes home with them. Be sure to tell your child ahead of time if this is the case. As you pack the clothes you can say, "As I told you, I'll keep your clothes at home until you are well and then I'll bring them back when it is time for you to go home again."

What Does Preparation Accomplish?

It cannot be overemphasized how much you can help your preschool child by this practical kind of preparation for hospitalization. Careful preparation has the double gain of giving you a realistic job to do. You forget your own anxieties for a moment in relieving those of your child.

The infant, the toddler, and the preschool child all face special emotional difficulties in hospitalization. It is safe to say that they should be spared all hospital admissions that are not *absolutely necessary*. It is a much simpler affair for the school-age child to go to a hospital. Even so, he will not find it exactly easy. But he is less emotional, is less dependent on his parents, and is now old enough to understand why it

must be. He also has available a wider range of interests to console him.

Life being what it is, emergencies arise and children of all ages must be hospitalized upon occasion. Parents and the medical staff together can take steps to lessen the child's fears. But they need to understand what specific hardships and special terrors lie in wait for the infant, the toddler, and the preschool child. Once the smallest child's behavior is understandable to the adult, his needs can be met more intelligently. And the harmful effects of hospitalization to the small child can be markedly reduced.

Safeguarding Emotional Health

If the child is to be operated on, the ideal procedure would be for him to have his pre-operative anesthesia in his own bed, in the presence of his parents. He should be asleep when he is wheeled up to the operating room. There is no question but that the parents should be on hand when he awakens from his anesthetic. Again, it is preferable that he be in his own bed. His parents should stay with him until they are quite sure that he knows, and will remember, that they have been there. This is the ideal arrangement.

Hospital policies vary widely in regard to the so-called "privileges" given to parents before and after surgery on their child. As the understanding of the child's needs increases, no doubt more hospitals will not just permit, but strongly urge, parents to be with their child before and after an operation is performed. In a real and deep sense, there simply is no substitute for the presence of the parents. To understand this is to practice good child care.

Why Is Playing "Hospital" Good?

The crisis of surgery passes and the child begins to settle down to convalescence. Good human relationships remain basic to his well-being, but he is not so desperate in his need for them now. He looks around him. If he is given the simplest opportunity to play, he usually will begin to live over again hospital experiences. Bandages are put on Teddy bears, just as they were put on him. Dolls get pricked with make-believe needles "to make them all well." Their temperatures are taken and they are given baths. It is a great treat to try the doctor's "telephone" in one's ears. Throat sticks are fun now to use on somebody else (of course with some respect for the rules of cleanliness). The spontaneity of this play should be respected and encouraged. Play is one way the child gets frightening experiences out of his system, and frees himself to return to his more usual interests. Such play should be a part of good

medical care in a hospital setting. Any mother knows that children play doctor after they come home from the hospital. There will be less need for this at home if they have already had their fill of it in the hospital.

How Shall We Handle Aftereffects?

An unhappy hospitalization may have unfortunate aftereffects. If the infant has not seen his mother, she must start to court him again with her love in order to rebuild a secure relationship. If the toddler has not seen his mother, he usually comes home angry at her for her "desertion." He will not forgive her completely until she can prove to him again her steadfastness and love.

If the preschool child has had a difficult hospital experience, his parents can expect some kind of temporary setback in his behavior. Each child has his own way of expressing his worries. There may be a temporary breakdown in toilet training. He may suddenly demand a bottle. Nightmares may appear. He may not let his mother out of his sight. No matter what form his behavior takes, his inner unsteadiness is the cause. His parents' calm acceptance of his sudden need for this babyish kind of behavior will do most to get him over it. He will get over it, never fear, as he feels surer of himself. Fundamentally, children flourish when their parents accept them as they are. This basic attitude takes on increased importance to a badly shaken and frightened child.

Thoughtful preparation of a child for hospitalization, followed by a hospital experience that takes his feelings into consideration, will do a great deal to lessen the all-too-common fear of going to the hospital. The well-known ounce of prevention is worth pounds of cure.

KEEPING A CONVALESCENT CHILD HAPPY

MARY R. OSBORNE, B.A., R.N.

Lecturer on Marriage and Family Life,
Sarah Lawrence College, Bronxville, N. Y.

CONVALESCENCE is that part of illness which follows the acute stage. The patient is regaining health and strength. After a slight illness, convalescence sometimes requires two to three days of extra rest and care. Following serious illnesses, it may involve bed rest of several weeks or months.

Take a look at convalescence from the point of view of the whole family. One mother, who had just seen a child through it, described the usual family situation in this way: "The whole house gets upset. They're still sick, only they don't seem to act sick, just naughty.

You're tired but you can't stop for a minute. You love them but you wish that just for one whole day they'd disappear, along with the rest of the family, and you could rest your feet." Perhaps you, too, know this feeling!

Convalescents Are Irritable

A child who is getting better after illness may be rebellious and unco-operative, or may whine and become more babylike than he has been for some time. He may express strong fears of the dark, of being left alone, of the doctor, or of ordinary sounds like doorbells.

- Davi Butts

Use your head to save your heels! Settle your youngster where he can hear and see you at work, where the fewest possible steps will be needed as you care for him and answer his call.

Quick fatigue, poor emotional control, and irritability are to be expected in convalescence at any age. The small child who is barely beginning to gain confidence, independence, and control in his healthy state is likely to have less of these qualities for a time as a result of the illness. The setback is temporary and calls for as much skill and patience in management as possible. It will gradually disappear as health returns completely.

Time out for a planning session can aid parents in meeting the kinds of problems that convalescence presents. Family members can be helped to understand the patient and the situation, and can then co-operate more effectively. Housework can be cut down and shared. Emotional strain and fatigue will decrease when a child is relaxed and happy. Best of all, children actually get well faster when they are helped to get over boredom, fear, and restlessness.

Good Care Speeds Recovery

Let's find out how Mrs. White managed to keep her twenty-month-old Tommy fairly quiet after a fever and sore throat. On his morning visit, the doctor said Tommy must be kept in bed until he had a whole day free from fever.

As Mrs. White said good-by to the doctor, Tommy was swaying on hands and knees and calling, "Mommy, me get out. Drink, Mommy. Potty, Mommy."

"The little dickens," thought Mrs. White, "he's trying everything to get me to come to him."

She tended to Tommy's needs and thought through her plans for the day. She reminded herself that if Tommy had reached the ten years of his sister, or even his brother's seven years, she could expect some co-operation and occasional solitary activity, if it were planned well. But she knew toddlers need to have a grown-up near them.

What Arrangements Reduce Work?

Understanding this, Mrs. White moved Tommy's crib into the dining end of the living room, where he could see and hear her in the kitchen. A screen of chairs and an old sheet kept off drafts and marked off a small area to keep the other children at a distance.

The tray with sponge-bath equipment was placed on a chair and covered with a towel. The potty was put under Tommy's crib, with a newspaper cone over it. With water and food and juices near at hand in the kitchen, Mrs. White knew that she could take good care of Tommy without running back and forth to the bedroom constantly.

She brought a string of colored beads and tied them to the side of the crib. A loved rubber duck was added, and a stuffed dog and picture books were kept near by. She began to work in the kitchen. When the youngster stood up

274

and asked to get out, she said nothing just then about lying down, but began a little made-up song about Tommy in his bed.

This did not work. Mrs. White felt a twinge of irritation, but reminded herself quickly that patience now would save time and worry later. She got a chair and sat by the crib, and showed the child his favorite pictures of a choo-choo, a doggie, and a big bus. As he sat more quietly, she said firmly, "Now Mommy is going to give Tommy a drink, and we'll tell Duckie to go to sleep. Let's sing Duckie to sleep." They put a blanket over the toy and, as she went back to the kitchen and started to wash dishes, she sang "Rock-a-bye-Baby" over and over, in a soft voice.

This time it worked. After Tommy had gone to sleep, Mrs. White was able to make beds and phone an order to the grocer. Most of her activities had to be carried on as near as possible to Tommy's crib. If she needed to leave him for a while and he was awake, she assured him, "Mommy will come right back." Cleaning was slicked over or neglected, and the cooking was kept simple.

The Whole Family Co-operates

There were several naps, a sponge bath, and some finger games with Tommy during the next few hours. When ten-year-old Lynn and her brother Stan came home, they were asked not to bring their friends in this afternoon, but to play outside. Later, their presence was helpful. As they listened to radio

A child recovering from an illness tires easily, but watching another youngster play amuses him without fatigue.

programs turned low, and as they set the supper table, a happily tired Tommy watched and talked to them.

Then, when Daddy came home, he and the children moved the crib back to Tommy's room. Mr. White put clean pajamas on his son while he told him how Daddy came home on a big bus. A few minutes by the child's bed were spent rubbing his back and telling him that Mommy and Daddy and Lynn and Stan were going to eat now. This helped Tommy to get sleepy and to know what was going to happen. He started to protest when his father left but was told firmly, "Tommy is going to sleep." A partly-opened door and a low night light also helped, because he could hear voices and did not feel alone. Soon Tommy was asleep.

Do We "Spoil" Convalescents?

Tommy's first day of convalescence will be sure to strike some parents as "spoiling" the child. If the whole family always planned activities around

Rae Russell

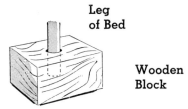

Keep your patient comfortable by giving him a change of position with pillows. You can avoid backache yourself, as you care for him, if you adjust the height of the bed to your comfort with a block of wood under each of its legs.

Leg
of Bed

Wooden
Block

Tommy, there might be some reason for such a fear. Actually, spoiling comes about quite differently, as explained in the chapter WHEN ARE CHILDREN SPOILED?, in this volume. Good, loving care during illness "spoils" nobody.

Remember that necessary firmness with Tommy was carried out in essential matters. He was not allowed to get out of bed and run around. He was not indulged by being allowed to stay with the family at dinner when he needed to go to sleep. But the planning and the understanding of his needs helped him to accept all this fairly calmly. There are many reasons why things do not always turn out as well as they did for Mrs. White on this day. Often several members of the family are ill at the same time. But, in any case, the principles Mrs. White followed tend to make things easier.

"If so much is done for children when they are sick, will they enjoy it enough to pretend illness?" thoughtful parents may wonder. A child who can count on at least some moments during the day when he gets a hug, or shares some talk and work and fun, will not need to play sick to be sure his parents are interested in him.

Planning for a Long Pull

During a period of convalescence running into several weeks or months, there is a greater strain on the morale of the family and on the patient, for recovery may proceed slowly. The choice of a room for the sick youngster will assume greater importance. The kinds of occupations and materials that make up his play are worth extra study, so that gradually more and more muscles come into use. The small, confined, sickroom world can perhaps be expanded to include people and ideas in the world outside. During a long convalescence, it is essential to foster any signs of independence.

In making plans to help everybody through a long recovery period, it may be wise to consider a complete rearrangement. The choice of the room can only be determined by the individual family. Advantages you can try for are attractive outlook, nearness to a bathroom, and convenience and step-saving. Then, too, provision for sociability without exposure to too much excitement and irritating noise is a point to consider. For the sake of the other members of the family, if possible there should not be too much sacrifice of their normal activities. Do not make the mistake of choosing the quietest room if that would give the child a feeling of lonely

276

isolation, or make many extra trips to a far corner of the house.

For Comfort and Convenience

The equipment of a room can also help or hinder recovery. If warmth is not sacrificed, a bed next to a window has many advantages. Trees and birds, or people coming and going, street activities, clouds, and airplanes provide diversion. Even watching somebody hanging out clothes can be interesting.

The equipment in the room should be simple but attractive, and as convenient as possible. A comfortable bed with some firm and some soft pillows is helpful. Sometimes families find it best to rent a high hospital bed, so that the mother is saved from the tired back which comes from stooping as she tends her patient. Four large blocks of wood, with holes to hold bed legs steady, can raise an ordinary bed to the proper height. Pillows may be used under the patient's knees and in various other ways to bring about a change of position without strain.

A wide, deep, wooden box which has had one side and the bottom removed can be put over the feet, under the covers, to relieve the steady pressure of bedclothes. Such a box may also have another side removed and be used as a bed tray, particularly if it is covered with oilcloth. A small rim can be added on three sides of the "tray" to keep objects from falling off. Or saw off the legs of an old folding card table to the length of eight inches, and you have a bed tray with a surface large enough for any kind of play.

A bedside table, or orange box, and a chest of drawers or bookshelves can hold toilet articles, bed linen, and extra clothes. A shoebag with several pockets can be hung near the patient or pinned to the mattress to hold extra toys and play materials not in use at the moment.

Cheerful, colorful prints on the wall add to the attractiveness of the room and may be changed from time to time. The bareness and neatness so helpful during severe illness is monotonous as the patient begins to recover. The aim is to have interesting, attractive things, but to avoid a cluttered look.

How About Lighting?

Lighting arrangements should be considered, too. The bed should be placed so that the patient does not face strong light from the window. If this is impossible to manage, the window should have adequate blinds. Eye doctors say that the contrast of pools of bright light and the surrounding darkness causes eye strain and irritation. Diffused light, with stronger but shaded light for close work, is ideal. An additional tiny bulb can be shaded and used as a night light. This makes things easier if care is needed in the night or if a child is bothered by those fears of the dark so likely to develop during periods of fever and pain.

What Makes for Restfulness?

If you have had experience with illness, you will have learned that a regular routine of meals, giving medicine or treatment, extra drinks, play, rest, and sleep is helpful to both you and the patient. If your child can tell time, a clock in the room will tell him how long he has to wait for his lunch tray, or how much longer he can play before rest time. These routines need not be so rigid that there is never any exception, but if a schedule is fairly well kept you can avoid needless arguments. You can adapt your other work to this schedule more easily if it is reasonably regular. If someone else takes over temporarily, the same routines can be carried out in a way that gives the child security. A youngster also profits by not being over-stimulated or bored by too long a play or rest period.

If sleep and rest times turn out to be sources of argument and rebellion, it is wise to try to provide as relaxing an atmosphere as possible before they are due. Reading aloud, music on the radio, or a quiet game with a definite end are better than a radio mystery murder. After exciting games, or a visit from a group of lively friends, give the youngster time to relax before he actually settles down to sleep. A quiet house, a darkened room, and a gentle back rub, with alcohol warmed by standing the bottle in hot water, are all conducive to relaxation.

Avoiding Eating Problems

During most convalescent periods, diets can be as full and as varied as the child's age permits. You are naturally eager to restore body weight and energy after illness, and this desire often makes you overanxious about your child's eating. You may feel that getting the egg or glass of milk into Mary is vital, but don't overlook long-term effects of forcing or coaxing a child who has little appetite.

Many feeding problems have started because children were forced to eat when they were not entirely well. The very success of getting a certain food eaten through threats or bribes gives the child the idea that one of the most important things in life, at least to his parents, is what he eats. This experience gives him a way of ruling his otherwise firm parents. If he is bored, he may enjoy the commotion he causes. He is likely to find satisfaction in the concern his mother shows when she returns from an outing and finds that he has not eaten. He may learn to say, when denied something he wants, "Then I won't eat," even though the thing wished for has no connection with his eating.

Understand Your Own Feelings About Eating

If you understand why your child's eating seems so important to you, you may be less anxious. Then you can tackle the problem sensibly. Like most mothers, you probably get deep satisfaction from seeing a child eat hungrily in sickness or in health. This is intensified after your child has been ill, since hearty eating is rightly considered a sign of returning health and vigor. Then, too, you have usually gone to a good deal of trouble to provide attractive, tempting dishes. If, after the work of preparation, your child either refuses to eat or only picks at his food, it is hard not to feel disappointed.

How Can You Tempt Appetites?

A little calm thought ahead of time will make clear what is really important in the situation. It will help you, when you are anxious and tired, to plan what you will say and do. Some help in eating can be given without hovering and coaxing and scolding. Tiny portions of food may be offered. When the child does ask for more, he really wants it, and no contest over eating has been set up. Let him have the foods he likes best if they are in his diet. In this way, good digestion is promoted through enjoyment, and the long-term goal of healthy eating habits is fostered. "MY CHILD DOESN'T LIKE TO EAT," in this volume, may have suggestions.

When a small child feels well, he needs playthings to keep him happy and out of mischief. Give him a few at a time and change the lot before he tires.

Keeping Him Occupied

Providing interesting, suitable play materials is an essential part of caring for a small patient. Through play, many things can be achieved. Undesirable activity arising from boredom can be partly or wholly avoided so that prolonged thumb-sucking or too vigorous bouncing on the bed will decrease. Emotionally satisfying occupations will stimulate digestion, elimination, and circulation. Well-chosen activities can gradually increase the use of muscles weakened by prolonged bed rest.

For Listening and Watching

During the early part of a long convalescence, it will probably be necessary to provide something requiring no more activity on the part of the child than watching and listening. A five-year-old's grandfather prepared a bedside garden of carrot tops, sweetpotato tops, and grapefruit seeds that kept his granddaughter quietly interested for a long time. Later, he brought a fishbowl with two goldfish that proved even more fascinating. As the child grew better, she fed the fish and took over the watering and sunning of the plants as well.

A prism hung where it will throw colored reflections on walls and ceiling, or a few bits of glass tied together so that the slightest breeze will bring musical tinkling sounds, can hold a small child's interest. Even a simple pinwheel placed on a windowsill can bring quiet satisfaction to the youngster who has no energy to move around. A record player with suitable records can be played for the child and later managed by him without help, if he is old enough. A singing canary is a delight to watch as well as to hear. Radios and television sets are helpful, too, if parental guidance can avoid an overdose, and if exciting programs are eliminated before rest and sleep.

Storytelling and reading aloud are well-tried and satisfactory ways of passing the time. Books for younger children, of course, should be simple ones with many colored pictures. The first three volumes of CHILDCRAFT are a special delight to the small child. The chapter STORIES FOR YOUNG CHILDREN, in this volume, has other suggestions.

What Play Materials?

Clay or plasticine, crayons, scrapbooks, and small construction blocks of wood or plastic are old stand-bys. In choosing good activities for your own convalescent child, you will bear in mind what is suitable at different ages. Remember, too, that in the first days of convalescence there is likely to be quick fatigue and boredom. This is particularly true of a child who is sitting up for the first time. A sick child often goes back to more babyish ways of playing. Toys he would scorn if he were quite himself may please him immensely now.

The fragile doll, the metal train that is flimsy, and the mechanical wind-up toy that does only one trick cause more difficulties than happiness. Homemade toys are often the most satisfactory. Cans may be smoothed and lacquered in bright colors and selected so that they fit into one another. Cigar and cheese boxes may be nailed tight and lacquered. During play they will become, magically, trains, houses, trucks, or whatever is wanted. Sturdy peg toys, stuffed or rubber dolls and animals, three- to five-piece picture puzzles, and the puppet head that can be put over fingers and made to nod or talk are other satisfying toys. The chapters TOYS AND PLAY MATERIALS, in this volume, and QUIET PLAY, in Volume 8, have more suggestions.

Even the Youngest Like Mail!

Relatives and friends may be asked to send funny drawings, picture post cards, photos, or cut-out pictures. These may be pinned or tacked up where the convalescent can see them and be reminded that Uncle Herb or Grandma sent them. Interest and variety are provided by frequent changes of these mementos.

One advantage in the last suggestion is that the child is helped to keep up his contacts with people outside the immediate family. Of course, the toddler has no capacity for a real give-and-take relationship with others, but the faint beginnings of such sociability are found even at this early age. He plays patty-cake or other finger games with his father or older sister. He watches and listens when Aunt Edie and Mother have tea, and he drinks his orange juice at the same time. If the convalescent youngster is four or five years of age, he has already formed attachments, and will be helped by short visits and messages to avoid too self-centered an existence.

Independence Through Play

Your goal is to increase activities and interests. You want your convalescent child gradually to become more and more independent and responsible, instead of needing so much done for him. His play activities are a natural means of leading him on through his own interests to this goal. You can foster any signs of interest in doing things for himself as he gains in strength. This may mean just washing his own hands and face at first, or partially feeding himself.

A sympathetic, matter-of-fact giving of help, while mentioning that you expect him to do it himself the next time, will bring better results than pushing too fast. It will take your own ingenuity in your own situation to provide a good atmosphere for getting well, but do not be discouraged if all that has been suggested cannot be carried out perfectly! As in other phases of family living, intelligent common sense plus living and learning together can make convalescence, with all its problems, an opportunity for the development of the qualities and relationships that make for fine human beings.

WHAT CAN I DO NOW, MOTHER?

Lucien Aigner

Sturdy playthings are a child's tools. He needs them to carry on his business, for play is indeed the small child's business.

Even the happiest, most inventive children occasionally need suggestions to stimulate their play. These suggestions often come from the playthings themselves.

Watching people or machines at work, or seeing new sights, enriches a small child's life and gives him new ideas for play, too. Stories, poems, and music suited to his years and his interests can extend a youngster's horizons in time and space and sharpen his use of his senses.

All these experiences with new sights, new sounds, new tastes and smells and feelings, can give a child richer resources within himself. Such experiences tend to cut down the unavoidable doldrums when he complains, "Nothing to do around here."

TOYS AND PLAY MATERIALS

ROWENA M. SHOEMAKER,
M.A.

Assistant Director, Play Schools
Association, New York, N. Y.

Shune Snow

BECAUSE play is a child's way of learning, and toys are learning tools, parents need to choose toys with care. We need to ask ourselves whether we are making the most of our homes and the material we have at hand to help our children play and learn and grow.

Planning for Play Life

Both short-range and long-range plans are necessary in selecting play materials. You can save time and money, and you can avoid much of the clutter caused by useless or broken toys, if you keep in mind what kinds of playthings lend themselves to the natural interests of children at each stage of development.

A child does not need a great number of playthings, but he does need playthings suited to his ability to use his muscles and his imagination. He needs a well-balanced variety of sturdy, durable, easily cleaned, safe toys that lend themselves to being used in many different ways. He needs some for playing alone and some for playing with other children.

Such a variety makes it possible to put away playthings that seem to have lost their charm for the moment. Bring them out again after a few weeks, and they may add new zest to the life of the doll family, the railroad-building, the store-keeping, or whatever may be afoot. Let the children choose what they enjoy doing. There is no harm in a little girl liking trains, or a boy liking housekeeping toys.

What Materials Are on Hand?

Many of the best toys are homemade from materials that would otherwise be thrown out. For the youngster who is two or more, collect odd bits of cloth,

Good play materials call for activity, challenge the imagination, and can be used in a variety of ways. Safe, sturdy, and easy to keep clean—these are the earmarks of a satisfactory toy.

colored wool, strings, buttons, old curtains, ribbons, lace, fancy paper, and cotton batting in a box. Rummaging in such a box is fascinating for the three- and four-year-olds. You can make dolls, stuffed animals, or puppets for the children from such scraps of material. Both boys and girls of four and a half or five can use the scraps for experiments in sewing. CREATIVE PLAY AND HOBBIES, Volume 8, has detailed suggestions along these lines.

Keep a "dress-up box" with a few discarded hats, men's vests, dresses, scarfs, purses, strings of beads, and some kind of small satchel. Such a collection can be a lifesaver on more than one rainy day when three-, four-, and five-year-olds are getting out of hand.

Discarded household utensils such as wooden chopping bowls, large wooden spoons, old pots, pie plates, pails, funnels, and egg beaters are excellent toys for infants and toddlers. Watch out that there are no sharp edges. Tin cans of different sizes, whose edges have been made perfectly smooth, have great possibilities. The three-year-olds like to fit them together. The four- and five-year-olds enjoy painting them.

A washtub of water will provide entertainment for simple splashing, for sailing small boats, for the dolls' laundry, or for making mud pies.

Doll furniture can be made of small milk containers or any small cardboard boxes. Orange crates and other wooden boxes can be made into real furniture that the children themselves will enjoy using. Here is a place where Father can be helpful, even though he is not especially gifted with a hammer and a saw. The chapter HE LEARNS THROUGH ACTIVITIES AND TOYS, in this volume, suggests ways the youngest children can use waste materials profitably.

What Materials Are Easily Found?

If you have a back yard, a family garden has real opportunities for children, for they like growing things. Gardening should not be made a burden to the small child. If he works along with Mother and Father it seems like play and he learns important lessons.

Large wooden packing boxes, barrels, and kegs (be sure there are no nails sticking in them) lend themselves to many uses in outdoor play, and are permanent equipment. These should be sanded, and can be painted.

Even small children have a natural interest in collecting things. Respect and encourage their collections, and, as they grow older, you will usually find that they look for more worth-while objects to gather and arrange.

Each family will find certain kinds of playthings easier to get, easier to store, and better adapted to the children's tastes. No child would need or would want everything listed here. Nor do these suggestions include all the toys small children can use.

The practice of passing toys on from one family to another as children outgrow them is often practical, but every child can be allowed to keep a few treasures long after you think they should be discarded. Some communities have toy exchanges run by a group of parents. When the youngest in a family has finished with a toy, this method of keeping equipment circulating is particularly valuable for expensive items like tricycles, skates, or the autos and fire engines that three- and four-year-olds can ride in.

Permanent Equipment

Some pieces of lasting equipment may be used by one family for ten or twelve years, or even survive for two generations. You can start with a few pieces for the two- or two-and-one-half-year-old in many cases, and add to the collection at birthdays and other holidays. Then the material keeps pace with the child's growth into later childhood.

For Indoor Use

Child's-size table, chairs, and rocker

Building blocks of natural hard wood in different sizes and shapes. Standard school blocks can be bought, or two-by-fours can be cut to desired shapes and sizes, and sanded smooth.

Dressing up adds to the fun, whether the youngsters are playing gardener, pirate, or Indian chief. Your discards may become their greatest treasures in such fun.

Press Syndicate

For supplementary block play—small cars, boats, trucks, planes, and block play figures. Block play figures and animals can be made at home by cutting pictures from magazines or catalogues, mounting them on heavy cardboard, and securing each figure to a wooden base.

Phonograph and record rack. The chapter YOUNG CHILDREN AND MUSIC, in this volume, has more suggestions for musical instruments for the early years.

Dollhouse and doll play equipment that can stand hard use

Adjustable easel, blackboard chalk, and bulletin board. CHILDREN NEED SPACE AND PLAY MATE-RIALS, in Volume 14, suggests how to make and store these.

Wooden steps or wooden box 5 inches high, 10 inches long, 10 inches wide. This step encourages independence, develops balance, and lends itself to many kinds of play.

The chapter PUPPETS AND MARIONETTES, in Volume 8, suggests ways of using puppets in play.

For Outdoor Use

Sandbox or sand pile, sand toys, and watering can. Discarded kitchen spoons, pans, molds, and strainers can supplement or take the place of sand toys to be found in the stores. Be sure discarded utensils have no sharp edges.

An 8-foot walking board and a sawhorse can be combined to make seesaw, slide, or inclined walk. Board should be cleated on both ends and in the center.

Wheelbarrow

Tricycle

Hollow blocks and stout boards to use as bridges from one block to another

Back yard gym-swing combination

Ladders or jungle-gym combinations

Wading pool

Toys for Infants

Many of the bright-colored "sound and feel" toys may be hung where the baby can watch them until he is able to grasp and hold them.

Toys That Delight Baby's Eye

Strings of large colored beads or colored spools

Balloons

Plastic dolls and animals or homemade yarn dolls

Toys That Make a Pleasing Sound

Pair of lightweight rattles. Can also be made of large beans securely enclosed in easy-to-hold containers.

Tone balls—set of three plastic balls, each making a different sound. Good as a bath toy, too.

Large metal bell on stick, or large rustproof bell sewed to long strip of cloth

Colored plastic disks on plastic chain, or loosely strung large wooden beads

Wooden or plastic blocks, each making its own rattling sound

Arrangements of plastic balls and bells, or wooden beads and bells, that fasten to play pen or crib. These can be found in infant's department in most stores.

Toys for Shape and Texture

Cloth doll or animals. Can be made from cotton stocking or terry cloth stuffed with sponge. Embroidered or painted features are a gay addition.

Rubber ball about 4 or 5 inches in diameter. Balls of different sizes are enjoyed all through pre-school years.

Cloth ball may be made with plastic covering filled with kapok or shredded nylon hose.

Hard rubber or plastic bath toys chosen for color and form

Large round wooden pegs that fit into wooden base. Colored balls fit on tops of pegs.

Various types of "cradle gym" that invite reaching and grasping

Toys for Toddlers

Some of the toys described in the section on *Permanent Equipment*, in this chapter, are useful for toddlers, too.

Toys for Activity

Wooden wagon with short rope pull. Can be made with smooth wooden box about 12 inches long, 4 inches deep, with 3-inch wheels and a rope pull.

—→

Blocks are the perfect toy, all through childhood. Different shapes and sizes can gradually be added to the collection as a child finds new uses for them.

Suzanne Szasz

Carton or packing case big enough to crawl into becomes cave, home, or fort, depending on what is afoot.

Push-and-pull toys that encourage walking

Kiddie car

Rocking horse

Baby swing to be attached to door frame

Rubber-head drum made by removing both ends of a can, covering top and bottom with pieces of inner tubing. Pad one end of dowel 8 inches long for striker.

Toys to Put Together and Take Apart

Blocks or cups that fit one inside the other

Stacks of blocks or wooden disks that fit on to a wooden spindle

Wooden spools colored with nontoxic paint may be threaded on long tipped strings, or shoelaces.

Bag of large wooden beads

Wagons or bags of wooden cubes and rods for building

Wooden boxes representing mailboxes, houses, etc., with openings of different shapes in top or "roof," blocks of wood that drop through the openings, and a door to release the blocks after they have been dropped in

Bag of large wooden nuts and bolts that fit together

Puzzles—wood inlay with simple pictures cut in 3 to 5 pieces. Can be made from large pictures mounted on heavy cardboard or plywood and cut into large pieces easy to fit together.

Toys for Imitating Adults

These toys are equally attractive to three-, four-, and five-year-olds.

Rubber doll, preferably of wetting and drinking type

Telephone with working dial and bell tone

Small corn broom with 28-inch handle

Doll drinking-bottle and nipple, or nonbreakable household bottle with nipple

Unbreakable or plastic play dishes and cooking utensils

Materials for Making Things

These materials are equally good for three-, four-, and five-year-olds.

Hexagonal crayons—large, easy to handle. Start with two or three colors and add to the collection.

Large sheets of manila paper

Finger paints to use on shelving paper or on 15-inch square of high-gloss oilcloth. Paint can be washed off oilcloth. For directions for mixing finger paints, see Volume 8, page 152.

Plasteline—oil-base clay. Use on board placed on large oilcloth square or on newspapers.

Toys for Three to Six Years

The sections in this chapter on *Permanent Equipment* and *Toys for Toddlers* have suggestions for the nursery and kindergarten years, too.

Toys for Imitating Adults

Mop with 28-inch handle and dustpan

Unbreakable doll that can be dressed and undressed

Doll bed or cradle. Can be made by attaching low blocks or rockers to smooth wooden box.

Doll carriage

Doll bathinette or water basin for bathing dolls

Doll high chair. Can be made from orange crate by removing one end, using middle section as seat, and covering seat with pad made of cloth or plastic material.

Washboard, basin for washing doll clothes, small clothespins, clothesline

Iron (not the kind that really works) and ironing board. Board shaped like ironing board can be attached to wooden box and padded to resemble real ironing board.

Small suitcase, wicker basket, or the kind of laundry case used for mailing

"Play store" equipment. Can be made from orange crates or heavy cardboard cartons. Empty cereal boxes, salt boxes, or the like, are the "stock."

Cash register, change maker, and play money

Equipment for playing conductor. Ticket punch, change maker, conductor's hat, tickets, and transfers.

Toys for Constructing and Fitting Together

Interlocking trains and interlocking boats can be made from pieces of wood 1 inch thick and 5 inches long, with large open screw eyes on each end to permit easy joining together.

Pegboards can be made at home if fathers or older brothers have brace and bits of various sizes. Use dowels cut to desired lengths for pegs.

Toys consisting of wooden wheels and rods, or plastic balls and tubes to be fitted together, are to be found in great variety in toy departments. Choose sturdy ones.

Large metal screws, bolts, and nuts countersunk into small wooden bench, with combination wrench and screw to loosen and tighten them. Variations of this toy can be made at home by setting collections of stone balls, nuts, and screws into a 1-inch-thick piece of wood. Use wrench and screwdriver to operate.

Puzzles—inlay puzzles of 15 to 25 pieces. Can be made at home as suggested in *Puzzles* under *Toys for Toddlers*, in this chapter.

Toys for Activity and Letting Off Steam

Hammer and pegboards

Hammer-and-nail sets. Can also be made with thick blocks of soft wood 2 inches thick and 10 inches long, with a composition board, or with pieces of soft wood, and large-headed nails to be pounded with light weight hammer.

Rubber balls of various sizes

Bean bags. Can be made by filling cloth or felt bags with cherry stones or beans.

Punching bag, or one of the large figures stuffed with soft material that can be punched, and is weighted so that it rebounds

Dump trucks, tow trucks, or trailer trucks with well-constructed metal cars and simple parts

Large metal trucks which can be sat upon and manipulated by rider

Beginners' skates

Rubber ring quoits

Sleds—if there is opportunity to use them

Toys for Making Things and Expressing Feelings

See also *Materials for Making Things* in the *Toddler* section, and the section on *Permanent Equipment*, both in this chapter.

Tempera paints or powder paints mixed with water. Start with red, blue, and yellow.

Paint brushes, ¾ inches wide with long handle

Newsprint paper—comes in inexpensive large sheets

Moist modeling clay—available in 5-lb. tin. Should be wrapped in moist cloth and stored in original container to prevent hardening.

Scissors with blunt end but good cutting edge, colored papers, and paste. Paste may be made at home with flour-and-water mixture, cooked to paste consistency. Save gift-wrapping paper for cutting and pasting activities.

Sewing projects can be carried on with blunt needle with large eye, heavy embroidery thread, and cloth marked at 1-inch intervals for stitches.

Tools for working with wood—7-oz. hammer, 12-inch crosscut saw, 4-inch screwdriver, 3-inch C clamp, scraps of wood, nails, and sandpaper. It is usually more satisfactory to buy good tools individually in a hardware store than to get one of the tool chests for children sold in toy departments.

Games for Quiet Times

Picture dominoes

Object Lotto, Things That Go Lotto, Good Things to Eat Lotto, House We Live in Lotto. Lotto games of any kind can be made at home by pasting pictures concerned with the chosen subject on several pieces of even-sized cardboard. Paste duplicate pictures on a set of cards.

The chapters CHILDREN NEED SPACE AND PLAY MATERIALS, in Volume 14, and MAKING THE MOST OF YOUR HOME, in Volume 8, have suggestions for using the available space and storing play materials.

Ellis O. Hinsey

STORIES FOR YOUNG CHILDREN

PAULINE HILLIARD, Ed.D.

Associate Professor of Education, College of Education, University of Florida, Gainesville, Fla.

THE young child is the center of his own universe. His early responses and interests are strongest when stories and poems are about himself and his things.

All kinds of everyday happenings may appeal in story and poem. In CHILDCRAFT, Volume 1, there are many poems that may be used playfully and that tell of simple activities.

Stories Help a Child Grow

Stories and poems can help the child distinguish between the real and the fanciful in the world. They can help him begin to see what his place is in the business of living. They can help him begin to understand what other persons in his world are like and what they do.

As the child's circle of experience and understanding spreads, he becomes interested in stories and poems about many kinds of people and things. The pattern of today's life becomes more apparent as he hears about children, animals, machines, and other things in the present-day world. Stories about trains, boats, planes, and all things mechanical have a strong appeal to most young children, particularly little boy listeners.

Stories Add to Understanding of the World

Virginia Lee Burton has given her machines real personality as they struggle to do their work to help people, Her *Choo Choo, Mike Mulligan and His Steam Shovel,* and *Katy and the Big Snow* delight the four- to six-year-olds. Lois Lenski's books about *The Little Auto, The Little Train,* and *The Little Airplane,* and such workers as *Engineer Small, Cowboy Small,* and *Farmer Small* explain the way people live and the things they do in our world,

Living today has become so complex that it is not easy for the young child to gain an understanding of whole episodes. Even so simple a thing as where we get bread or milk means to many children only the loaf from the store or the milk bottle at the front door. *This Is the Milk That Jack Drank* by William R. Scott tells the story of milk in a way the young child can understand.

Stories Add to Self-Understanding

Stories and poems can help the young child begin to understand himself and his own feelings. In stories he hears of the feelings, the joys, and the disappointments of other children. Although he does not put his understandings into words, he begins to see how they have solved their "problems."

It is not always easy to be the kind of child adults want. Even Peter Rabbit could not do it! Through the years, children have responded with excitement to the escapades of the rabbit, so much like a little boy, who went out to explore his world and almost ended in Mr. Mac-Gregor's rabbit pie. But young readers are reassured to learn that home and Mother Rabbit were waiting for him, in a matter-of-fact way, with their safety and security.

Children are inevitably going to get into trouble, and sometimes be punished. Stories that tell good-humoredly and gently of such experiences can help a child understand that he is not particularly bad, even when he has displeased his parents.

In *Dorcas Porkus*, Tasha Tudor tells of a little brother and sister who try to give their pet pig a bath on the afternoon when their mother is entertaining with a church quilting-bee party. Young listeners will understand the embarrassment the children feel when Dorcas gets loose and runs through the party. Nor are they surprised when Dorcas Porkus has to go live with the other pigs, and the children must do extra chores for a week. But at last the children in the story know their mistake is fully forgiven.

In selecting stories, be sure that the characters are forgiven and loved, and not treated harshly, or the effect will not be desirable.

Stories Can Reduce Worries

Relationships with older brothers and

Books are a source of pleasure. These little girls know the stories almost by heart and like to recite them, even though they are not yet readers.

291

No need to point a moral when stories fascinate eager listeners. All kinds of lessons sink in, as children become acquainted with storybook friends.

A. Devaney

sisters and their playmates can be trying for three-, four-, and five-year-olds. *Wait for William* and *Tag-A-Long-Tooloo* are two stories telling of little ones' successful struggle to gain a place with older children.

Having a new baby in the family is sometimes hard for a young child. Dorothy Baruch's *I Know A Surprise*, or Harold and Ruth Shane's *The New Baby*, let the children know that annoyance at baby brothers and sisters is universal and acceptable.

When you are afraid of the dark, it could be good to hear about *Boo, Who Used to Be Scared of the Dark* by Munro Leaf, or *Who Likes the Dark* by Virginia Howell.

Stories Become a Part of Living

Stories and poems can be woven into daily life in ways that make them a part of family living. Help your children make friends with the characters in the stories and poems in the first six volumes of CHILDCRAFT. As you read these well-loved favorites over and over again, you will find that the Three Billy Goats Gruff, the Little Red Hen, and the Three Little Pigs become as much a

part of their life as the children next door.

No delightful story or poem should be weighted down by pointing out the lesson to be learned. Children, like adults, will identify themselves with the characters in stories and poems. If children are exposed to a wide range of people and situations in stories, they will draw their own meanings from them.

One mother tells how her children frequently refer to themselves or each other as "Simple Simon" when something foolish has been done.

In another family, when the six-year-old has exaggerated greatly, her nine-year-old sister will say, "You must be on Mulberry Street." Dr. Seuss' fanciful tale *And to Think That I saw It on Mulberry Street* is a prime favorite here.

Stories Add Meaning to Events

Stories and poems can never take the place of firsthand experiences in children's lives. But certainly they can add meaning and pleasure to a child's firsthand experiences. How thrilling it can be to find in a story or poem something "just like what happened to me."

The poem "The Umbrella Brigade"

(Childcraft, Volume 2) may make umbrellas and boots fun instead of a chore. A trip on a ferry boat or train can give new meaning to James Tippett's little poems about "Trains" and "Ferry Boats" in Volume 1.

Laughter in Stories and Poems

Nonsense, fun, laughter, rhythm, repetition, and beauty of expression can greatly enrich a child's imaginative life and are part of the heritage of all children.

You can encourage in, and enjoy with,

A. Devaney

young children their exploration of words and sounds, by means of many kinds of verse and stories. Mother Goose is probably one of the richest poetical sources for word experimentation, rhythm, and nonsense fun. The poems of A. A. Milne, Walter de la Mare, Dorothy Aldis, Eunice Tietjens, and many others you will find in Volumes 1 and 2 of Childcraft frequently make use of words and rhythm patterns which fit the mood and messages of the poem.

The nonsense poetry of Edward Lear and Laura Richards provides not only play with words but also the kind of fun and sense of the ridiculous so appealing to many children.

From about the age of three on through kindergarten and early school years, children usually respond with great zest to stories exaggerated just for fun.

Laughter is a special gift to the human child. Whether the fun and laughter come from the repetition of words that tickle or surprise, or from the nonsense of the story or poem, it is mentally healthy for children and adults to laugh together.

Stories Parents Make up

Fortunate indeed is the child whose parents enjoy making up stories to tell him. Jane's father began this adventure

Some of the best stories are the ones you make up for the children yourself. Your young audience enjoys occasional exaggeration for the sake of effect.

with his three-year-old daughter by telling bedtime stories about Paddle, a little duck. Each evening's story recounted pleasant and interesting happenings of Jane's day, told as the adventures of Paddle. Two other parents developed a similar continued tale but used the child's name, and she herself became the main character in the story of "Linda's Day." As Linda grew in understanding she shared in the telling, and would add what Linda said or thought.

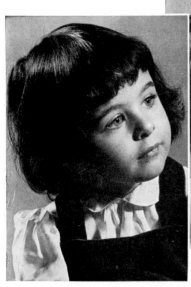
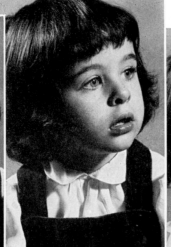
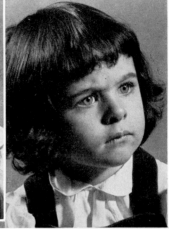

F. P. G.

Once upon a time there were three Billy Goats. On their way to graze, they had to cross a bridge over a river.

Under the bridge lived an ugly Troll. When the tiniest Goat crossed the bridge, Troll said, "I'll eat you up." "Wait for a bigger goat," said Billy.

The Past Comes Alive

You can share happenings of your own childhood with your children. These stories help children to see their mothers and fathers as real people. There is courage and strength to be gained, as well as fun, in realizing that even such wise, grown-up ones as Mamma and Daddy sometimes got into trouble but were able to live through their adventures and grow up.

One kindergarten teacher tells of the five-year-old who shares with zest and a sense of importance incidents and bits of information prefaced by, "In the olden days when my daddy was a boy." Once it was when they had made ice-cream at school in a hand-turned freezer; again it was about the first time he heard a radio program.

Regardless of whether Mother and Daddy grew up on a farm, in the center of a crowded city, or sailed the seas from another country, the everyday doings of their lives can be a source of real pleasure and interest to their children. A careful backward look into any parents' childhood will bring forth some pleasant, comforting, or exciting episodes that will delight their children and help them to see their parents as real people. It may be the time Mother got lost, or

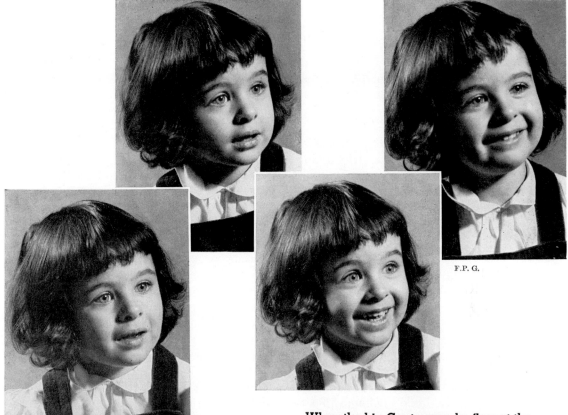

F.P. G.

When the big Goat came, he flew at the Troll, tossed him into the river and went on up the hillside where the three Goats grew so fat they could hardly walk.

When the Troll said he would gobble up the second, Billy Goat said, "Wait for the big one." So Troll let him go, too.

Daddy's first day at school, or the kitten that was found on the doorstep.

Guideposts for Storytellers

You need only listen and watch your children's responses to know when you and the children are communicating with pleasure and interest.

If you do not feel you are a champion storyteller, select an experience that is simple enough for the young listener to understand. Tell a story about a situation a child can cope with. Skip the frightening or the tragic. You will be rewarded if you read ahead and look around for the kind of stories that will appeal to your family.

What Situations Are Frightening?

Young children sometimes worry about losing Mother or Father. Often children fear some terrible unknown punishment. Until they understand the difference between what is real and what is make-believe, it is usually safer not to use the grim stories of wicked witches or giants, and ugly, evil animals or people. One might well avoid stories where adults, who are supposed to be the children's friends, mistreat or severely punish them.

Certainly most children should not

have frightening stories just before bed-time, or at any time when they may already be anxious or troubled by some upsetting event in their normal living.

When children are older, most of them can and usually do relish stories with exciting and even frightening themes. Certainly fairy tales are a part of the rich heritage due children. Wise parents can judge by their children's responses when they are ready to take the "stronger" stories. Perhaps you have wondered about when to introduce fairy stories. This question is discussed in the chapter READING TOGETHER, in Volume 12.

How Early Can You Start Stories and Poems?

Mothers through the years have known that their babies have responded to the bodily rhythm of rocking and patting, accompanied by the rhyming words of a lullaby. It is fun to chant or recite little poems as you care for the baby.

Finger and toe plays such as "Pat-a-cake," "This Little Pig went to market," and "Forehead-bender, Eye-winker" have long served parents as playful rhythmic communications with their young children. Mother Goose rhymes are perhaps the most widely used and universally loved poems for little ones. Parents who need help to refresh their memories of Mother Goose, and to become acquainted with other well-selected new and old poems for the young child, will find CHILDCRAFT, Volumes 1 and 2, helpful.

How Do You Cultivate Good Taste?

Children will listen to practically anything adults read to them. The story is told of one bachelor uncle who experi-mented with reading the telephone book in an expressive voice and found his three-year-old niece entranced! Because young children cannot select, the adults who choose stories and poems have a real responsibility.

As children grow in strength and understanding, they need books of their own. At first you can turn the pages, read, and talk about the pictures. A little later the children want to handle the books themselves. The size of the book seems to be of slight consequence, so long as the child can handle it easily. Children respond best to books with clear, colorful pictures or photographs of objects and happenings not too far removed from their experience and understanding.

Stories Strengthen Family Ties

There are rich values in reading and telling stories to young children, and, with the first six volumes of CHILDCRAFT on hand, you will always have a source of story material. A child who learns to like stories, poems, and books is building readiness for learning to read in the beginning school years. The enjoyment of good stories and poems in the earliest years opens the way for developing discriminating taste for a wide range of reading interests throughout life. Probably the most important gain is the close, friendly bond which is being formed between children and their parents, as parents give of their time and attention to share stories and poems with their children.

Memories of good times together with stories and books can be a means of communication that will endure through the years. Memories of these experiences can contribute to the stability of individuals and of families.

YOUNG CHILDREN AND MUSIC

EMMA DICKSON SHEEHY, M.A.

Author of "There's Music in Children,"
New York, N. Y.

MUSIC is made up of sound and rhythm. If we are aware of sound and rhythm in our day-by-day living with children, we shall have a good start in understanding, appreciating, and guiding their musical growth. Children are constantly experimenting with these musical elements and are continually making their own kinds of "music."

Sometimes it is hard for our adult ears to hear their music or to respect it. It is important for us to examine our own feelings about music and what it means to us. Perhaps our musical horizons need stretching. Perhaps we may even have the idea that we are not musical. The wrong kind of instruction or some unfortunate experiences with music when we were young may have turned us away from it.

Again, we may have a highly developed musical skill and may be willing to accept only the usual ways of making music. Or we may just be "naturals" in this business of sound making. We may never be bothered by what others think, and go merrily on our way. If we belong here, we are lucky.

Music Is for Everyone

There is no such thing as a completely unmusical person. There are many degrees of competence. There are many varieties of music for many occasions, but do not let yourself be downed by the cult of "best music." It is a lucky child who lives in a home where singing is part of living, even though Father or Mother may occasionally go off pitch. The child who grows up in a home where every bit of music must be perfect may turn his back on music completely. If we can feel comfortably at home with music, we can explore the sound and rhythm all around us with the children. Then we have in our possession the fundamental skill for helping young children grow musically.

Exploring the World of Music

The small baby enjoys babbling. It is not long before he tumbles into a satisfying rhythmic repetition of certain sounds such as "da da da da." He is sure to get enthusiastic approval from his parents, who encourage him by repeating what he is doing. They probably try a few sound tricks of their own for his amusement. Even in repeating what the baby says, one can offer variations such as calling back "da da" in a different pitch, a high or a low voice, or changing the rhythm by going fast or slow.

The baby also shows awareness of the music that goes on in the home. He is soothed by Mother's lullabies. He responds to the radio or to Father's and Mother's favorite recordings. If they sing or play an instrument, he usually listens. Some music soothes him and some may annoy him, but he is getting something from these experiences and associations with music.

This play with syllable and sound develops rapidly. As the toddler grows, he becomes highly skilled in the use of his voice. If you do not think the imitation of sirens, the engine roars, and the animal sounds the four- or five-year-old makes are skills, try making these sounds yourself!

Experimenting with Voices

Young children love to chant a phrase over and over. To them it is music, although to us it may be sheer annoyance.

Most mothers find that when a small person starts a chant, "I don't want supper, I don't want supper," the best thing to do is to get in on the game by answering good-humoredly, "We're going to have cocoa. Guess who likes cocoa?" If you add variation in words and rhythm, you can contribute to the child's fun and make a "sound game" out of what

When the smallest children want to beat the drum, and the "drum" is a kitchen pan, give them wooden spoons and padded sticks to dull the noise.

started out to be a difficult situation. These chants seem to be the same in any language around the world.

Now is the time for parents to acquaint themselves with simple nursery songs and Mother Goose rhymes. You will find these in Volume 11. You can rediscover the folk songs with their nonsense refrains. Children also enjoy nonsense poetry for its sound play. Such rhymes as those of Edward Lear and Laura Richards in Volumes 1 and 2 al-

Experimenting with the sound and the feel of a piano is a good way to develop an interest in playing it.

ways delight children of all ages.

A happy, contented child will often accompany his work and play with singing talk. Sometimes this will be directly related to what he is doing—"I'm helping Mommy. We're going to the store." How much fun it is when Mother sings along and makes up short song bits herself!

The simple, easy expression of feelings is a good foundation for a healthy personality. What is more, there is lifelong value in these early, pleasant associations with singing. This is a good time to get acquainted with the songs about playing traffic or tugboat, having a parade, or being an animal. You will find such songs in Volume 11.

Experimenting with Instruments

Children explore the world of music as they experiment with "instruments," too. Probably the rattle is the first instrument that is given to babies. It is important to choose pleasant-toned rattles. As far as babies are concerned, any spoon or tin pan that makes a sound will be welcomed. Many mothers allow their toddlers to amuse themselves with the pots and pans. A wooden spoon or a padded stick will make these sessions a little easier on your ears. It is worth taking an occasional minute or two from your own work to lend your interest to what is going on.

Simple musical instruments can provide other ways of playing with sound. A large homemade drum with a pleasant resonant tone is always enthusiastically received. MAKING MUSICAL INSTRU-MENTS, in Volume 8, has helpful suggestions. A collection of pleasant-sounding bells, rhythm sticks, and homemade rattles has great possibilities. An accurately-tuned xylophone or resonator blocks will offer to children an opportunity to find out about melody. Be careful not to spoil the child's way of learning by expecting him to play certain songs. The chances are strong that he is interested in playing his own "make-ups."

If the family has a piano, a youngster has another way of finding out about melody and rhythm. When he is very young he enjoys sitting on your lap while you play or sing, but he soon begins to want to explore for himself. Sometimes his playing will be pretty vigorous. If you are certain he is listening to what he is playing, bear with him for awhile. Respect his experimenting and be willing, now and then, to listen with him. Perhaps you can play back to him what he has been trying to play. Your patience and interest will pay big dividends when you feel the time is ripe for him to listen to you.

How Should You Guide Musical Interest?

Making pleasant-sounding instruments available and allowing the child to use them are first steps in musical guidance. Lending your interest and encouragement are next. Here you must be careful that you do not take the situation out of the child's hands and try to teach him how you think music should be made. More is gained when the teacher is willing to take cues from the child. If you are sensitive to what a youngster is trying to find out, you can help him do a better job. There may be times when showing him will be the answer, but these times are rare. Too much "showing" is likely to result in the child depending entirely on the adult.

Experimenting with Rhythm

The use of rhythm is a constant part of musical sound play. A secure and happy child just naturally uses his whole body rhythmically. His rhythm depends upon his temperament, his size, and his feelings. Usually it is different from yours! Too often you may tend to associate rhythm only with response to music. If Junior cannot keep time to the music you play, you are likely to think he is not rhythmical. Grownups need to be more sensitive to the child's natural rhythm. Let him know you feel his rhythm when you supply a simple accompaniment. You can catch his rhythm as he moves by clapping your hands, tapping your feet, singing a simple song in the same rhythm, or playing an instrument, but you must always be careful to play his way. If he has plenty of opportunities to build up pleasant associations with accompaniment, he will respond easily to music when it catches his mood and tempo.

Lessons in Music and Dancing

Dancing is movement. It can go on with or without music.

As children experiment with their voices, with instruments, and with rhythm and dancing they are having "lessons." These lessons can go on day by day in a happy home and may provide the most rewarding musical learning the child will ever have.

In these early years the child learns rapidly. Parents are the ideal teachers because they are with him most of the time. Children's interests are unpredictable and sometimes do not last long. It is for you to make the most of opportunities as they present themselves.

Philip Gendreau

With bells and blocks, tambourines and triangles, they shall have music wherever they go, for they can make it.

F. P. G.

When the band strikes up, let children keep time in their own way. Let them dance for the sheer joy of it.

Children's natural growth and development can be blocked easily by forcing them to take formal lessons in dancing and music. You may even "train" the real music out of them by giving them set forms. Too often the emphasis is on performance and not on the joy and emotional security that result from the right kind of experiences in music and dancing. You need to ask yourself why you are eager to give your young children formal training. Perhaps you believe you have a potential star and are willing to sacrifice your child's normal development to his later success. It is still questionable if formal early training is the way to reach that goal.

Family Music

There is no age level in music. Children respond to what pleases them, and their choices are frequently unpredictable. Their ears are wide open to a great deal that goes on musically besides the singing, the drums, and the piano playing you may provide for their special enjoyment.

For one baby, a pre-bedtime session on Dad's lap, while he sings snatches of gay songs, is a "must." Another child's mother grew up in a home where there was a great deal of hymn singing. She unconsciously sings or hums hymns much of the time while she is working. Her five-year-old can carry most of the tunes, at least in part. Still another father, a college music professor, entertains his youngster with Bach, Bartók, and be-bop. This dad earned his way through college by playing be-bop, and he was quick to recognize the relation between his son's early boos, goos, and gurgles, and be-bop! A five-o'clock chamber-music hour on the radio is a mother's favorite while she is preparing dinner. She is astonished by her four-year-old's awareness of and interest in this music.

How Shall We Choose Records?

Phonograph records and radio have turned us in an incredibly short time into a nation familiar with many kinds of music. Records bring variety and the opportunity to hear what we want when we want it. The growth of the children's record field is phenomenal. We are exposed to the good, bad, and indifferent. How do you choose records for children? Certainly you cannot make selections on the basis of an attractive envelope! Many excellent records are in artistic folders, but a beautiful folder does not guarantee the worth of what is inside. Is the music pleasing, is it well played, is the surface of the record free of scratches? If it is a story record, is the story likely to be of interest to your child? Is the story told in a simple,

Lullabies and lively tunes, folk songs and waltzes, nursery rhymes and opera become a part of the child who has the opportunity to listen often to good records.

straightforward fashion without talking down to children? Consider, too, the quality of voice, the pace, and if the words are spoken clearly. Does the music support the story or does it tend to drown out the narrator's voice? A number of good records for the use of children are listed in Volume 11.

Children can be exposed to a great variety of records. Folk music, short selections from the great classics, the familiar "light" classics, and band music may all be enjoyed. Modern music is likely to have an unusual appeal. Songs, and even a few better-known operatic arias, have a place in a youngster's musical diet. Small children enjoy making selections from the family record collection. In many communities, the town library has a record-lending service.

Children should be allowed to make their own choices, for there is no better way to develop taste. You can add a few of your choices from time to time to widen their tastes. Records should never take the place of "homemade" family music, but they *can* and *do* extend music experiences. They can give young children a unique opportunity to explore independently. Children can learn to know great music and the stories that belong with it.

Music in Nursery School

All the things that can be done at home can be enjoyed with fresh stimulation in nursery school and kindergarten, because there are more children to learn with and from. The informality of the program respects the individual needs of each child and takes account of what all like. More musical equipment is available than in most homes. The teacher sees to it that children are exposed to many kinds of musical experiences, both indoors and outdoors. Children have time to get acquainted with such instruments as a number of different-sized drums, resonator bells, and the piano. Much of the fun is in making music with a friend. We are not talking here about showing off the children through rhythm-band performances, where the emphasis is on the product and not on the musical development of each child. The best musical growth of each child is seldom contributed to by this kind of performance.

The teacher is also familiar with many songs and other music usually enjoyed by children. Her "music group" in nursery school may consist of three or four children free to come and go according to their interest. In kindergarten, the music group is likely to include the majority of the children, who have fun dancing, skipping, and singing together. A good portable record player, together with a selected group of records, is also available for individual children's use. How they love to sit close to the player and watch the record go round and round.

Concerts in Kindergarten

In one school, the teacher brought in additional experiences that were contributed by parents, friends, other teachers, and older children. These extra little "concert times" in this kindergarten grew into a short series of concerts each winter, planned especially for the younger children. They were a success because the program was limited to one-half hour. Each child had a ring-side seat and some personal experiences with instruments before the concert. The program included children's favorite pieces and offered new experiences in listening.

Above all, great respect for the children was shown by artists and managers both. They recognized that children approach music directly and should not be tricked into it by stories and explanations. In concerts, informal contacts with music, and the many experiences children may be exposed to from day to day, we must never forget the right of the child to respond to music in his own way. We cannot experience for him, but we can be responsible for seeing to it that he has a rich musical environment in which to grow.

Edith Loder

EXCURSIONS FOR YOUNG CHILDREN

ETHEL WRIGHT KUNKLE, M.A.

Author of "Saturday Walk"; Winnetka, Ill.

A N EXCURSION need not be a big expedition. Little children enjoy watching, or taking part in, the simplest, everyday occurrences. Even these simple events can be more rewarding if plans are made and some preparations are carried out.

Small Children Like to Watch

Children like to watch people at work. In the city or in the country, one can always find some sort of workman just around the corner, a few blocks away, or right in one's own home. Plumbers, painters, or handymen are often under your own roof. Children love things that move. Any kind of transportation—trains, boats, trucks, cars, steam shovels, steam rollers, tractors, combines, bulldozers—fascinates them.

Animals have great appeal to a child. The neighbor's cat, the dog in the next block who just had puppies, the angleworm that came with the warm spring rain, the tadpole fished out of the ditch at the end of the street or meadow are as wonderful as strange beasts at the zoo. Guinea pigs, white rats, white mice, rabbits, doves, and hamsters all delight the small child and are good pets, too.

The tiniest tots love the things that are near home. The more grown-up preschoolers can be taken a little farther afield. Children do not like to be hurried. They will stand a long, long time, just waiting for the streamliner to go by. But usually they do not like to be in large groups, where it is too noisy, or where they have to keep still too long. Still, we need to remember that some children seem to relish crowds and noisy things. Most little children seem tireless when one watches them play all day, but they tire easily when situations or people are new, or when excitement runs high.

Where Shall We Go?

For the youngster in a city neighborhood, the store, the mailbox, the firehouse, any kind of building project under way, or even a garage where cars are being repaired is satisfying. There are parks, zoos, greenhouses, and conservatories to be visited. A ride on an elevated, a subway, a ferry boat, a bus, or a streetcar is as good as a trip to a foreign country would be for you. Railway stations and airports, if they are not too noisy and confusing, are never dull! If you live near a body of water, the beach is endlessly attractive in warm weather. In winter, watching skaters on the pond or making first attempts at skating can be fun. Farm life opens a new world to the city child.

The child who lives in a small town is particularly fortunate. The railway station is not overwhelmingly big, and perhaps there is even a turntable to watch, as well as the trains that bring passengers and mail. In a small town the child can be taken to the shops to see what is in them, in addition to being an onlooker when Mother goes to the store. Woods or beaches are likely to be near at hand, and hills suitable for coasting

"Men at work here" means something worth watching is afoot. Youngsters are spellbound when concrete mixers, bulldozers, or steam shovels perform.

in winter are usually not far away.

Grain elevators, canneries, and creameries are usually within reach of the youngster on a farm. Looking for polliwogs or fishing in ponds and brooks, "exploring" in woods and meadows are all special delights for the country youngster. A model farm with its machinery makes an interesting trip, and, because everyone likes some variety, a trip to the nearest town is always a great event.

Excursions Are Good Teachers

Children need many kinds of experiences to help them understand the world about them. From these experiences, the child gets the beginnings of a love for nature and its pattern, and a feeling for machines and what they do. He begins to realize what labor contributes, as he sees people at work. Best of all, these experiences give him a feeling for people and human relations. He grows up to be a better-informed individual, better able to take his place in a

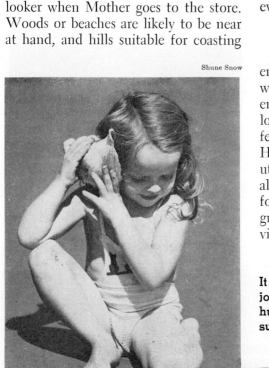

Shune Snow

It is a fortunate child who knows the joys of spray and sand, the thrill of hunting shells and hearing in them the surge and thunder of a mighty sea.

democratic society, if, from his earliest days, he has had the chance to get the feel of the life around him.

Excursions or small trips also help the present development of the child. But the fun the youngster has on the way is the most important part. Going alone with Daddy even for an hour gives a new feeling of independence. Putting his own dime in the slot on the bus makes a three- or four-year-old feel grown up. All young children ask questions. Excursions give a child many good questions to ask. You have a chance to teach him a great deal as you answer his questions, too. Going on excursions and talking about them afterward stimulate a child's interest in gaining new knowledge. He becomes interested in new places and is less afraid to try new things.

New Ideas for Play

What children do and see on these little trips often carries over into their daily play. Block structures will be more interesting, dramatic play more exciting, stories more full of meaning to a child because of what he has seen and heard.

On the basis of an excursion, adults can make casual suggestions that encourage new activities. All the joy could be taken out of the trip if the children were forced to make something, but a hint is helpful. "Oh, that looks like the new building where we went to see the cement mixer," or "I think you could draw some pictures about that farm we visited yesterday."

In school, we often see a clay product

For city children, a field of daisies is the finest kind of show, and being allowed to pick flowers is a treat.

or a picture showing up weeks after the trip. You will find that children who have been on frequent excursions and who have had many experiences seem to have more ideas for play. They also seem more creative and get along better with other children. Primary teachers will tell you that the children with wider experiences are usually the first to read. These children tend to have more curiosity about things, and curiosity is a good incentive for reading. We also know that the more good, interesting experiences a child has, the more ready he is to read. His familiarity with the world about him helps him in every way.

Do Not Overdo the Teaching

There is danger in overemphasizing what you want the child to learn. Usually the less said about what a youngster will get out of the trip, the better. The most important thing is that children and adults really enjoy the entire excursion. No matter how much you talk, a

Elizabeth Hibbs

Fishing, or even just dreaming by the side of a pond, makes a thoroughly satisfying excursion for small fishermen.

Keystone

child will get out of a trip just exactly as much as he can easily absorb.

Sometimes it is fun to make a remark about something you are seeing, or, occasionally, to draw attention to something. You can overdo such comments as, "Did you see this?," "Let me explain how this works," and "Now, I don't want you to miss this." You will be amazed at what a child will enjoy and learn if he is left to his own devices, but his idea of what is interesting and educational may not be the same as yours.

Sometimes an excursion falls flat because the adult has planned it without taking the child into consideration. Sometimes it is hard for the adult to remain in the background and let the child take the lead. A three- or four-year-old knows how fast he can walk, how long he can stand, when he is hungry, and when he needs a drink. He is a good judge of how much he can take, too.

Let the Children Lead

A walk down to a dock to look over a small boat can be a great adventure, and an educational experience as well. When Mrs. Grayson took Hugh and Marlene to the dock she explained to them beforehand about staying away from the edge of the pier. Because Hugh was barely three and exceptionally lively, she put a life jacket on him, just to be on the safe side. When four-year-old Marlene forgot and stepped near the edge of the pier, Mrs. Grayson took her gently by the hand and began talking about how you could smell the salt water and the fish down here.

When the owner of the boat invited them on board, Mrs. Grayson followed the children around as they explored eagerly. She asked once or twice "What do you think that is for?" or "Do you know what this is called?" instead of constantly telling them about things. She was surprised to find that Marlene knew the names of many things on the boat. When the owner of the boat commented on how well the children behaved, their mother answered, "I just try to put myself in their place when we do things like this, and try to imagine how they feel about it. There's no wear and tear on the nerves when the children take the lead some of the time, and it's much easier to get them to do as I ask."

The next day Mrs. Todd brought Penny and Fred to see the boat, but the experience was not a happy one for anybody. She held both the children tightly by the hand and kept after them every minute—"Don't touch that." "Now stay away from the water." "Don't go there, come over this way." "Hurry up, we've got to get back." The owner of the boat was not surprised that the Todd children whined and complained and asked few sensible questions.

Why Do Some Excursions Fall Flat?

Children may become cross if you have attempted too much. Maybe this is something that they are not particularly interested in at the time. You may have taken them when it was convenient for you, even though one or more of the children was overtired or not quite up to par physically. Perhaps you expect too much of a child for his particular stage of development. Complicated processes tend to confuse him. If too much has been said to him about how he must behave on the trip, he may not be able to enjoy himself for fear he will do something wrong, or not be "good."

Sometimes, teasing a child can ruin his whole experience. One family could not imagine why their three-and-a-half-year-old had terrible nightmares for weeks after a short trip to the zoo. They finally recalled a passer-by saying to their little boy, "That's the bear that comes at night and eats up children who are not good." Careful reassurance and some good stories about bears that lived only in the forests finally helped the little boy to sleep through the night. A simple thing like that can throw a child off. Often a child will try to state his worry or fear to his parents. If your child tells you of his worries, listen and reassure him without laughing at him.

Simplicity Is the Keynote

At what age a child is ready for fairs, carnivals, and magic shows depends on his family, his neighborhood and friends, the things he has already seen, and most of all on the child himself.

Until a child reaches his sixth birthday, he is so interested in the things around him that he is usually much happier with simple everyday events, even as a treat.

A child of four will find more magic in planting a garden and watching it grow than he will in a magician cutting up a handkerchief and having it come out all in one piece. If you watch most young children at one of these performances, you will see that they wriggle and twist, crawl under the seats, talk out loud, ask for a drink, and get up to go out to the bathroom two or three times. There are rare occasions when a special performance of such shows might be all right. Such performances given for small children's birthday parties are entirely unnecessary. Eight-, nine-, or ten-year-olds love carnivals, magic, and other entertainment of that kind. The edge is taken off the thrill if they are exposed to such entertainment too early.

Making the Most of Excursions

Be sure to make plans before you start, if you are only going to go across the street or down to the next block. The excursion that is organized in the parent's mind will be the most successful. But be flexible about plans. Follow the child's interests and plan things that he can take at his own stage of development. You will have more fun, and so will your child, if you have planned the excursion for *him*, not for yourself.

When you get home, put some books, stories, and pictures about the things you have seen where the children will find them easily. They will use the materials if they need them.

Remember that all the world is exciting to a little child. You can have the pleasure of discovering it with him.

WILL MY CHILD BE READY FOR FIRST GRADE?

CELIA BURNS STENDLER, Ph.D.

Professor of Education, University of Illinois,
Champaign, Ill.

Technically, all children are ready for the first grade once they have reached the legal entrance age. Schools do not say to parents, "Keep your child at home until he is ready," but only, "Keep your child at home until he is five years, nine months," or six years, or whatever the legal entrance age may be.

Expect Differences

There is Dick. He sits up in the front seat and greets all his friends as they come in the door with a loud "Hi!" He explores his desk, raises the cover, and lets it come down several times with a loud bang.

Sharon walks in slowly. It has been hard for her to leave her mother at the door. Roger enters the room eagerly and curiously and greets the teacher with a friendly smile.

Noisy children, mousy children, aggressive children, friendly children—all variations of character and personality come to first grade. Which ones are ready for it? How can parents help prepare children for this new experience?

First-graders may resemble one another in age, but they will differ in their readiness for experiences in school. They will differ in the relationships they will establish with the teacher. Some will form a friendly relationship with her easily and quickly and be eager, within limits, to please. Others will see the teacher as a forbidding creature of whom one must be wary. First-graders will differ, too, in their approach to learning. Some will be quick, curious, confident of their own ability. Others will be slow, timid in their approach, lacking in confidence.

A child's rate of growth, his intelligence, and his personality determine how ready he is for first grade.

Differences in Readiness

A quick glance around a first-grade room will reveal differences in the rate at which children grow. There is Roy, who at six is a big-boned, fast-growing child with three of his second teeth already in sight. There is Susan, not so big, but also mature-looking. She is a fast-growing child who proudly displays

There are different kinds of first graders

. . . Some seem to be born "greeters"

. . . Some look mature

. . . While some still look babyish

. . . And the "fast growers" tower over them

her new second teeth. There is Tom, still with a baby cast to his features. His milk teeth are still firmly in his mouth.

All three children were born in the same month in the same year. There is some evidence that a fast-growing child physically will also be a fast-growing child intellectually. All aspects of growth seem to be intertwined. If this is so, other things being equal, Roy and Susan will learn faster than will Tom in the first grade, although all three children may have the same mental ability. Tom may be as much as a year behind in his beginning reading rate. But, because he is as bright as Roy and Susan, he will catch up with them eventually and will continue to grow after they have stopped. But this will be true only if Tom is permitted to grow in reading at his own rate. Let us hope teachers or parents do not try to force him into a faster rate of growing! Then Tom might develop attitudes toward school and learning that would stand in his way. Learning is not simply a matter of willpower and work. Individual children have individual patterns of growth. Allowing a child to grow at his own rate insures his best development.

How Does Intelligence Affect Learning?

Children vary in their mental ability, and of course mental ability affects their work in school. We attempt to measure this ability with intelligence tests. The usefulness, the limitations, and the ways of using intelligence tests are discussed in detail in MEASURING ACHIEVEMENT AND ABILITY, in Volume 14. Most first grades today recognize the fact that there are individual differences in intelligence. They attempt to adjust their programs to these differences. A good first-grade teacher will not expect the

Going to school means meeting new playmates and new experiences. Some children take this as a challenge; others find it difficult, even frightening.

Lucien Aigner

same achievement from two children if one has unusual ability and the other less-than-average mental capacity. But she does try to help every child use effectively what ability he has.

If parents, too, accept differences in intelligence, the child is helped to use his native ability to the best advantage. If a parent continually puts pressure on a child to be in the "best" reading group and to bring home the "best" report card, the effects upon the child may be bad. The child may not be constitutionally equipped to do this. He may not be able to use effectively the mental ability he has if pressures are severe.

How Does Personality Affect Readiness?

Whether or not a child uses his intelligence to learn what the school teaches depends upon the personality he brings with him to school. Personality affects learning to get along with other children, learning good work habits, or learning the three R's. Knowing the alphabet, being able to count to 100, or being able to read does not make a child "ready" for first grade, but the personality he has developed in his preschool years plays a great part in his readiness. Personality includes a child's attitudes, his understandings, his values, his goals. Perhaps most important of all, as far as readiness for the first grade is concerned, is his picture of himself. The kind of person he thinks he is, the feelings about himself that he brings with him to school, vitally influences his readiness and his ability to learn.

The child who looks upon himself as a worth-while person, who can take success and failure in his stride, can tackle new problems with confidence. He feels he can eventually master what he has to learn. He is likely to use effectively what ability he has.

Five-year-old Patty is eating breakfast. Her mother keeps up a running stream of conversation.

"Patty, you sit right up at that table and finish your breakfast . . . Patty! Look what you're doing! You're spilling

311

First graders are expected to look after themselves in dressing, and to hang up coats and hats. A well-prepared youngster has been away from Mother before going to school.

your oatmeal all over your clean dress. Can't you do anything right?"

By this time Patty is in tears.

"Stop that sniveling. I won't *listen* to your carrying on like this."

Four-year-old Mary has been setting the table. Her mother inspects:

"Mary, I like the way you've done your job. You remembered everything. That was a hard job, to remember the salt and pepper and extra spoons and to count everything out. You've done it beautifully."

If Patty's mother consistently punishes her for behavior she cannot help, Patty is going to learn to regard herself as a person who does not amount to much. She is likely to approach new learning situations with insecurity and even fear. Mary, whose mother continually points out to her that she is a worthwhile person, has good feelings about herself. As a result, she is likely to ap-

proach new learning situations securely and confidently, able to take failure in her stride. A child tends to live up to what others expect of him.

Good Preparation for First Grade

There are some ways of working and playing with others that the sixes are expected to know. As a supplement to the feeling "I am the kind who can do it," these specific ways of behaving are valuable.

In our society we expect a six-year-old to be able to tie his shoelaces, to dress himself, to hang up his clothes, to follow simple directions, to wash and toilet himself, and to leave his mother. Although we do not expect him to do these things perfectly, we do expect him to do them with some degree of ease. The good first-grade teacher will not hold it against the child who does not know these things, but the child who has learned them is at an advantage. He can use his energies for new learnings.

How About Foundations for Reading?

There are many things you can do that will make reading easier for your youngster. Many things he does by himself lay the groundwork for reading. In one sense, your child has been preparing himself and has been prepared for reading since infancy. At six weeks he was able to follow a moving object placed before his eyes. At six years he will be able to follow the printed word across the page. At two years he pointed in his picture book and said, "Baby go bed." At seven he will look at a picture for a clue to an unknown word. Throughout infancy and early childhood, your child has been developing skills which are necessary for reading. You can help this development by reading to your child. Listening to him as he pretends to read, sitting down with him to look at and talk about pictures in magazines and books, lets him know that books are a source of pleasure and something you value. In these ways you make early experiences with stories satisfying. You help to extend your child's vocabulary.

A visit to a farm, trips to different kinds of stores, watching trains come in at the railroad station, watching a steamshovel at work, visiting the fire station, all are experiences that will extend your child's horizons. He builds up his background of general information and further enlarges his vocabulary. A story involving a tractor or a tender will have more meaning for the child after he has seen a tractor or a tender in operation.

It Is Useful to Read and Write

Douglas and his mother were going to the store. "Let's leave a note for Daddy," said Mother. "He may get home before we do. Tell me what to say."

Douglas dictated while his mother wrote on the small blackboard in Douglas' room: "Dear Dad, We are going to the store. If you get home first let Chipper out. Love, Douglas." Douglas proudly signed his name at the end of the message.

When Larry was playing train he told his mother, "I need a sign for my railroad station. Make me one that says 'Springfield.'" Larry watched interestedly while his mother printed the sign.

Another mother asked her five-year-old daughter to get a box of rice from the storeroom. "See if you can find a box that looks like this, Judy. It will have the word 'rice' on it. Here's what the word is like." Judy's mother pointed to the word on the box and Judy proudly went to get the rice.

Ewing Galloway

Make books and stories a pleasure, and your child will have a background for learning to read more readily.

These are the kind of activities the good kindergarten or first-grade teacher uses to introduce her children to "book reading." The child who has a rich experience at home should not find books too difficult.

How Do Children Learn to Read?

An enjoyment of books, an interest in reading, and a good speaking vocabulary are essentials of reading readiness. Your child must also want to learn to read. He must have the feeling that reading is something he can do. A boy or girl must be mature enough to concentrate on a task. Learning to read takes close concentration and attention to detail. The child must be able to grasp the thought that a group of printed symbols stand for an idea. He must be able to tell one such group of symbols from another. Gradually he grows in this ability. First he may know vaguely that a word shaped like ▬◢ means *monkey*. Later he may know that a word beginning with a letter formed with rounded hills, with a tall letter in the center and a letter with a tail at the end, says *monkey*. At this point he may be able to recognize the word regardless of where he sees it. He has learned the cues so well that he can tell likenesses and differences, from one word to another.

All this takes time. It is conceivable that such growth could be speeded up with intense drill, but a child learns more easily and quickly when he is ready. That is the idea behind "reading readiness." A child tends to like reading, rather than to fear it, if we wait until there is reasonable assurance that he will be at least moderately successful. Meanwhile, a good teacher uses the time saved for other important experiences.

A child does not need to know the alphabet before he learns to read. Learning the alphabet will come later in Grade I, or in Grade II. Nor does he need to know the sound of the letters. It probably will not harm a child, but neither will it help him much, to learn the alphabet before he begins school. Nor will it help to drill him on sounding words. He is much more likely to learn words in the beginning if they are part of an interesting story. You will find more about this question in the chapters WHAT READING MEANS TO A CHILD and WRITING AND SPEAKING THE LANGUAGE, in Volume 14.

How About Teaching Reading at Home?

A few parents of five-year-olds may find their children eager and anxious to try book-reading months before they enter first grade. A child who is sufficiently able to distinguish likenesses and differences might enjoy a picture book with a simple vocabulary. A preprimer, preferably from a different series than those the school uses, might appeal to him, too. Read a page or two to the child and let him repeat. If he tackles the job with zest, if he remembers the words easily, if the reading experience is pleasurable to him, he can go through a few simple books.

Many parents have been told that schools frown upon teaching reading at home. They say that the child may be confused by different methods, or that he may be bored in first grade if he already knows how to read.

Schools are justified in cautioning parents. Some well-meaning parents have handicapped their children by pushing reading at them. But it is just as foolish to keep reading from some children as it is to push it at others. Five-year-olds who are ready for reading

School is a larger, perhaps a rougher world. When life seems hard, steadying encouragement from you will bolster your child's self-confidence.

Elizabeth Hibbs

can and should learn to read. They may even be more successful at five than if reading is postponed until they are six. Beginning reading materials may challenge a child when he is five, but be pushed aside as boring when he is six. None of the activities proposed in this article will handicap a child later on in school, provided the parents' attitude is good.

As first grades recognize that some children learn to read before entering school, they adjust their programs. The good teacher will provide reading materials that will challenge the more mature children and allow them to proceed from where they are. Just as the school should provide for those children who will not be ready for book-reading until late in Grade I, so the good school also provides for those who can read when they come to school.

Your Attitude Gives the Cue

For most six-year-olds, going to school is a big and important event. "Big kids" go to school. Adults indicate by their tone how important this step is when they say, "So you're going to first grade in the fall!" The event is further dramatized by the new clothes and special privileges.

You can help your child like school. Take him to visit the first grade the spring before he enters. See that he knows the way, knows the teacher, and knows the building. Inviting some of his fellow first-graders to your house to play is a real help. Familiar faces on the

first day make the transition from home to school easier. Presenting the school as it will really be is also important. Many children expect to learn to read and write and figure almost immediately, and are disappointed when they do not "learn" anything.

Don't make it appear that teacher and school are strictly disciplinary. "You just wait till the teacher gets you. She'll make you mind" is taboo to all right-minded parents! Children should know that they will be expected to behave with some consideration for others in school, but extreme statements or threats should never be made. If they have learned to consider others at home, school will present no problem along that line.

What if a Child Fears School?

A few children do not want to enter first grade. Almost all children balk at going back after lunch at least once during the first year. The reasons for these

315

refusals may be difficult to discover. Some children find it hard to break the home ties and need to be weaned away from mother gradually. In such cases it helps when a parent can bring the child to school and stay there until the youngster feels comfortable in the situation. It may be easier for a boy or girl to leave home if Father or an older neighbor child can accompany him to school. Sometimes reluctance to begin school may be due to jealousy over a younger brother or sister. A child may dislike the thought of going to school and abandoning the home field to a rival for his mother's affections. Occasionally a child may be frightened by older children's remarks about what will happen to him when he goes to school.

In any event, discovering the cause is important. Sometimes it will help to let the child know that you understand his worries. The situation may improve if you listen to his troubles sympathetically.

One mother play-acted Roger's going off to school. Roger dressed up in his "school" clothes, said good-by to his mother, and was greeted at school by the teacher (also played by his mother). Then the mother took Roger's part while Roger played at being the teacher.

Taking something from home to school also helps to bridge the gap. Garden flowers for the teacher, some pretty autumn leaves, a favorite book from which the teacher can read may make the classroom seem friendlier. Don't hesitate to tell the teacher about the child's fears. Then she can give him a little extra attention until he is over the hurdle.

If a child refuses to return to school after lunch, he frequently has had an unhappy experience that morning. If a child cries on the playground and the rest of the children jeer and call him crybaby, he will hardly be eager to return. If a child was scolded by the teacher and dissolved in tears, returning seems too difficult. If he is picked on by other children on his way to and from school, he may need some extra protection. Almost all first-grade children have these kinds of difficulties.

You can comfort your child, but at the same time help him to see that he is strong enough to take such situations in his stride, if that is true. You will not say, "You're too big to be a crybaby," or "You're in first grade now and you should be more grown up." But you may say, "I know it makes you feel bad when the teacher scolds. But it isn't that she doesn't like you. She *has* to scold sometimes to make children mind;" or "Bigger children like to tease smaller ones. Try not to let them see that they bother you and they'll stop;" or "Let's get Jerry (one of the teasers) over for lunch soon. You can walk back to school together and he'll help you."

Getting children together at lunch or for a snack sometimes changes feelings on both sides. It's worth trying.

In a few cases, more parental action is necessary. Have a conference with the teacher if a child persistently refuses to return. Notifying the school if the "big" boys are really being bullies may be in order.

But, for the most part, wise parents realize that growing up brings its difficulties. You cannot, nor should you attempt to, take all life's blows for your child. The best preparation for first grade is, after all, the best preparation for life, a readiness to face the task of growing up with courage and a conviction that one can master it eventually.